W9-APY-448

LEARNING THROUGH
SUPERVISED PRACTICE
IN STUDENT AFFAIRS

LEARNING THROUGH SUPERVISED PRACTICE IN STUDENT AFFAIRS

Diane L. Cooper
Sue A. Saunders
Roger B. Winston, Jr.
Joan B. Hirt
Don G. Creamer
Steven M. Janosik

Routledge
Taylor & Francis Group
New York   London

Published in 2002 by
Routledge
Taylor & Francis Group
270 Madison Avenue
New York, NY 10016

Published in Great Britain by
Routledge
Taylor & Francis Group
2 Park Square
Milton Park, Abingdon
Oxon OX14 4RN

© 2002 by Taylor & Francis Group, LLC
Routledge is an imprint of Taylor & Francis Group

Printed in the United States of America on acid-free paper
10 9 8 7 6 5 4

International Standard Book Number-10: 1-56032-879-7 (Softcover)
International Standard Book Number-13: 978-1-56032-879-7 (Softcover)
Library of Congress Card Number 2002020522

The author wishes to acknowledge permission to reprint the following:
A Four-Stage Cycle of Learning. From Arthur W. Chickering, **Modern American College: Responding to the New Realities of Diverse Students and a Changing Society**, copyright © 1981 by Jossey-Bass, a division of John Wiley & Sons, Inc. Reprinted by permission of John Wiley & Sons, Inc.

No part of this book may be reprinted, reproduced, transmitted, or utilized in any form by any electronic, mechanical, or other means, now known or hereafter invented, including photocopying, microfilming, and recording, or in any information storage or retrieval system, without written permission from the publishers.

Trademark Notice: Product or corporate names may be trademarks or registered trademarks, and are used only for identification and explanation without intent to infringe.

Library of Congress Cataloging-in-Publication Data

Learning through supervised practice in student affairs / Diane L. Cooper...[et al.]
        p. cm.
    Includes bibliographical references and index.
    ISBN 1-56032-879-7 (pbk.)
    1. Student affairs services—Administration. 2. College student personnel
administrators—Training of. 3. Student counselors—Training of. I. Cooper, Diane L.
LB2342.9 L43   2002
378.1'01—dc21   2002020522

Taylor & Francis Group
is the Academic Division of T&F Informa plc.

Visit the Taylor & Francis Web site at
http://www.taylorandfrancis.com

and the Routledge Web site at
http://www.routledge-ny.com

CONTENTS

PREFACE

For prospective higher education administrators, most comprehensive, graduate-level, professional preparation programs use multiple tactics or strategies for teaching content material. Generally, the prescribed program of study at the master's level includes one or more supervised practice experiences, typically known as practica or internships. Most doctoral programs require supervised practice as well. Future higher education and student affairs administrators are called on to perform entry-level work under the guidance of seasoned practitioners. During the experience, students' knowledge, application skills, attitudes, and values are deployed and evaluated. Many administrators view this as the acid test of students' aptitude and readiness for life as student affairs practitioners.

From the earliest days of professional practice in medicine, law, and other professions and later in higher education administration, the principle of supervised practice or "learning by doing" (Dewey, 1916) has been widely used in professional education. In its early forms, this approach might have been called *on-the-job training, clerkship,* or *apprenticeship*; later, when it found a place in the curriculum of higher education it became known as *internship* or *practicum*. By whatever label, hands-on supervised training has been an historical component of preparation for a variety of professions.

This text has been developed for use by graduate students, preparation program faculty, and functional area site supervisors in higher education and specifically in student affairs. Higher education administration requires a balance of knowledge and skills grounded in professional values. Successful practice demands that professionals understand students' background characteristics and their modes of learning coupled with knowledge of higher education environments and principles of organizational effectiveness. The supervised practice experience is the place where theory, application skills, personality attributes, technical knowledge, human foibles, institutional resources, and politics come together. Astute, reflective students can learn much about themselves as persons, as future student affairs professionals, and as participants in the social, educational, and political institution known as higher education.

Most of the principles and applications presented in this book are pertinent to a variety of areas of higher education administration, yet examples, ethical standards statements, and historical references have been restricted to student affairs because it is the only administrative specialty with a well-defined professional preparation curriculum and explicitly stated values and canons of professional practice (Miller, 2001). One should also note that this text is *not* intended for, or suitable for use in, practica or internships where the primary purpose is to train counselors, psychologists, social workers, or other clinical professionals. There are a number of excellent texts in the literature intended for students who are undergoing training to provide psychological services (e.g., Boylan, Malley, & Reilly, 2001; Chiaferi & Griffin,1997; Kiser, 2000). Their focus is on working with individuals who are experiencing interpersonal or intrapersonal problems; intervention is generally through working therapeutically with individuals or small groups of clients. Administrative internships, on the other hand, focus on activities such as needs assessments, program development, implementation, and evaluation, and organizational management and administration. Although generally concerned with organizational interventions, working with individual students to address developmental problems or issues is well within the purview and ethical responsibility of competent student affairs practitioners (Winston, 1996).

CORE VALUES

This book is grounded in several core values related to the purposes of higher education and the professional practice of student affairs administration. We hold that successful professionals must possess the skills of teaching, administration, advising, leadership, conflict management, planning, programming, working with students from diverse backgrounds, and individual and group interpersonal facilitation. Members should approach their work with energy and enthusiasm, but also with tolerance and patience. They must care about students' learning and development as unique human beings, citizens, and members of the academic community. They should ground their practice in sound theory and the findings of relevant research, but within the context of the dynamics, and sometimes conflicting, goals and values of higher education. Professionals should operate from a base of carefully considered values including an appreciation for individual worth and social justice.

These broad requirements for successful professional practice can be fully met only through the integration of theory, an understanding of research, a grounding in professional ethics and humanitarian values, and a full appreciation of the intricacies of higher education administration and organizational maintenance and change. This integration can best be realized by providing students opportunities to: (a) observe the daily activities of functional units within a higher education institution; (b) experience the details of administrative life in a structured, supervised context; (c) apply what has been learned in the classroom to real problems and situations; (d) receive candid feedback about performance; (e) receive emotional and tangible support as students experiment with new behaviors and acquire new knowledge; and (f) reflect on and make personal meaning from that experience.

WHAT'S IN A NAME?

From the time the authors began discussing this book, we have struggled to find an unambiguous and generally used term to describe the supervised practice experience in higher education. As we talked with colleagues, reviewed curriculum documents, and read student handbooks, we discovered that there is no generally accepted vocabulary to describe the supervised practice experience in student affairs professional preparation. *Internship, practicum, field observation,* and *fieldwork* are commonly used terms. Some institutions use *practicum* for master's level programs and *internship* for doctoral level programs, with the primary distinguishing feature being the level of the student. Other programs seem to use the terms interchangeably, reflecting perhaps some historical institutional vestiges, frequently for unknown or forgotten reasons. Still other programs use a single term to describe all supervised practice experiences.

Consequently, in this book *internship* is the generic term used to describe supervised practice in professional preparation no matter the level or location for which one receives academic credit. Readers at institutions that have different terminology will need to translate from this book to their local usage.

PURPOSES OF THE BOOK AND INTENDED AUDIENCE

This text has been developed primarily for students who are enrolled in internship courses at the master's level. It also should be useful for site and faculty supervisors and doctoral level interns. For master's level students, this type of experience typically represents a new approach to learning. By the time they get to graduate school, students know how to succeed in traditional classes. They are familiar with the learning that comes from attending lectures, completing class assignments, writing papers, and taking exams. The educational value of supervised experience, however, is somewhat elusive for many students. Making the connection between what has been learned in the classroom and what occurs in professional practice requires some new skills and understanding. It also requires more self-direction than may be required in more traditional classroom-based courses.

The intent of this book is to assist students in comprehending this approach to learning. First, the text describes the role of supervised learning in the curriculum so students gain an appreciation of the purpose of supervised experiences. The subsequent chapters are designed to help students construct an experience that contributes to their learning and professional development. They are prompted to consider practical issues such as working with supervisors and the legal liabilities they may face as practitioners. The chapter on learning and evaluation helps them make connections between theory and practice and enables them to identify learning outcomes and assess the degree to which they achieve those outcomes as a result of their experience.

Those who supervise graduate students in practice settings typically confront very different challenges from classroom-based teachers. These supervisors are in administrative roles, so they are familiar with the managerial tasks associated with such classes. However, they typically have been out of the classroom for a number of years and may not be as comfortable with the learning component of the class. They question how to promote learning and wonder about what kind of experiences lead to designated learning outcomes. These supervisors are constantly called upon to make decisions on what is appropriate and inappropriate for practicum/internship students to deal with and how to explain to students the history of issues and the politics of organizational life in such a way that confidences are respected and professional decorum is maintained. The material presented in this text is intended to assist site supervisors as they explore ways in which to make the experience more meaningful to students, as well as, contributory, or at least not distractive, to the ongoing operation of the administrative unit.

This text can prove useful to doctoral level students who need guidance or who did not receive a good internship experience during their master's programs. By using this book, they may be able to ascertain what went wrong previously and it can help them create a better learning experience during doctoral study. Furthermore, because many site supervisors—while well qualified to discharge their administrative responsibilities—may not have had the benefit of training in structuring and implementing internships, the intern may need to help them provide the needed experiences and assistance, something for which this book can perhaps be helpful.

KNOWLEDGE BASES

Several distinct knowledge bases form the foundations for this book. Theories and applications of experiential education and self-directed learning are essential to understanding and structuring the supervised practice experience. In addition, theories of college student psychosocial, intellectual, and moral development and theories of learning and pedagogy are essential to understanding college students' growth and learning. Theories of environmental influences and organizational functioning are also important to gaining an understanding of higher education as an organization and social entity. Finally, theories and models of organization development, human resource development, interpersonal facilitation, program development, needs assessment, program evaluation, and management techniques, are needed for successful professional practice in higher education administration. This text highlights these bodies of knowledge and focuses students' attention on how these somewhat distinct bodies of knowledge find application in the everyday operations of colleges and universities.

STRUCTURE AND CONTENTS OF THE BOOK

This text is designed to follow the logical stages experienced within the supervised practice experience, beginning with the foundation and rationale for the experience and ending with the final evaluation and departure from the site. As the means of addressing this goal, each chapter has two distinguishable features with different purposes. Each chapter contains instructive material based on established theory, research, and the authors' experiences as student affairs administrators and teachers. Interspersed within this material (enclosed in boxes) are questions and exercises intended to help students reflect on or personalize the material. These boxed sections can be thought of as worksheets or structured assignments written in the second person. Faculty or site supervisors may want to encourage interns to attend to these sections and to discuss their responses with others (such as fellow interns or supervisors).

Each chapter is briefly described below.

Chapter 1: Foundations of the Supervised Practice Experience: Definitions, Context, and Philosophy

This chapter introduces the concept of supervised practice as an important part of professional preparation for work in higher education settings. It provides historical and theoretical foundations for the experience, explores the multiple learning goals that may be pursued through this experience, and explains how this experience fits into the student's total program of study and possible career goals. Students are asked to (a) consider multiple conceptual views of supervised practice; (b) examine their experiences through the eyes of their supervisors and faculty members; and (c) note the presence and malleable effects of cultural dimensions of the work environment.

As a means of assisting students to understand the complexity of professional practice and the supervised practice experience, Creamer and Winston present a model of the integrated student affairs professional, which includes (a) applied knowledge; (b) theoretical knowledge; (c) practical and technical skills; (d) social and interpersonal skills; (e) professional ethics; (f) life experiences; and (g) personal and professional attitudes and values. Building on this model, they detail how supervised practice fits within the Council for the Advancement of Standards in Higher Education (CAS; Miller, 2001) standards for professional preparation of student affairs practitioners at the master's level, which leads to a definition of supervised practice and an explanation of how, through reflection, it contributes to the education of student affairs professionals. Students are further asked to engage in reflective learning with their site supervisors, student colleagues, and faculty supervisors.

Chapter 2: Structure and Design of the Supervised Practice Experience

This chapter by Hirt and Janosik is organized around six design principles: (a) assessment, (b) expectations, (c) goals, (d) structure, (e) resources, and (f) responsibility.

In the assessment segment, students are provided with guidance about how to assess the skills they currently possess and the skills they need to develop in order to succeed professionally. The text then describes ways to evaluate the different environments in which they might work on campus and the types of competencies that can be developed in those settings. In the expectations section, students are offered suggestions about strategies to assess the realism of their expectations. Guidance is proffered about how to determine what they can be expected to contribute in the setting, and what they can expect the setting to contribute to their learning. Through the development of a contract between the student and the site supervisor (with the approval of the faculty supervisor), students identify goals, establishing objectives that are linked to those goals, and estimating the time necessary to accomplish them. The chapter then identifies different pedagogical approaches that might be employed by faculty and site supervisors and explains the roles of the student in each of these approaches.

Next, students are informed about the resources they should expect to find in their work settings in terms of personnel, facilities, and equipment and the assets that students may need to bring to their settings. The chapter concludes with a discussion of the overall management of the internship. One example of the guidance provided to students discusses how to balance the responsibilities of the internship with the workload of other classes and outside responsibilities.

Chapter 3: Supervision: Relationships That Support Learning

More than any other single factor, the nature and quality of the relationship between the intern and the site supervisor usually determines the overall quality of the learning experience. A caring and honest relationship between the two can often overcome serious deficiencies in a site as a learning venue.

In this chapter, Winston and Creamer address both conceptual and practical aspects of this relationship. First, the realities of the site are explained; for example, sites do not exist exclusively for the purpose of educating interns. Second, characteristics and potential pitfalls of a good site supervision experience are enumerated and a developmental model to describe the optimum supervisory relationship is explained. Third, working with others, such as support staff and students, is discussed, and means of dealing with or avoiding potential problems are suggested. Fourth, the roles of the site supervisor and faculty supervisor are explained and distinguished. Finally, advice on troubleshooting the internship site is given to the student.

Chapter 4: Application of Theory in the Supervised Practice Experience

This chapter by Saunders and Cooper discusses theories and models that can be particularly useful in understanding student-clients and higher education organizations as students begin their internships. First, the focus is on the intern as learner; this is explicated by a discussion of experiential learning models, such as Astin (1984) and Kolb (1981), use of reflection journals, ways in which one can become constructively involved in the internship site, and conditions that foster effective learning through practice. Next, the chapter addresses the organization: its politics, structures, and ways that one can scan the environment and respond appropriately. Particular attention is focused on providing suggested ways by means of which interns can come to understand the organizational dynamics operating within the institution and how to influence, or at least avoid hazards (obvious and hidden), in dealing with them. Finally, the chapter focuses on process models that explain how theories work, and psychosocial and intellectual development theories, as well as the concepts of mattering and marginality (Rosenberg, 1979; Schlossberg, 1984). The chapter concludes with a discussion of cautions to be observed in applying theory to practice in the internship site.

Chapter 5: Legal and Ethical Issues

There is no escaping the fact that on a daily basis, every area of higher education faces issues of legal liability and legally mandated rules and regulations, as well as a multitude of ethical issues. It is through the internship site, contend Janosik and Hirt, that students can learn the practical consequences of these realities of administrative life in higher education.

This chapter instructs students about the potential liability they face while working in the settings and offers suggestions of ways to recognize and minimize it. Students are also guided through processes for evaluating the work setting's legal issues and parameters and for initiating investigations of how the institution has chosen to respond. Professional ethical standards are introduced, and students are offered strategies for identifying ethical issues in their own conduct, the conduct of others in the setting, and in institutional policy and procedures.

Chapter 6: Evaluating the Supervised Practice Experience

Evaluating supervised practice provides students with the feedback necessary for their personal and professional development. For many, this will be their first work experience in higher education. Students need to take an active role in the evaluation of the: (a) actual site; (b) supervision received at the site; (c) supervision received by the faculty member; and (d) their own performance.

Students need to receive evaluative information throughout the supervised practice experience. In this chapter, Cooper and Saunders focus on how students should approach this process. Methods are offered to interns so that they can constructively reflect on their experience, review their desired outcomes and actual results, and articulate how they will use the insights and skills gained in the supervised practice in their future role as an administrator in higher education. Learning to receive and give proper feedback provides them with important skills to use in their personal and professional development.

Ending the supervised practice experience can be an anxiety-provoking time for some students. Close relationships have often formed between them and workplace colleagues and must now be modified. Projects assigned as part of the supervised practice experience must now be completed or appropriately passed on to the new person responsible. In addition, students in sites serving clients must learn how to properly terminate those relationships.

Finally, students need to learn how to give appropriate feedback to supervisors about the supervised experience. Both site and faculty supervisors need to receive an evaluation from the student that will help improve the relationship for students in the future.

ACKNOWLEDGMENTS

All six of the authors contributed to conceptualizing the project and to supplying ideas and suggestions to all chapters. Each chapter, however, is the work of a pair of authors. We have done our best to integrate the materials and to keep duplication to a minimum. This book was a true collaborative effort. To the best of our knowledge, this is the first comprehensive, nationally available text specifically addressing supervised administrative practice in higher education settings.

Finally, we would like to thank our many students through the years who have taught us much more than they sometimes realized and who helped us help them become contributing professionals. We also wish to acknowledge the many higher education administrators who as site supervisors made time in their busy work lives to accept interns and teach them how to be effective student affairs professionals.

Diane L. Cooper
Sue A. Saunders
Roger B. Winston, Jr.
Joan B. Hirt
Don G. Creamer
Steven M. Janosik

REFERENCES

Astin, A. W. (1984). Student involvement: A developmental theory for higher education. *Journal of College Student Personnel, 25,* 297–308.

Boylan, J. C., Malley, P. B., & Reilly, E. P. (2001). *Practicum and internship: Textbook and resource guide for counseling and psychotherapy.* New York: Brunner-Routledge.

Dewey, J. (1916). *Democracy and education: An introduction to the philosophy of education.* New York: Macmillan.

Chiaferi, R., & Griffin, M. (1997). *Developing fieldwork skills: A guide for human services, counseling, and social work students.* Pacific Grove, CA: Brooks/Cole .

Kiser, P. M. (2000). *Getting the most from your human services internship: Learning from experience.* Belmont, CA: Wadsworth/Thomson Learning.

Kolb, D. A. (1981). Learning styles and disciplinary differences. In A. W. Chickering (Ed.), *Modern American college: Responding to the new realities of diverse students and a changing society* (pp. 232–255). San Francisco: Jossey-Bass.

Miller, T. K. (Ed.). (2001). *CAS: The book of professional standards for higher education.* Washington, DC: Council for the Advancement of Standards in Higher Education.

Rosenberg, M. (1979). *Conceiving the self.* New York: Basic Books.

Schlossberg, N. K. (1984). *Counseling adults in transition.* New York: Springer.

Winston, R. B., Jr. (1996). Counseling and advising. In S. Komives & D. D. Woodard, Jr. (Eds.), *Student services: A handbook for the profession* (3rd ed., pp. 335–360). San Francisco: Jossey-Bass.

Chapter 1

FOUNDATIONS OF THE SUPERVISED PRACTICE EXPERIENCE
Definitions, Context, and Philosophy

Don G. Creamer
Roger B. Winston, Jr.

Looking from the outside in, higher education in the United States appears to be a paradox, wrapped in ambiguity, and influenced by shifting, sometimes contradictory internal and external social and economic forces and educational philosophies. Unlike most of the world, in the United States there is no national higher education authority that determines mission, sets policy, promulgates standards, dictates organizational structure, or allocates resources. For public institutions those functions are primarily fulfilled by the states. A variety of board structures govern higher education, ranging from a single state board for all institutions, within the state to separate boards for individual colleges and universities to boards for categories of institutions, such as research universities, regional colleges, and community colleges. For private institutions those responsibilities are discharged by governing boards of private citizens who may or may not be affiliated with a sponsoring organization such as a religious entity.

Because of the unique U.S. educational system of strong, relatively autonomous public and private colleges and universities, one of the few things that can be said with certainty is that there is scant constancy in the higher education cosmos. For virtually any practice that *appears* universally applicable in higher education, one can find an exception. Likewise, there is no *standard* organizational structure in higher education. Consequently, one may find student affairs divisions that encompass only three or four functional areas and others that may include as many as 20 or more. The senior student affairs administrator may be known as a *dean, vice president, associate provost, director,* or *coordinator* (to name only a few titles). She or he may report directly to the president and be a part of the executive cabinet or may be several administrative levels removed and considered a midlevel manager.

Student affairs practitioners may hold master's or doctoral degrees in disciplines directly related to fulfilling the mission of student affairs and may be intimately involved in the work of the field's professional associations, or they may hold advanced degrees in any field from Russian literature to quantum physics. In rare instances they may possess no graduate degree at all. They may or may not be associated with student affairs or higher educational professional associations. Student affairs may be thought of as central to the educational mission of the institution or may be seen as ancillary or peripheral in a category analogous to parking services—necessary, but of little educational consequence. Because of this wide diversity, which can never be entirely captured in textbooks, in-the-field experience is essential if professionals in training and neophyte practitioners are to acquire the basic knowledge and skills needed to function successfully in student affairs.

In this chapter, we provide an overview of the supervised practice experience and lay theoretical foundations for its implementation. First, we present a model of an integrated student affairs practitioner. It is important for students to have a clear conception about what professional preparation programs are trying to produce. Next, we present a broad sketch of the types and approaches to professional preparation in student affairs that are currently offered. The supervised practice experience is analyzed from several different perspectives—including elucidation of types of internships and kinds of applied learning. Finally, we present a model of the internship experience and relate it to the practicalities of the internship experience.

THE INTEGRATED STUDENT AFFAIRS PRACTITIONER

Student affairs practitioners are expected to fulfill a variety of roles within their institutions; paramount among the roles are educator, leader, and manager (Creamer, Winston, & Miller, 2001). These roles carry with them certain values, a need for knowledge, ethical strictures, applied knowledge, and skills that enable professionals to facilitate formal and informal processes of learning in higher education. Such professionals may be seen as combination educators who are well grounded in liberal or general education yet not firmly fixed on any single discipline as a way of knowing and inquiring. They are administrators yet their principal purposes are accomplished largely through out of class teaching. They are humanists who seek the full release of human potential in the people with whom they work, yet they are managers of resources and of people who must maximize institutional as well as individual efforts. All of these courses of action must be conducted in an ethical environment where all educational activities are firmly and directly targeted to achieve the most basic purposes of education: individual and community development.

Figure 1.1, which derives from the authors' experiences, depicts the comprehensive nature of knowledge, skills, attitudes, experience, ethics, and values that are required of the fully functional professional in student affairs. A quick survey of them makes it obvious why it would be difficult to acquire all of them *after* taking a job. That is why most graduate preparation

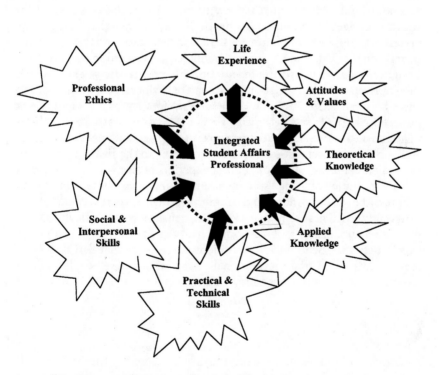

FIGURE 1.1. Model of the Integrated Student Affairs Professional.

programs intentionally include all of these elements in their curriculum.

To be a fully functional and integrated student affairs professional, one must bring together a wide array of knowledge, skills, and experience. These are also the areas to which students should attend while in their supervised practice experiences.

Figure 1.1 identifies seven large clusters needed for successful practice. In no particular hierarchy, they include: life experiences, attitudes and values, theoretical knowledge, applied knowledge, practical and technical skills, social and interpersonal skills, and professional ethics.

LIFE EXPERIENCE

Fried (1995) argued that America, higher education, and student affairs must undergo a paradigm shift to be able to comprehend a multicultural world. She pointed out that America's cultural lenses are shaped by cultural norms and values that place great importance on (a) "emotional control, individual autonomy, and achievement; (b) the written word over the spoken word; (c) youth over age; (d) an emphasis on the future rather than the past or present; . . . (e) the right of humans to dominate nature; and (f) monotheistic religion" (p. 10). The American paradigm also is rooted in the European Enlightenment that laid the foundation for positivistic science, which "downplayed the role of emotions in human behavior and the value of differences between people" (p. 11). Who one is shapes one as a student affairs professional; that is, one's ethnicity, gender, sexual orientation, religious affiliation and practice, physical appearance, upbringing, and other experiences and personal characteristics. One does not come to the field a tabula rasa; the individual brings all his or her past experiences (as interpreted by one's culture) to the job of being a student affairs professional. Certain life experiences assist in understanding and communicating with certain kinds of students and staff. These same experiences also make it more difficult to work with others because of a lack of commonality or deficit in certain kinds of experiences and the implicit assumptions made about that deficit. It is essential that student affairs professionals engage in careful self-exploration to identify their cultural biases and frames of reference.

Attitudes and Values

As noted, one's values are influenced to a large degree by one's culture. All cultural institutions have certain implicit and explicit values embedded within them. Young (1993) reviewed historic documents that advanced a philosophy for the field and conducted a survey of practitioners (Young & Elfrink, 1991) to identify the fundamental values of the student affairs profession. Four broad categories were identified:

- Human dignity, which is functionally defined as the inherent worth and uniqueness of individuals;
- Freedom, which is linked with responsibility (freedom must be disciplined), altruism (the worth of the student affairs professional is determined by her or his sincere and intelligent interest in individual students and ability to respect the student's fundamental right to reject or disregard the professional's attempts to be helpful), and truth (expressed through candor and findings derived from research on students and the learning process);
- Equity (which in the early days of the profession emphasized holistic education of the student that recognized the significance of personal development in addition to intellectual development; later in the 1960s the concept of equity was extended to civil rights for all people, including students, without regard to race, sex, religion, or national origin);
- Community, which Esther Lloyd-Jones (1989) elucidated well when she wrote: "The condition of community is the binding together of individuals toward a common cause or experience. Individuals both enlarge and restrict their freedoms by joining such a community. But whatever restriction results is far surpassed by the individual's and the group's ability to achieve established goals while at the same time creating mutual support and pride" (pp. 2–3). Justice is also related to community. Young (1993) explained that "Students need just treatment in order to be empowered by the college" (p. 11).

An attitude may be thought of as a manner of acting, feeling, or thinking that shows one's disposition, opinion, or mental set. The late legendary Dean of Men at the University of Georgia, William Tate, was fond of saying that "working with a boy who refuses to try is like going hunting and having to carry the dog." By that he meant that a student with a poor attitude was difficult, if not impossible, to help. Poor or negative attitudes by staff members are equally problematic. Staff members who have positive, enthusiastic, cooperative, and responsive attitudes accomplish much more than those with negative and oppositional attitudes, and are much more enjoyable to work with and be around. Disgruntled staff members are not only generally ineffective, they can also infect coworkers to the extent that they too no longer put forth maximum effort. Probably one of the most problematic attitudes to deal with is the passive–aggressive staff member or student. Because they cannot or will not verbalize their discontent or opposition to persons in positions of authority who have the power to effect change, they become disruptive forces that undermine programs and services intended to provide help.

Students in an internship setting need to be careful not to allow discontented staff or students to interfere with their relationship with the unit supervisor or to diminish their ability to take advantage of learning opportunities. Students should enter the site with a positive, goal-oriented attitude and take precautions to maintain that attitude.

Theoretical Knowledge

One of the defining characteristics of a profession is the existence of a body of knowledge that informs and guides what practitioners do. As Argyris and Schön (1974) observed, theories are vehicles for explanation, prediction, or control. An explanatory theory explains events by setting forth propositions from which these events may be inferred; a predictive theory sets forth propositions from which inferences about future events may be made; and a theory of control describes the conditions under which events of a certain kind may be made to occur. The CAS standards (Miller, 2001) for professional preparation specify a number of areas in which students should have a command of theories, including student development; individual, group, and organizational diagnosis and intervention; assessment, evaluation, and measurement; and behavior change and learning.

An important area about which all student affairs professionals must be knowledgeable is the law. Although one need not be an attorney, competent practitioners must be knowledgeable about current laws and regulations that govern the operation of higher education institutions and the ever-evolving case law that interprets statutes and regulations. They also must adjust their practice to conform to the law.

Theoretical knowledge is acquired through reading the literature and through conducting research that tests theories. Student affairs professionals have both an obligation to be informed about theory and a responsibility to contribute to the advancement of knowledge through conducting rigorous research and evaluations of theory-based interventions. They also have an additional responsibility to share the results of their investigations with others through the publication of findings.

Applied Knowledge

Applied knowledge comes through experimentation and repetition. It comes about through the application of theoretical understanding and practice. For instance, one can study the physical dynamics involved in riding a bicycle, but the first time one attempts to mount and ride a bicycle the experience is somewhat frightening when the "rider" discovers the difficulty of maintaining balance, steering, and pedaling simultaneously. With practice, under a variety of conditions and terrains, one acquires an applied knowledge that enables one to navigate in difficult circumstances with little conscious thought about the physical dynamics of riding a bicycle. Through practice and careful attention to detail, bike riding eventually becomes second nature.

Applied knowledge in student affairs is acquired through extensive contact with students within an academic context while discharging one's responsibilities as an institutional agent. When this experience is combined with an understanding of the developmental processes experienced by students and theories of organization and management, the student affairs practitioner is able to contribute to students' academic and personal growth and to the institution's organizational effectiveness.

Argyris and Schön (1974), Schön (1987), and Argyris, Putnam, and Smith (1985) term this theories-in-use. "When you know what to do in a given situation in order to achieve an intended consequence, you know what the theory-in-use for that situation is. You know the nature of the consequence to be attained, you know the action appropriate in the situation to attain it, and you know the assumptions contained in the theory" (Argyris & Schön, 1974, p. 7). It includes one's espoused theory of action (often based on research findings and research-based theories) and one's informal theory of action, which includes assumptions about "self, others, the situation, and the connections among action, consequence, and situation" (p. 7).

Practical and Technical Skills

Student affairs practitioners are expected to possess a wide array of skills, some of which are acquired directly through professional preparation and others that are acquired prior to beginning a professional preparation program. Examples of some technical skills that today's student affairs professional is expected to possess include, computer skills (such as use of word processing and spreadsheet programs, e-mail, and web page construction), program intervention design, group leadership, active listening, goal setting, needs assessment, program evaluation, and use of pedagogical devices. Other skills may be acquired through informal means and include, for instance, how to run a meeting, recruit student participation, create flyers, devise publicity campaigns, and negotiate fees for services with tradespeople. Many of the latter skills may have been acquired while functioning as a student or community leader.

Through observation of practitioners and through assuming responsibility for tasks, projects, and activities associated with the ongoing operation of the site, students have multiple opportunities to acquire technical and practical skills needed to become a fully functional student affairs professional.

SOCIAL AND INTERPERSONAL SKILLS

Most successful student affairs professionals possess good people skills; that is, they are able to communicate effectively and to build harmonious, amicable, cooperative relationships with students and people in general. Most student affairs practitioners bring well-developed social and interpersonal skills with them to the field. They also possess basic personality characteristics that attract them to working with others and have a desire to be of service. Through training, education, and practice, students can sharpen their interpersonal skills and build effective counseling skills; but they must already possess a desire to be helpful and have the ability to convey empathy, respect, and personal warmth in their interactions with others before entering professional preparation.

Sandeen (1991), in discussing the chief student affairs officer (CSAO), argued that successful CSAOs must establish trusting relationships with students, which he maintained is accomplished by (1) being honest; (2) demonstrating personal concern; (3) involving students in policy decisions; (4) following through on programs; (5) maintaining confidences; and (6) setting a good example. We maintain that this is true for practitioners at all levels.

PROFESSIONAL ETHICS

Student affairs practitioners are faced daily with situations that involve conflicting personal interests, values, belief systems, and goals. Practitioners must determine what is "right" or what "ought to be done" within legal and institutional policy parameters. "Ethical beliefs and belief systems are intended to serve as guides to action in confusing and difficult circumstances" (Fried, 1997, p. 5). Thus, professional ethics serve to sensitize student affairs professionals to circumstances that have a high probability of producing ambiguous situations in which the "right" course of action is unclear. In a few instances, ethical standards statements provide explicit strictures about behavior or actions to eschew, but in most instances the standards serve to remind practitioners about the profession's moral principles, such as *do no harm* and *act to promote justice.* Ethical standards are based on (1) maximum competence; (2) lack of self-interest as a motivator; (3) colleague relationships characterized as cooperative, egalitarian, and supportive; and (4) freely sharing new information with colleagues, rather than using it to gain a competitive advantage as is true in commercial enterprises (Greenwood, 1957; Winston & Saunders, 1991). Because of the overriding concern regarding the appropriate application of moral principles in student affairs practice, ethical issues are discussed more fully in chapter 5.

The internship experience allows students the opportunity to observe situations that have moral import and to see how practitioners deal with, or perhaps fail to deal with them. During the internship experience, students may also find themselves involved during activities in which they must analyze and determine the appropriate course of ethical action.

---

*ℛ*eflection *𝒫*oint

- What attributes of the fully functional, integrated professional appear most vital to you? Why? Put them into a rank order list based on your beliefs and values.
- Should some of these essential attributes be developed before others? What is your reasoning?
- What are the likely consequences of action not grounded in a clear sense of values?
- In what ways might cultural background influence the way an individual sees others—perhaps, for example, who is seen to be easy and who is seen to be difficult to work with?
- How do attitudes affect practice? How can one confront examples of "poor attitudes" without invading a student's or staff member's personal privacy?

GRADUATE PROFESSIONAL PREPARATION

There are multiple approaches to graduate professional preparation. Approaches used in most student affairs preparation programs, however, almost always include supervised practice (Winston et al., 2001). The context for this practice will be disclosed here.

Work in student affairs is different from holding administrative positions in most other areas of leadership within colleges and universities. For example, in academic affairs positions the customary career route is (1) obtain a terminal degree in an academic discipline (e.g., English, biology, engineering, or education, the field of study is unimportant); (2) teach in the academic field and distinguish one's self as competent; (3) show interest and/ or ability in administration and be selected for either a part-time or full-time administrative post (frequently, academic department head). If one proves adept at performing the tasks assigned and wishes to pursue an alternative career to teaching or research, then the academic administrator career ladder can lead to positions of increasing responsibility (such as college dean or division director, assistant provost, or vice president) and ultimately to being a college or university president.

On the other hand, most practitioners in student affairs envision a different kind of career ladder that typically entails (1) completing a master's degree in a student affairs professional preparation program; (2) working in an entry-level student affairs position and showing success in performing assigned responsibilities; (3) after 3 to 5 years of successful entry-level work experience, moving to a midlevel management position or enrolling in a doctoral program in student affairs administration, higher education, or counseling/counseling psychology; (4) continuing through positions of increasing responsibility, such as department head in areas such as housing, student activities, or career services, perhaps to assistant/associate vice president or dean, and ultimately to vice president or dean for student affairs. Student affairs practitioners' vision of appropriate preparation and relevant experience for positions of senior leadership sometimes collides with the experience of academic administrators who reached their current positions through on-the-job training (OJT). They reason that if OJT was adequate for becoming knowledgeable, effective academic administrators, why is student affairs any different? They fail to appreciate fully student affairs administrators' arguments about the need for specialized professional preparation and capacious work experience in student affairs (Blimling, 1993, 2000).

Preparation Programs

Graduate preparation programs generally assume the task of formally preparing student affairs practitioners to enter the field. Student affairs preparation can be seen as professional education in a larger sense. Hoberman and Mailick (1994) assert that:

[P]rofessional education is directed toward helping students acquire special competencies for diagnosing specific needs and for determining, recommending, and taking appropriate action. Professional education is also expected to socialize students in the 'thought processes' of the profession and to inculcate them with its customs, ethics, working relationships, and the behaviors expected from members of the profession. (pp. 3–4)

Student affairs clearly is part of the applied sector of professional education rather than research-oriented sectors and, as such, seeks to "adapt and use the theory and techniques developed [in the research-oriented sector] for the purpose of providing services for people and organizations" (Hoberman & Mailick, 1994, p. 9).

Professional education may be distinguished from professional training in a number of ways. The goal of professional education is to assist students in (1) acquiring necessary background knowledge; (2) devising and critically evaluating theories; (3) developing the analytical skills needed to diagnosis situations and people; (4) devising strategies for applying theories appropriate to the situation and people involved; and (5) conducting research that tests theories upon which professional practice is based.

Professional training, on the other hand, is much more limited in scope. Its purpose is to instruct students in the application of predetermined or preestablished strategies, interventions, or programs. The difference between education and training can be illustrated with the example of learning to drive an automobile. First, one must learn the mechanics of how to operate the vehicle and to coordinate manual activities, awareness of one's surroundings, and awareness of applicable traffic laws and regulations. After having been trained to operate a car, one can then use that information combined with goals to actually make a trip. Making a trip is much more complicated than just learning to operate a car. In the course of reaching one's destination, the driver must be aware of operating his or her vehicle, but must also be aware of other drivers, pedestrians, road conditions, weather, traffic signals and signs, and perhaps the passenger. Successful professional practitioners need both training and education to fulfill their responsibilities within an institution.

This book is concerned mainly with the experience component of graduate preparation programs. Experience as a part of a professional preparation incorporates all the other aspects of the *integrated student affairs professional*. It is through the practical experience component of preparation that students are able to observe the attitudes, skills, knowledge, and values that successful professional practitioners incorporate into their work lives. This component of the curriculum is referred to as *supervised practice, supervised experience*, or simply the *internship*. We will use these terms to mean experiences purposefully provided in the program to meet specific aims that are supervised by both a faculty member in the preparation program and by an on-site practitioner who has direct oversight of the duties being performed by the student.

Scientist-Practitioner Model

Many professional preparation programs in the helping fields such as counseling, psychology, and social work are based on the scientist–practitioner model (Schroeder & Pike, 2001). This model asserts that professional practitioners have dual responsibilities, to the client and to the field or profession. If one accepts the argument that in order to qualify as a profession, practitioners must base their work on sound, well-tested theories, then practitioners have an ethical obligation to contribute to the advancement of knowledge within the field. If the client is defined as either students or higher education organizations or both, then student affairs professionals, in the course of regular practice, should both remain informed about theoretical developments in the field and be involved in ongoing programs of research that test accepted theories, resulting in the modification of theories or development of new ones.

If one accepts the scientist–practitioner model of professional practice, then professional preparation programs must assist students in acquiring theoretical knowledge, application experience, and research skills.

---

*ℛ*eflection *𝒫*oint
- The scientist–practitioner model of graduate preparation places application experience squarely in the mix of education for theoretical knowledge and research skills. What is the best balance between these three essential areas of learning? On what do you base your answer?
- Not all student affairs practitioners subscribe to the scientist–practitioner model. Some view it as all practice (application of common sense and learning by trial and error) with little regard for theory or research. Does this approach make sense to you? If this view is accepted, what then would be the best preparation for work in student affairs?

Just as there is no universally accepted understanding about the nature and scope of student affairs within institutions, there is wide variety among preparation programs.

Variations among Preparation Programs

Within student affairs preparation programs, there is considerable difference in orientation, intensity, and breadth. Program orientation is determined to a certain extent by the academic department within which the program resides. Most commonly, programs are housed in one of three departments: counseling or educational psychology, educational leadership and policy studies, or higher education, and perhaps adult education. (The exact configuration of programs within departments varies considerably depending on the size of the college of education, the degree to which programs other than K through 12 teacher education are supported, and an institution's historical development.) One may not necessarily infer that the content of a program's curriculum is based on the department within which it resides. From our observation, there are three general approaches taken to curriculum: student affairs as a stand-alone program; student affairs as a concentration or major within a broader program; and student affairs as a minor emphasis within a broader program.

In stand-alone programs, student affairs is viewed as the central focus of the program; most courses (at least two-thirds) are designed specifically for students preparing to enter the professional practice of student affairs. The curriculum in these programs differs considerably from that offered to students in other programs within the same department. Practicum and internship courses are exclusively for students in the student affairs program and are always in student affairs settings in postsecondary institutions.

In programs where student affairs is a concentration, about one-third to one-half of the courses are specific to student affairs theory and practice; the remainder of the courses are generally focused on counseling, general educational administration, or higher education administration and history. Usually, there are practicum and internship courses specifically designed for student affairs settings. Often students are required to have a cognate outside the department (e.g., in sociology, psychology, or business).

In programs where student affairs is a minor concentration, the bulk of the courses in a student's program of study do not focus specifically on student affairs or college students. Generally, courses particular to student affairs theory and practice number no more than three or four; there may or may not be practicum or internships specific to the student affairs "program."

Standards for Master's Level Preparation

Consensus has been sought for more than a quarter century on essential requirements for student affairs preparation. Some historical perspective on this provides a foundation for later explicit development of preparation standards by Council for the Advancement of Standards in Higher Education (CAS).

Historical Development of Standards

Delworth and Hanson (1980) provide a good example of historic proposals for graduate preparation programs. In their view, the core components of a comprehensive curriculum in student affairs were:

- *History* (of higher education and student affairs) and *Philosophy* (of education)
- *Theory* (of human development and person–environment interaction)
- *Models of Practice and Role Orientations* (patterns of organization and ethics)
- *Core Competencies* (including counseling, assessment and evaluation, consultation, and instruction)
- *Specialized Competencies* (including program development, environmental assessment and redesign, and paraprofessional training)
- *Administration and Management* (management tools)
- *Practicum or Field Work* (including practical experience, supervision, reflection, integration of academic and practical experiences)
- *Additional Theory and Tool Courses* (e.g., behavioral science, management, social learning theory)

Other views, such as those advocated in an early publication devoted to describing experimental graduate preparation programs (Knock, 1977), also expressed strong support for an experiential component of student affairs preparation. Greenleaf (1977), for example, calls for practice skills in management, counseling, and other student affairs responsibilities. In brief, these proposals are similar in their structure for recommended preparation of higher education and student affairs professionals and always include supervised practice as a main component of the process. All of these proposals and programs tend to include three components: foundation studies, professional studies, and application of learning (McGlothlin, 1964). This application of learning component is sometimes referred to in different language, such as was found in Creamer and Shelton (1988) in their synthesis of literature about preservice education programs for the field. Their study pointed to the goal of preparing scientist-practitioners in graduate preparation programs. Achieving this balance naturally requires a significant experiential learning component in the preparation programs.

CAS Standards

The most recent and universally accepted standard for providing supervised experiences in graduate preparation programs in student affairs can be found in the standards and guidelines of the Council for the Advancement of Standards in Higher Education (Miller, 2001), which promulgates standards and guidelines for practices in higher education. Practices such as academic advising, new student orientation, career development, housing and residential programs, and campus activities are examples of functional areas of student affairs for which CAS has written standards and guidelines in close consultation with affiliated professional associations of the respective functional areas. CAS also has prepared standards and guidelines for master's level preparation of student affairs professionals.

CAS operates on a philosophy of self-regulation and self-assessment. It is not an accrediting agency; rather, it is a consortium comprised of representatives of professional associations in higher education. These representatives promulgate and then maintain standards and guidelines for practices in approximately 30 different areas of service provided in higher education institutions. Standards and guidelines are prepared using a collaboration model wherein the representatives write the standards and guidelines in consultation with many colleagues in a professional association, then collaborate with all other association representatives to eventually agree on the standards and guidelines that will be published by CAS. Following publication, functional areas of service in higher education can voluntarily use the materials for program assessment and improvement.

The CAS standards and guidelines for master's level preparation of student affairs professionals include three curricular components—foundation studies, professional studies, and supervised practice. It is instructive to examine the CAS standard for a student affairs preparation curriculum:

> All programs of study must include the three components of (1) Foundational Studies, (2) Professional Studies, and (3) Supervised Practice. Foundational Studies must include the study of the foundations of higher education and student affairs. Professional Studies must include the five related areas of (a) Student Development Theory, (b) Student Characteristics and Effects of College on Students, (c) Individual and Group

Interventions, (d) Organization and Administration of Student Affairs, and (e) Assessment, Evaluation, and Research. Supervised Practice must include practica and/or internships consisting of supervised work involving at least two distinct experiences. Demonstration of minimum knowledge in each area is required of all program graduates. (Miller, 1997, p. 174)

In the guidelines associated with the supervised practice standard, curriculum designers are advised that, "One of the purposes of supervised practice is to add both breadth and depth to the student's professional experience" (Miller, 1997, p. 175). These experiences should include opportunities for direct work with students, program planning, implementation, and evaluation, staff training, and administrative functions associated with the areas of supervised experience. The guidelines continue by encouraging exposure to diverse settings and clientele, and, as was noted in the standard, suggesting that experiences should be carried out in at least two distinct settings.

A representation of graduate preparation programs using the CAS standards and guidelines can be seen in Figure 1.2. At the heart of the CAS recommendations for supervised practice in preparation programs is

Foundation Studies	Professional Studies	Supervised Practice
• History • Philosophy • Psychology • Anthropology • Sociology • Research methods	• Student development theory • Student characteristics and effects of college on students • Individual, group, and organizational interventions • Assessment, evaluation, and research strategies and techniques	• 300 hours of supervised practice consisting of at least two distinct experiences • On-site supervision • Prepration of students for supervised practice • Compliance with ethical standards

Professional Practices and Standards; Institutional Mission; Curriculum Policies

FIGURE 1.2. CAS Standards: Elements of a Masters' Level Curriculum for Student Affairs Professionals.

opportunity for translation of academic knowledge into practical tools, receiving supervision, and instruction in ethics of the profession.

$\mathscr{R}$eflection $\mathscr{P}$oint

- Does the structure of the CAS standards and guidelines for master's level preparation in student affairs—foundation studies, professional studies, and supervised practice—adequately mirror the scientist–practitioner model of graduate preparation? Where might there be differences or omissions?
- Should more or different kinds of practica be included in these graduate education programs? Why?
- If, in your view, there is insufficient supervised practice experience available in your program of study, what can you do?

Supervised Practice

Supervised practice experiences are called many things. They often are called *practica* (courses emphasizing the practical application of theory in which a student gains on-the-job experience) or *internships* (practical experiences of serving as an intern under the supervision of a seasoned practitioner). They sometimes are called *field experiences, externships, shadowing programs,* or *work-study* programs. In other fields generally outside of higher education, these training experiences might likely be called *apprenticeships* and would be associated with preparation for trades or crafts and often are legally required in order to join trade union organizations. Supervised experience in graduate preparation programs in student affairs on the other hand are obligatory only in the context of program curriculum policies, common sense about professional requirements, and sometimes specialized program accreditation that is either mandated or self-imposed. In any form, supervised practice in these preparation programs generally is included to help professionals in training prepare themselves fully for the work that will be required of them on the job. In this book, we are somewhat arbitrarily calling these applied experiences *internships*, even though they may be known by many other names.

"Training and preparation for professional practice, historically and continuing to this day, are rooted both in experience and practice (an apprenticeship model) and in formal graduate work" (McEwen & Talbot, 1998, p. 127). In fact, until the 1960s and 1970s, most preparation for practice in student affairs was conducted on the job. New staff members assigned to duties in student affairs learned their responsibilities from more experienced staff or through processes of trial- and-error or imitation of others. This situation has changed dramatically since the mid-1970s.

Educational benefits of supervised practices, such as practica or internships, have long been recognized in education. They are, in fact, a subset of an educational concept called *experiential education*. Scannell and Simpson (1996) hold that:

> [The purpose of such experiences as a part of formal education is] to encourage more understanding, interests, and participation in . . . [appropriate functional units] to observe operating processes; to undertake extensive research; and to gain knowledge of relationships between theory and practice. Successful internships are most often based in and administered by academic departments, strongly supported centrally with requirements linked to the academic enterprise. (p. 18)

In addition to the direct educational benefits of supervised practice, Scannell and Simpson assert that students who participate in such activities during their formal education are more attractive candidates for employment and are more likely to be satisfied with work in the field.

Engaging in supervised practice in graduate preparation programs is an intentional effort to infuse experience into formal education, a component absolutely essential to quality learning, according to Dewey (1916), one of education's most influential philosophers. Dewey believed that learning was enhanced by experience, a doing or practice component, and by thinking, an active and a cognitive component. "When we experience something we act upon it, we do something with it; then we suffer or undergo the consequences. We do something to the thing and then it does something to us in return" (Dewey, 1916, p. 163). There is reciprocation in doing; it reinforces cognitive learning and makes the experience complete and meaningful. Experience is an organizing force for all learning, according to Dewey, and is most effective when it is self-directed, guided by theory, and includes reflection. Other educators who have demonstrated the effectiveness of experiential learning, such as Hutchings and Wutzdorff (1988, p. 3) of Alverno College, have synthesized major learning issues from their work and from the work of educational theorists. In their view:

- Learning must be active, involving, engaging.
- Learning involves not only the cognitive but also other dimensions.
- Knowing and doing must be pursued together in an ongoing integrative way, whereby each activity redefines and transforms the other.
- Self-reflection, or examination of oneself as a learner, is crucial to linking knowing and doing.

- Learning by experience is a concept that must permeate the curriculum in a systematic and developmental way.

These issues serve to justify the use of supervised practice in graduate preparation programs such as student affairs. They are organizing principles for insuring effective learning.

Kinds of Internships

In the area of student affairs, there are two distinctly different kinds of practical experiences—administrative and counseling/therapy. Even though both kinds of internships share common goals in terms of the integration of theory and practice, they differ in a number of significant ways. The most obvious difference relates to the kinds of activities in which students are expected to engage. In a counseling/therapy internship, students see clients (individually or in small groups) and engage in activities designed to assist individuals in identifying and solving personal problems and changing behaviors, attitudes, or beliefs. In an administrative internship, students' focus is more on the organization, administration, and operation of programs or services. The theoretical base in a counseling internship comes primarily from psychology and counseling. In an administrative internship, the theory based is broader, drawing from the disciplines of sociology, social psychology, anthropology, and management and from theories of organization development, leadership, student development, learning, and person–environmental interaction. A counseling internship requires close supervision involving audio and/or videotapes of interactions with clients; an administrative internship does not require such minute supervision and generally does not require a critique of tapes.

In this book, we are concerned with the administrative type internship only. Programs that are counseling based or require a counseling internship are best served by using one of the well-established models for the counseling or psychotherapy applied experience (e.g., Boylan, Malley, & Reilly, 2001; Chiaferi, R. & Griffin, M.,1997; Kiser, 2000). .

Levels of Applied Learning Experiences

There are many different types of applied learning in which students may engage. They may be classified by the amount of purposive learning that is likely to occur and is directly determined by the intensity of involvement and psychic engagement required of the student. In the context of student affairs, we have identified five levels of experience resulting in increasingly rich opportunities for purposive, applied learning.

The levels are cumulative in that each successive level incorporates and supersedes the levels below it. As one moves from level 1 to level 5, the potential amount of purposeful, applied learning increases. Successive levels are distinguished by increased (1) amounts of personal investment required of the learner; (2) amounts of individual responsibility assumed; (3) levels of sophistication utilized in applying theory and professional knowledge; and (4) emphasis on personal reflection and integration and application of theory (see Figure 1.3).

Level 1

Level 1 is made up of experiences such as field observations and job shadowing. Field observations are events, usually relatively short in duration, that permit students to observe practitioners performing in their usual work set-

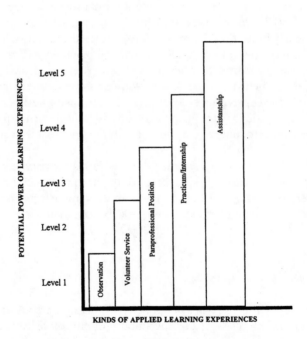

FIGURE 1.3. Kinds of Applied Learning Experiences.

ting. These events may range from a visit to a campus by a whole class to meet with student affairs practitioners, to individual visits to functional areas for interviews or short-term observations as a class assignment.

In job shadowing, the student spends extended periods of time (1–3 days usually) with one or two practitioners as they perform their usual duties. In a sense, students are allowed to see a "day in the life of" an activities advisor, or career counselor, or admissions director.

At level 1, students learn vicariously. They observe what is going on and are permitted to ask questions to gain a better understanding of what they have seen. They also have the opportunity to visualize themselves working as professionals in the setting.

Level 2

Level 2 requires more active involvement by students than at level 1. The kinds of experiences that comprise level 2 include volunteer services and student leadership experiences. Examples of volunteer services include supporting philanthropic causes such as working at a homeless shelter or soup kitchen, visiting residents of a nursing home, raising money for a charity, providing service to the college or university by being an usher at graduation, leading campus tours for prospective students and their families, or working on telephone banks to raise money from alumni for a capital campaign.

Another kind of experience at this level is filling leadership positions in student or community organizations that require the organization and delivery of programs or services to others. These activities may range from membership on student programming boards, residence hall associations, or religious groups, to leadership in social or service fraternities or sororities. The principal goals of activities at this level are accomplishment of the objectives of the organization or program; individual learning of participant-leaders is often secondary to "getting the job done." Valuable learning may occur while involved in these kinds of activities, but learning is frequently secondary unless there are mechanisms in place for giving students critical, constructive feedback and processing of the experience.

Level 3

The next level of experiences includes serving in student paraprofessional positions such as resident assistant, peer tutor, orientation leader, peer counselor, peer educator (about topics such as sex, health and wellness, or drug and alcohol use), peer academic advisor, or peer career assistant. In this context, a paraprofessional is defined as "a student who is selected, trained, and supervised in assuming responsibilities and performing tasks that are intended to . . . directly promote the individual personal development of his or her peers [or] . . . foster the creation and maintenance of environments that stimulate and support . . . [the client-student's] personal and/or educational development . . . " (Winston & Fitch, 1993, p. 317). It should be noted that not all students who work for a college or university are paraprofessionals by this definition. Students who work in offices making copies, filing, or answering the telephone, or who serve as security officers, bus drivers, or maintenance workers, fulfill important support functions. These positions, however, do not fit the definition of paraprofessional positions.

At level 3, students are performing some of the duties that would be performed by a professional in the absence of paraprofessionals. The latter are called upon to exercise considerable independent judgment and often exert appreciable authority on behalf of the institution. For these reasons it is imperative that paraprofessionals be carefully selected, extensively trained, and given access to immediate supervisory support as they perform their duties.

Paraprofessional positions that meet these standards offer students rich learning opportunities. Service learning experiences also fall under level 3. For service learning activities or projects to quality, the following criteria must be satisfied: (1) the service activity has a direct connection to classroom instruction or an academic discipline; (2) the activity is of sufficient duration to challenge the student intellectually and/or affectively; and (3) students complete activities/assignments that require reflection on their own learning.

Level 4

Level 4 experiences include practicum or internship experiences. Characteristics of this level include: (1) explicit learning goals that govern the form and content of the experience; (2) activities, assignments, and projects that are related to classroom learning; (3) numerous opportunities for students to ask questions and explore the subtleties of what is happening around them and receive frequent, candid feedback about their performance; and (4) award of academic credit.

Level 5

Level 5 includes positions that are characterized as professionals in training, also sometimes known as assistantships. Professionals in training may be distinguished from student paraprofessionals by the greater autonomy allowed and usually the greater amount of authority and responsibility associated with the position. Professionals in training are often graduate students who are enrolled in programs of study that are directly related to the responsibilities of the positions. If the work assignments are directly related to academic study, supervisors may appropriately have higher expectations about the level of performance expected of the student and the kinds of professional skills the student will possess (at least during the later stages of their academic programs).

Assistantships as a level of applied learning experiences are assigned to level 5— unlike most internships which were assigned to level 4—because of several factors. (1) Frequently, assistantships are much longer in duration (generally one or two years), thus allowing the assistant to gain more detailed, varied, and in-depth knowledge about the functional area and the student clientele involved than is possible in the usual one- or two-term internship. (2) The longer duration generally assures that the graduate assistant is able to observe and participate in the full range of cyclical activities, which may occur only once a year—such as new student orientation or selection and training of paraprofessional staff members. (3) Assistantships frequently place greater responsibility on the holder's shoulders and have more exacting accountability than internships. For these reasons, assistantships *can be* more powerful learning experiences, closely approximating professional work experience, than internships.

Not all assistantships, however, qualify as level 5 experiences. Only when there is a symbiotic relationship between work assignments and academic preparation can assistantships reach this level. If the work assignments do not qualify as "professional level" or if there is no opportunity for the student to apply theory learned in the classroom or practice skills required of professionals, then the assistantship is just work, resulting in less than optimal learning. Often the quality and frequency of supervision provided to students make the genuine difference in the quality of the learning experience.

---

*ℛ*eflection *𝒫*oint
- At what level of experience should supervised experience be directed for students in master's degree programs in student affairs?
- In doctoral degree programs?
- What kind of assessment is required to match students with their appropriate level of supervised experience?

A MODEL OF SUPERVISED PRACTICE IN STUDENT AFFAIRS

In our view, supervised practice in graduate preparation is composed of five major components. These components are shown in Figure 1.4 picturing supervision as the integrating feature of direct experience, translation, applying ethics, and reflection.

Each of the model's components is essential to a meaningful learning experience for graduate students. Students must be able to participate in direct experience in the practices of the field and translate the theories, research, and models of practice learned in academic settings to direct application. They must conduct professional practice ethically and think about or contemplate what they are doing under the watchful and nurturing eye of the on-site supervisor of the functional area in which the student is working. Any one of these components is helpful to students learning about professional practice; however, it is the supervision component that links all other experiences to the purposes of supervised practice and makes the experiences predictably educational.

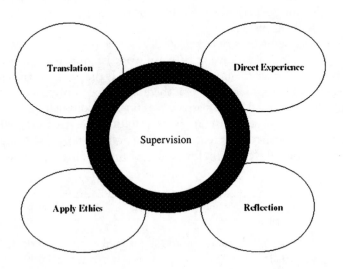

FIGURE 1.4. Model of Supervised Practice in Student Affairs Graduate Preparation Programs.

Direct Experience

Students in supervised practice should have opportunities for doing student affairs work first-hand. Making arrangements for participating in student affairs work in this manner will be explained elsewhere in this book, but, regardless of the procedure used to get the student to the scene of practice, the student should be involved in day-to-day activities that routinely engage student affairs practitioners.

Student affairs practitioners conduct their business of shaping and sustaining environments for student learning in many ways. They very often are involved in direct service to students. They meet students face-to-face to advise them about campus life and how to take full advantage of it, or to help them assess personal strengths and limitations and devise strategies for accomplishing goals. They also guide them in planning and executing educational programs. Practitioners often oversee the activities of students and student groups to ensure compliance with campus policies and procedures. Practitioners counsel students and consult with them on multiple topics that affect the quality of life on campus. They sometimes discipline students, but, even then, are doing so in a helpful, developmentally stimulating manner.

Additionally, student affairs practitioners conduct their business on campus indirectly; that is, they work through others or through other media to reach students. Practitioners may write educational materials for students or guidebooks for student conduct. They may prepare manuals for uniform functioning of very complex operations such as residential education programs or campus activities programs. They reach individual students indirectly through, for example, a cadre of trained paraprofessionals such as resident assistants (RAs) or through media such as the Internet where specific instructions for conducting organized programs in student organizations may be posted. These practitioners also prepare visual materials, such as videos to teach about campus culture, for example. Student orientation programs often rely upon videos, as one case in point, to communicate to new students the nature of the campus cultures. In an effort to get them up to speed quickly and enable new students to take immediate and full advantage of the learning opportunities afforded by the institution, some form of electronic communication is the only feasible approach on large campuses or campuses, such as community colleges, where it is virtually impossible to convene meetings of all students. In all of these forms of professional–student interactions, student affairs practitioners seek to teach and to facilitate student learning. These are the activities, at least by type, in which the graduate student practicum or intern student should be engaged.

It is most crucial that the graduate student engagement be centered on direct service to students. Because practicum and internship requirements typically demand at least two formal supervised experiences (Miller, 2001; Winston et al., 2001), at least one of them should include direct service to students. It is in this form of practice that professionals in training get immediate feedback about the effects of their work. They learn the value of listening and of communicating clearly and directly to other students. They feel the power of influence and the vulnerability of weaknesses in knowledge and skill. They internalize this information and learn from its consequences. It is in this context that students in training know what they really know and whether they can impart their knowledge to others.

Internship students should negotiate assignments with on-site supervisors that allow them to have these direct service contacts with students. Again, the procedures to arrive at these arrangements are discussed elsewhere in this book, but graduate students should strive for this type of opportunity to supplement their academic education rather than settling for back room duties that do not allow for assessment of the impact of their interactions with students.

Translation

Graduate students in student affairs preparation programs are exposed to wide-ranging and complex subject matter in the Foundation Studies and Professional Studies areas of their plans of study, as is shown in Figure 1.2. Both of these areas of academic study require that the student learn extensive knowledge and skills related to the theories, research, and models for practice of the field. Further, there are associated values, beliefs, and attitudes that are included in these baseline arenas of study that may fundamentally alter the way the graduate student sees his or her world. Both the cognitive and affective aspects of these complex plans affect internship students and cause them to question prior beliefs and knowledge. It is during this period of sometimes severe questioning of self that the practical experiences afforded through supervised practice can have their most profound and lasting effects.

Learning and development are related to span of time of knowing, opportunities to apply knowledge, and intensity of experience associated with knowledge acquisition. Though students may learn a concept it may fade from cognitive competence without opportunities to apply the concept—to see for oneself how it works in professional life. The more frequent and the more varied the opportunities to apply concepts the more likely the learner will retain and possibly enrich or extend the concepts. Learning also is related to the power of experiences. Routine, humdrum activities (and there are plenty of these that are necessary, but not especially enriching to the professional) may offer little opportunity for fully integrating concepts. On the other hand, rich, powerful, and challenging experiences not only allow for application of knowledge and skill, but also provoke professionals to reach within their inner selves for creative solutions. This process often yields learning and skill development that "sticks to the ribs"; that is, the learner owns new behaviors rooted in greater cognitive complexity as a result of such intense experiences.

Sometimes learners never really grasp intellectual or cognitive ideas and concepts until they use them in practice. Students go through the motions and they even say that they understand the ideas and concepts, then, later, after they have used them, confess that only then do they fully understand them. Such learners are not faking what they know; they simply have not completed the necessary cycle of cognitive maturation that often comes only through experience that allows them to really "see" the meaning of the ideas and concepts.

Applying Ethics

Students in supervised practice are expected to participate in professional practice. They will see or observe behaviors, attitudes, and values in action that are carried out according to the ethics of the profession. These ethics hold professionals to the highest standard of conduct and competence to enable the greatest benefit to students' learning and development.

Canon (1996) discusses "doing ethics" in a very practical manner. He is, of course, referring to the multiple approaches in which the profession encourages ethical behavior of its members. He sees the application of broad principles of ethics, the provision of formal codes of ethics, and the development of informal consensus among community members with common values as the principal methods of "doing ethics." In the first act of doing ethics, Canon is referring to principles such as respecting autonomy, doing no harm, benefiting others, being just, and being faithful. These principles are widely accepted in student affairs and are attributed to the milestone work of Karen Kitchener (1985). Her work serves, in fact, as the foundation for the formal code of ethics published by the American College Personnel Association (American College Personnel Association, 1992). The association's commitment to ethical standards is evidenced by the fact that the official statement is published in every edition of the member directory.

Applying ethics means that each professional is fully aware of the ethical standards of the profession and actively seeks to fulfill the expectations of the published statements by respective associations. Students in supervised practice should be vigilant in their own behavior and watchful of the behavior of others. The ethics statements of all professional associations re-mind us to work together to deal with ethical issues when they arise.

Ethical issues most certainly will arise. They may not be blatant, such as a professional seeking personal gain from relationships or from the work of others. They are more likely to occur when competing demands place an individual in direct conflict. An example of this latter situation might occur when a staff member is aware of information gained in confidence and is requested by a supervisor to reveal the information. Overlooking unsatisfac-tory performance, perhaps even incompetence, is another example of ethical conflict in which professionals frequently find themselves. In these cases, professionals must weigh the consequences of competing courses of action. Making such decisions never is easy, but to avoid them almost always is un-ethical.

Applying ethics is a very practical matter. In fact, Canon and Brown (1985) assert that "being ethical in itself is a very practical pursuit. Individuals . . . [who] place a high premium on respecting autonomy, avoid-ing the doing of harm, benefiting others, being just, and being faithful estab-lish a degree of credibility with others that tends to earn loyalty, trust, and respect in return" (p. 84). Achieving the kind of credibility referred to by Canon and Brown is exactly why students in supervised practice should ap-ply ethics in all that they do (see chapter 5 for a more extensive discussion of professional ethics and their relationship to the integrated student affairs professional model).

Reflection

The learning cycle is complete when the learner reflects on knowledge and uses it in practice. Providing an opportunity to complete this learning cycle is one of the more obvious reasons for including supervised practice in aca-demic preparation programs.

Reflection takes many forms. Students under supervision might be asked to interpret, analyze, speculate, evaluate, compose, contrast, discover, weigh, recognize, and remember important knowledge and skills. Green (1997) says that these actions, collectively or in part, may be included in re-flection that takes the form of journals, logs, critical incidents, seminars, spe-cial assignments, independent study, task analyses, and portfolio development. It also should occur in oral exchanges with colleagues and es-pecially with the site supervisor.

Reflection is crucial to learning and simple intuition suggests that re-flection that requires the construction of knowledge will be more effective than recognition tasks alone. Therefore, supervised practice that includes writing and analysis may be more potent than reflection conducted orally, especially if the reflection is informal. On the other hand, frequent oral reflection—particularly with one's supervisor—may have an equally positive result.

Supervision is a key to successful performance of higher education and student affairs professional roles. It is the lynchpin of all staffing practices, according to Winston and Creamer (1997). Once staff are hired and properly oriented to their jobs, supervision becomes most responsible for other crucial staffing practices like staff development and performance appraisal. Winston and Creamer argue that supervision should be conducted synergistically and this concept will be more fully devoted in chapter 3 of this book. Fundamentally, however, synergistic supervision is based upon mutual reliance and reciprocity in the relationship between supervisor and staff member and it is ongoing. All interactions between staff member and supervisor play a crucial role in synergistic supervision.

Synergistic supervisors will want to establish a relationship with students in supervised practice that will enable meaningful interactions about both personal and work-related issues. It is in this context that effective supervisors will engage students in oral and written reflection activities. From casual conversations on the job to formal written assignments, supervisors ask for reflections that lead to clearer and deeper insights about important concepts and tasks and that lead to more permanent and stable learning.

Expectations for Learning from Supervised Practice

Thinking, doing, experiencing, reflecting, and achieving—all fundamental behaviors in supervised practice—lead to awareness, sharpened skills, and a sense of industry for students. In other terms, they lead to change in the way students see themselves, the institution or organization, professional life, and education itself.

Views of Self. A graduate student who recently completed her practicum requirements said of the experience, "Practicum is a time to evaluate yourself." This comment represents a synthesis of many outcomes of supervised practice that change the way students see themselves. They learn that they can assume responsibility and take charge of important projects in the field. They can demonstrate professional behavior and receive feedback that helps them understand themselves as professionals. They come to feel that they possess a great deal of knowledge and skill and that they can use both in practical ways. Sometimes they also are faced with the reality of skills deficits or realization that that they are unwilling to make the personal sacrifices that certain positions require.

Graduate students often see their professional selves as if in a dream. They form mental images of being a professional, but until they are allowed to perform professional activities, their view of self-as-professional is only a fantasy. Supervised practice permits students to say, "I can do this for myself. I can function as a professional. I am not dreaming."

Confirmation of this insight is available all around students in supervised practice. They can witness the behavior of others and even come to see shortcomings in those they observe. They can compare themselves with others who have been judged reasonably successful in the field, and they often come away from these comparisons feeling good about themselves. "I am, or can be, as good as those who currently function in the field," is a sentiment often felt by students who have completed their supervised practice requirements in a professional preparation program.

Students in supervised practice also come to understand what they know at deeper levels than when their knowledge was confined to academic or intellectual interactions only. They fully grasp concepts in actual practice that were only known abstractly in the classroom. They "see," sometimes for the first time, what they said they "saw," but in fact did not, in purely intellectual exchanges. Thus, the learning cycle is closed, and they finally learn concepts and practices that they knew about but did not own until they exercised an option to use them in supervised practice.

A bottom line feature of these new views of self is that students gain confidence in their professional preparation. They come to know and to feel that what they have been taught is important, and maybe essential, for them to practice successfully in the field. They gain a sense of well-being about having learned "the right stuff."

Views of the Institution or Organization. Frequently, students in supervised practice tend to mature during, or as a result of, their experiences. They see the institution and its organizational units more realistically than they did before supervised practice. They achieve a form of organizational sophistication, which in turn suggests that those student views of divisions of student affairs and the units that compose the division become more realistic. They gain insight into the actual purpose of the organizational patterns that make up a unit in a division of student affairs. They see both the distinctions among organization unit missions and the way these units and missions fit together to accomplish major institutional purposes.

After supervised practice, students seem to possess a better idea of institutional or office cultures because they have experienced them directly.

They also may be able to describe dysfunctional aspects of organizational culture that prior to their supervised practice experiences were only text-book knowledge and realize how important it is to overcome such impediments to effectiveness.

At a more simplistic, but equally important level, students in supervised practice gain a familiarization with work sites. They "bump into" real world experiences in their day-to-day work in various sites. They observe daily what work is being performed in many offices of a division of student affairs and come away from these experiences a more fully informed professional. They often encounter people doing work of which they were previously unaware. They see how complex a college or university really is and how many "cogs" it takes to run the entire "machine."

Views of Professional Life. Looking up at the long professional ladder from the ground level may give the student a distorted vision about the overall process. Both views of professional behavior and the routes professionals take to succeed in the field may be contorted from the perspective of someone who has not even begun the work. Supervised practice enables students to begin the real world practices of a professional. Figuratively, they move to the first step of the metaphorical ladder, and things begin to look different.

Views from this first step often look so different from earlier views that students may reassess whether actually entering the profession is what they want. Most students have their earlier views confirmed by the new vision and proceed to complete their formal preparation with renewed vigor and enlightenment. On the other hand, some corroborate their worst fears and these few may take alternative actions to find another more suitable career. Supervised practice is a reality check. At its conclusion, students generally "know," both in their heads and in their guts, whether they have chosen the right professional field.

There is a certain demystification of professional life that occurs as a result of supervised practice. Students often are given opportunities to participate fully as colleagues in the offices where their experiences are located. This may mean discovering the teaching role of student affairs practice. It may mean discovering the research and assessment role of practice (that heretofore they believed was only harassment inflicted upon them by overly demanding professors!). Many students become involved in professional activities with full-time staff and are invited to professional conferences to make presentations and to begin an association with colleagues from other colleges and universities that will last a lifetime.

Views of Education. As a part of the process of completing the learning cycle through supervised practice, students often see education itself in a different light. Educational philosophers assert that education is everywhere; it is ubiquitous. It is a part of everyday life, in families, businesses, churches, synagogues, temples, and mosques, and in ordinary exchanges with other people. In these ubiquitous activities, students come to know themselves, to reach for goals and even to expand them, and come to understand their role in a community as citizens in a democratic society. That part of the process that occurs in educational institutions may be more properly called schooling (only one example of education).

It is too often the case that students see education as something being done to them by others. They often do not see themselves as actors in the process. Supervised practice can change this shortsightedness. Through supervised practice, students can become aware of their role as learners, but also of their role as teachers in the grand ubiquitous realm of education.

Reflection Point

- Make a list of the most important learnings *you* should seek from an internship experience.
- Is your list different from the other students' lists in a student affairs preparation program? How?
- What does your list say about you as a future student affairs practitioner?

REFERENCES

American College Personnel Association (1992). Statement of ethical principles and standards. *Journal of College Student Development, 34,* 89–92.

Argyris, C., Putnam, R., & Smith, D. M. (1985). *Action science: Concepts, methods, and skills for research and intervention.* San Francisco: Jossey-Bass.

Argyris, C., & Schön, D. A. (1974). *Theory in practice: Increasing professional effectiveness.* San Francisco: Jossey-Bass.

Blimling, G. S. (1993). The context of conflict in the academy: An educational dialectic on faculty and student affairs educators. *College Student Affairs Journal, 13*(1), 4–12.

Blimling, G. S. (2000). Trusting student life and learning to a vice president with less experience. *Journal of College Student Development, 41,* 377-379.

Boylan, J. C., Malley, P. B., & Reilly, E. P. (2001). *Practicum and internship: Textbook and resource guide for counseling and psychotherapy.* New York: Brunner-Routledge.

Canon, H. J. (1996). Ethical standards and principles. In S. R. Komives & D. B. Woodard, Jr. (Eds.), *Student services: A handbook for the profession* (3rd ed., pp. 106–125). San Francisco: Jossey-Bass.

Canon, H. J., & Brown, R. D. (1985). How to think about professional ethics. In H. J. Canon & R. D. Brown (Eds.), *Applied ethics in student affairs* (pp. 81–88). New Directions for Student Services, No. 30. San Francisco, CA: Jossey-Bass.

Chiaferi, R., & Griffin, M. (1997). *Developing fieldwork skills: A guide for human services, counseling, and social work students.* Pacific Grove, CA: Brooks/Cole.

Creamer, D. G., & Shelton, M. (1988). Staff development: A literature review of graduate preparation and in-service education of student affairs practitioners. *Journal of College Student Development, 29,* 407–414.

Creamer, D. G., Winston, R. B., Jr., & Miller, T. K. (2001). The professional student affairs administrator: Roles and functions. In R. B. Winston, Jr., D. G. Creamer, & T. K. Miller (Eds.), *The professional student affairs administrator: Educator, leader, and manager.* New York: Brunner-Rutledge.

Delworth, U., & Hanson, G. R. (1980). Conclusion: Structure of the profession and recommended curriculum. In U. Delworth & G. R. Hanson (Eds.), *Student services: A handbook for the profession* (pp. 473–485). San Francisco: Jossey-Bass.

Dewey, J. (1916). *Democracy and education: An introduction to the philosophy of education.* New York: Macmillan.

Fried, J. (1995). *Shifting paradigms in student affairs: Culture, context, teaching, and learning.* Washington, DC: American College Personnel Association.

Fried, J. (1997). Changing ethical frameworks for a multicultural world. In J. Fried (Ed.), *Ethics for today's campus: New perspectives on education, student development, and institutional management* (pp. 5–22). New Directions for Student Services, No. 77. San Francisco: Jossey-Bass.

Green, M. E. (1997). *Internship success: Real-world, step-by-step advice on getting the most out of internships.* Lincolnwood, IL: VGM Career Horizons/NTC/Contemporary Publishing.

Greenleaf, E. A. (1977). Preparation of student personnel staff to meet flexibility and diversity in higher education. In G. H. Knock (Ed.), *Student Personnel Series, No. 22. Perspectives on the preparation of student affairs professionals* (pp. 151–165). Washington, DC: American College Personnel Association.

Greenwood, E. (1957). Attributes of a profession. *Social Work, 2,* 45–56.

Hoberman, S., & Mailick, S. (1994). Introduction. In S. Hoberman & S. Mailick (Eds.), *Professional education in the United States: Experiential learning, issues, and prospects* (pp. 3–6). Westport, CT: Praeger.

Hutchings, P., & Wutzdorff, A. (1988). Editor's notes. In P. Hutchings & A. Wutzdorff (Eds.), *Knowing and doing: Learning through experience* (pp. 1–3). New Directions for Teaching and Learning, No. 35. San Francisco, CA: Jossey-Bass.

Kiser, P. M. (2000). *Getting the most from your human services internship: Learning from experience.* Belmont, CA: Wadsworth/Thomson Learning

Kitchener, K. S. (1985). Ethical principles and ethical decisions in student affairs. In H. J. Canon & R. D. Brown (Eds.), *Applied ethics in student affairs* (pp. 17–30). New Directions for Student Services, No. 30. San Francisco: Jossey-Bass.

Knock, G. H. (Ed.). (1977). *Student Personnel Series, No. 22. Perspectives on the preparation of student affairs professionals.* Washington, DC: American College Personnel Association.

Lloyd-Jones, E. (1989). Forword. In D. C. Roberts (Ed.), *Designing campus activities to foster a sense of community.* New Directions for Student Services, No. 48. San Francisco: Jossey-Bass.

McEwen, M. K., & Talbot, D. M. (1998). Designing the student affairs curriculum. In N. J. Evans & C. E. Phelps Tobin (Eds.), *The state of the art of preparation and practice in student affairs: Another look* (pp. 125–156). Washington, DC: American College Personnel Association.

McGlothlin, W. J. (1964). *The professional schools.* New York: Center for Applied Research in Education.

Miller, T. K. (Ed.). (1997). *The book of professional standards for higher education, 1997.* Washington, DC: Council for the Advancement of Standards in Higher Education.

Miller, T. K. (Ed.). (2001). *The book of professional standards for higher education, 2001.* Washington, DC: Council for the Advancement of Standards in Higher Education.

National Association of Student Personnel Administrators. (1998). *Membership directory.* Washington, DC: Author.

Sandeen, A. (1991). *The chief student affairs officer: Leader, manager, mediator, and educator.* San Francisco: Jossey-Bass.

Scannell, J., & Simpson, K. (1996). *Shaping the college experience outside the classroom.* Rochester, NY: University of Rochester Press.

Schön, D. A. (1987). *Educating the reflective practitioner.* San Francisco: Jossey-Bass.

Schroeder, C. C., & Pike, G. R. (2001). The scholarship of application in student affairs. *Journal of College Student Development, 42,* 342–355.

Winston, R. B, Jr., & Creamer, D. G. (1997). *Improving staffing practices in student affairs.* San Francisco: Jossey-Bass.

Winston, R. B., Jr., Creamer, D. G., & Miller, T. K. (2001). *The professional student affairs administrator: Educator, leader, and manager.* New York: Brunner-Routledge.

Winston, R. B., Jr., & Fitch, R. T. (1993). Paraprofessional staffing. In R. B. Winston, Jr. & S. Anchors (Eds.), *Student housing and residential life: A handbook for professionals committed to student development goals* (pp. 315–343). San Francisco: Jossey-Bass.

Winston, R. B., Jr., Lathrop, B. J., Lease, J., Davis, J. S., Beeny, C., & Newsome, K. (2001). Supervised practice in student affairs: State of the art. Unpublished manuscript.

Winston, R. B., Jr., & Saunders, S. A. (1991). Ethnical professional practice in student affairs. In T. K. Miller & R. B. Winston, Jr. (Eds.), *Administration and leadership in student affairs: Actualizing student development in higher education* (2nd ed., pp. 309–345). Muncie, IN: Accelerated Development.

Young, R. B. (1993). The essential values of the profession. In R. B. Young (Ed.), *Identifying and implementing the essential values of the profession* (pp. 5–13). New Directions for Student Services, No. 61. San Francisco: Jossey-Bass.

Young, R. B., & Elfrink, V. L. (1991). Essential values of student affairs work. *Journal of College Student Development, 32,* 47–55.

Chapter 2

STRUCTURE AND DESIGN
OF THE SUPERVISED PRACTICE
EXPERIENCE

Joan B. Hirt
Steven M. Janosik

Historically, supervised practice or internships have played an essential role in the preparation of student affairs practitioners. Most graduate preparation programs have offered such experiences for decades, and they are generally viewed as a fundamental component of the curriculum (Winston et al., 2001). Indeed supervised practice experiences are a core component of the CAS master's level preparation standards (Miller, 2001; see chapter 1 of this volume for a more detailed discussion of CAS standards).

When intentionally designed and clearly focused, supervised practice experiences can be one of the most powerful learning and socialization tools for aspiring professionals. Students can gain personal insights into the operation of an office on campus and hone their skills in a variety of contexts. Site supervisors have an opportunity to pass along their expertise about a functional area in which they have a proven track record. Faculty members are provided with the chance to assist students in translating classroom instruction to professional practice.

On the other hand, when such experiences are not clearly defined, they can limit the amount of learning that occurs and can be frustrating for students, supervisors, and faculty. The key to maximizing the effectiveness of an internship, then, is in the design of that experience (McCormick, 1993). Featherman (1998) argues that as higher education has become a mature industry it has undergone a transformation that has resulted in an increased emphasis on service and learning through that service. Others have identified more specific outcomes associated with such experiences. For example, Carter, Cooke, and Neal (1996) suggest that internships should enable students to make and justify decisions, plan and control activities, evaluate the results of activities, communicate effectively, work with people effectively, and continue their personal development (p. 66). Other specific objectives of field experiences include: research, career exploration, community service, and intercultural experience. These are not necessarily mutually exclusive, and they can be combined when designing an internship (Van Aalst, 1974).

The consensus of many scholars is that internships should offer students insights into the world of work, develop professional skills, develop interpersonal and social skills, link theory to practice, and enhance employment prospects for students (Carter, Cooke, & Neal, 1996; Harcharik, 1993; Ryan & Cassidy, 1996; Toohey, Ryan, & Hughes, 1996). They should also socialize students to the professional roles to which they aspire (Fernald et al., 1982; Wolf, 1980) and allow them to integrate theory, research, and practice (Joslin & Ellis, 1990).

Even though these shared objectives may be applicable to a variety of supervised practice experiences, some are related to discussions of undergraduate internship experiences and others come from disciplines such as psychology, speech communication, or political science. In this chapter, we emphasize how supervised experiences can be designed to maximize learning for those aspiring to careers in student affairs administration. To this end, we recommend a six-component model for designing successful internship experiences in higher education.

1. It is important for students to conduct a personal assessment of their skills in order to identify areas they wish to develop through the experience.
2. Students need to establish realistic expectations about what the supervised experience can offer.
3. Students need to develop a contract for the experience. This involves identifying specific goals for the experience and linking those goals to objectives and activities that will enable them to realize those goals.
4. Students should consider the structure of the experience, the different players to be involved, and the different approaches faculty coordinators may take with respect to the class associated with the experience.
5. The resources necessary to conduct the experience need to be identified. These include resources provided by the site to the student and those provided by the student.

6. It is important to examine overall management issues associated with supervised experiences and the role students play when balancing the experience with other components of the curriculum and their lives.

Each of these six components is addressed in this chapter but it is important for students to note that they need not address the internship without assistance and direction. The faculty member who coordinates the internship program is an invaluable resource to students planning supervised experiences. We encourage students to consult with their faculty supervisor throughout the planning process (see chapter 3 for a discussion of the roles of the on-site and faculty supervisors).

ASSESSING SKILLS

Given the extensive literature about supervised experiences, there is surprisingly little written about assessing students' skills prior to the internship. Green (1997) touches upon the topic by suggesting that those seeking internships identify basic skills they might bring to the experience such as technical skills, clerical skills, organizational skills, or artistic skills. In our opinion, however, this type of minimalist approach to assessment is not likely to result in an experience specifically designed to improve skills.

The internship should be carefully and purposively designed if students expect to maximize learning from the experience. This requires students to conduct a thorough assessment of the skills they bring to potential sites and the skills they believe they need to improve in order to develop their professional craft. This assessment should be sufficiently broad in scope to enable the student to see potential gains that could be achieved in any number of settings. If students only examine the skills required to succeed in a single setting, they limit the potential that a given internship may afford them. If students consider skills in a broad array of areas, they may identify a number of potential sites where supervised practice could contribute to their development.

It may be helpful to conceptualize these skills in six distinct areas (Stewart, 1994):

1. *Articulation skills.* No matter what functional area students wish to pursue professionally, they will need to have an ability to articulate issues about higher education and student affairs. At times, the ability will focus on describing the field in general or the philosophy and theory that guide professional practice. At other times, professionals are called upon to articulate student concerns to colleagues on campus, or to explain campus policies

and procedures to students. In all cases, the ability to speak about the profession in knowledgeable, articulate ways is important.

2. *Process skills.* All practitioners in higher education need to understand the dynamics of the college campus and to act in ways that promote the mission and goals of their institution. To successfully meet these responsibilities, administrators need to be able to process the information they possess or can acquire and utilize that information to solve problems. This can range from working cooperatively with others to mediating conflicts between individuals or recognizing group dynamics. If students understand where their skills lie at the outset of a supervised experience, they can target development of other talents in this area as part that experience (Stewart, 1994).

3. *Functional area–specific knowledge.* Acquiring knowledge and background specific to an administrative area on campus is also an important outcome of the supervised experience. Those who wish to work in judicial affairs, for example, need to have an understanding of the policies and procedures related to the campus conduct code. Those seeking positions in the housing arena need to master an understanding of how to manage facilities. Most professionals have budgetary responsibilities, but many students do not have experience developing or managing budgets. All those who work in higher education need to develop abilities to work with nontraditional students, including ethnic minorities, students with disabilities, or commuter students. So, assessing skills related to specific career objectives is another component of assessing overall skills (Stewart, 1994).

4. *Research skills.* Perhaps one of the most overlooked skill areas for those who desire to work in the academy relates to research skills. Higher education is driven by data and grounded in the production of new knowledge. Those who wish to work in this enterprise need to be able to read, interpret, understand, and make use of data if they are to succeed. Additionally, practitioners should be able to design sound research studies and generate new information from those projects. Such studies can range from designing surveys that evaluate the outcomes associated with participation in a particular program or using a specific service on campus, to in-depth studies that advance theoretical foundations for the profession. Possessing research skills is essential to becoming a good professional (see chapter 1). Even though research may be a skill that is more fully utilized later in a professional career, the internship setting and experience can be an excellent venue for acquiring or refining research and evaluation skills (Stewart, 1994).

5. *Programming.* Entry-level professionals, in particular, are frequently assigned responsibilities that focus on identifying students' needs and designing and implementing programs to meet those needs. But even more experienced administrators need strong programming skills. They frequently need to develop programs for staff and other constituencies on campus. Suc-

cessful programming involves the ability to identify needs, design appropriate activities that relate to those needs, and implement programs in an efficient and effective manner. At times, it also requires practitioners to develop manuals about the programs they sponsor or to evaluate their programmatic efforts in report format (Saunders & Cooper, 2001; Stewart, 1994).

6. *Teaching.* Most administrators who work on college and university campuses need to serve as trainers and instructors in some context. For some, these activities focus on designing and implementing staff development programs. For others, it might include teaching a class for student leaders (e.g., resident assistants, orientation leaders, or peer tutors) or undergraduate students in general (e.g., a continuing orientation course or a student leadership course). Practitioners are also expected to participate in professional activities like presenting sessions at conferences and consulting with other campus and noncampus groups. In all cases, the ability to assume the role of trainer or instructor is critical to professional success (Saunders & Cooper, 2001; Stewart, 1994).

Reflection Point

- Think about your own skills and abilities. How would you rate yourself on each of the six skills areas described above?
- What other skills would you like to develop during your time as a graduate student?

Although there may be other areas that should be assessed by those considering an internship (for instance, technology), the six areas of expertise described here comprise a sound basis for students to evaluate their knowledge and skills. Moreover, the way in which the assessment is conducted is important if the supervised experience is to be intentionally designed. That is, it is important for students to assess their current levels of skill in each of the six areas, but it is equally important to assess how significant each area is to their professional aspirations. For those who seek careers in admissions, for example, developing skills to promote relating to nontraditional students or creation of web sites might be more important than developing programmatic skills. Others who seek careers in residential life, student activities, or Greek life may find developing programmatic skills more important to their immediate professional goals. In the long run, however, developing skills in all six areas is essential for professional advancement. Indeed, there may be other skills that students seek to develop through supervised experiences. If so, they should make a concerted effort to design an internship that will enable them to develop those talents. Students also should keep in mind that because of changing personal interests, societal expectations and demands, and personal circumstances, it is difficult to accurately envision one's career path at this stage of development.

To assess skills, Stewart (1994) has developed an instrument that addresses abilities in all six areas. The Skills Analysis Survey for Graduate Students in Higher Education and Student Affairs Graduate Preparation Programs (SAS) asks respondents to rate their abilities on 60 items. Additionally, the instrument calls on respondents to rate the extent to which they hope to develop each skill by the time they complete their graduate program. Those who have identified other skills they would like to develop through their internships might create additional questions like those on the SAS relevant to those additional skills. By completing the SAS, students are provided a profile of current skill levels and of needed skills to be acquired before completing their program of study. This enables students to critically evaluate their options with respect to supervised practice experiences. The goal here is to provide students with a comprehensive picture of their current abilities as well as a detailed understanding of the skills they wish to develop while in graduate school. Given this understanding, they can design supervised experiences that enable them to work on some of the skills that they believe they will need to succeed as professionals. A copy of the SAS can be found in Appendix A. This assessment provides the groundwork needed to consider the next component of the design process, setting realistic expectations.

SETTING REALISTIC EXPECTATIONS

Once students have an understanding of their current abilities and the skills they wish to hone while in graduate school, the next step in designing the supervised experience is to set realistic expectations for that experience. Research findings suggest that those who successfully complete internships are more likely to be deemed qualified for entry-level positions than those who have not worked in a professional setting. They are also more likely to report greater satisfaction with their positions and to earn higher salaries than those who did not complete a supervised experience (Taylor, 1992). But these expectations are not likely to be achieved if the experience is not intentionally designed. Furthermore, if students are to be intentional in designing their supervised experiences, they must have a good grasp of the skills on which they wish to concentrate while in the internship. This information is best elicited via a thorough assessment process.

It is likely that the assessment process will reveal a number of skills that students have already developed quite fully. That process is also likely to have identified a number of skills that students have not yet developed but which will be important to their future success as practitioners. It is unrealistic to expect that any given internship experience is going to enable students to develop all the skills they will need as professionals. Indeed, it is important to consider all the mechanisms available to students to develop the skills they will need to succeed in the profession.

For example, skills can be developed through other classes offered in the graduate curriculum. If students want to develop skills that enable them to articulate theory, they might use assignments from a class on organizational or student development theory to sharpen their skills in this area. Students seeking to develop programmatic skills might take advantage of assignments in an intervention design class to develop a program on a particular topic. Those who wish to develop research abilities may enroll in a research design class that would enable them to focus on developing a research project on a topic of their choosing. The point is that students can develop their skills through didactic-type classes as well as internships.

A second opportunity to practice and enhance skills is provided in graduate assistantship positions (GAs). Many graduate preparation programs in higher education and student affairs administration work in conjunction with other campus administrators to offer students GA positions. These positions can be in any number of offices, including, admissions, financial aid, academic advising, career services, housing and dining services, student activities, or judicial affairs, among others. In exchange for working 10 to 20 hours per week in a given office, students in GA positions are provided with a stipend, and, in some cases, tuition remission. Many administrators and students view GA positions as a way of funding graduate education and, in fact, GA positions are a form of financial support for graduate students. But GA experiences go beyond merely funding a student. They are opportunities for students to develop and practice skills they will need in their professional careers. In that sense, GA positions can serve as mechanisms for students to hone their skills, and students should use these opportunities accordingly (review chapter 1 for a discussion of the assistantship and similarities and differences between it and the internship).

Finally, it is important for students to consider opportunities to develop their skills that fall outside the campus. Professional associations are a prime example of such opportunities. Most professional associations in higher education and student affairs administration offer reduced membership rates for graduate students, and we urge students to take advantage of those rates to further their professional development. Joining associations not only provides students with regular member benefits such as receiving journals and other publications, but also provides students opportunities to develop other professional skills. For example, those who wish to develop training and instructional skills may wish to submit proposals to present programs at professional gatherings. Students who wish to gain experience in programming might volunteer to serve on a committee responsible for developing an association's annual conference. At issue here is the notion that there are opportunities to learn professional skills beyond those offered through formal supervised practice courses. Even though it is unlikely that any single internship will provide students with opportunities to address all the skills they would like to develop, it is incumbent upon students to make use of all the opportunities provided by the graduate education process. By conducting a careful assessment of their abilities, and identifying those skills they already possess and those skills they believe they need to develop, students can take full advantage of the various options they have to develop those skills while in graduate school. In this manner, students are more likely to have their expectations of professional preparation fully met.

Setting realistic expectations plays a role in the process of designing the supervised experience, and expectations are more realistically established if students conduct a thorough assessment of their skills before considering their options with respect to internship settings. If students used the SAS (Stewart, 1994) to assess their abilities, they might use the results of that assessment to identify all the skills they hope to develop before completing their degree program. Then, they can approach development of those skills through the various opportunities available during graduate school. Some may be best developed through coursework, whereas other skills might be honed through GA positions or work with professional associations. The remaining skills on the list might be addressed through the supervised practice experiences.

Indeed, respondents to the SAS (Stewart, 1994) are asked to identify the five skills they most want to develop through a single supervised experience. This list of skills and concomitant knowledge areas can then be used to identify a site that might promote the development of such skills to the greatest extent. For example, suppose that the student has identified the following as the skills she or he would most prefer to work on during the experience: articulating the special needs of minority or nontraditional students; articulating the needs of one student population to another student population (for instance, Hispanic students to white students); recognizing and evaluating group dynamics; writing public relations materials; and conducting independent research. The next step in the process is to identify one or more supervised experiences that would provide opportunities to work on these skills. There may be several options for the student to combine the development of these skills in some form.

One option would be to work with a multicultural center on campus on a project to incorporate Hispanic student events into a campus calendar. This would enable the intern to work with a cultural minority group and, by incorporating their plans into other campus activities, to articulate the group's interests to other student groups. Such an experience might also enable the intern to work on identifying group needs by working with both the minority student group and the other groups on campus vying for calendar time. Finally, the experience might enable the intern to develop some public relations materials for the Hispanic student group, highlighting the programs they plan to sponsor. Such an internship would enable the student to gain experience related to four of the five skills areas identified in the assessment process. The final skill area, conducting research, could then be addressed in another supervised practice setting or through other curricular avenues.

Another option for a student seeking to develop skills in these five areas would be an assignment in a service learning center. Perhaps the intern could work with a group of undergraduates who serve as tutors for disadvantaged high school students. Such an assignment might require the intern to conduct an initial assessment of the high school students' skills, and represent their interests to the student tutors. This experience might meet four of the five designated goals for the experience. By working with disadvantaged high school students, the intern would have an opportunity to work with a nontraditional group. By systematically assessing those high school students' skills, the intern would be able to develop research skills. By explaining the needs of the high school students to the undergraduate volunteers, the intern would practice articulating the needs of one group to another group. Finally, the intern would be able to observe and evaluate the group dynamics among the tutors. In this case, working on public relations materials might have to be postponed, but the other four objectives of the intern could be met.

Finally, there may be an internship that could address all five objectives. Consider the opportunities that an office that serves students with disabilities provides. Interns may design an experience that would allow them to advise an organization for students with disabilities in the annual student government budgeting process. In this case, the intern would conduct an assessment of the organization's needs, assist the students in developing a budget proposal that addresses those needs, and develop that budget proposal in written format to present to the student government's budget board. Such an experience provides for working with a non-traditional group, conducting research, developing PR materials about the group for presentation to the student government, and articulating the needs of students with disabilities to the student government group. Throughout the process, the intern would have the opportunity to observe and evaluate the group dynamics among members of the students with disabilities group. Hence, all five of the intern's objectives could be met.

These three examples suggest typical activities in which students may engage through an internship. They also typify ways in which students can target the development of certain skills when designing supervised experiences. Students, however, need to be realistic when designing internships. They are well served if they identify a limited number of realistic goals and intentionally design experiences to achieve those goals. They are less well served if they try to accomplish so many goals through a single experience that they are unable to fully develop any of the skills they seek to cultivate. Once realistic goals for the experience have been identified, the next step in the process is to design the contract for the experience.

DESIGNING THE LEARNING CONTRACT

The learning contract represents the clearest expression of what the student hopes to achieve in a supervised experience, what the student plans to bring to the site, and what the student expects the site to contribute to the experience. As a result, developing the contract is an essential component of designing a meaningful internship. Interestingly, few scholars have addressed the issue of the contract when writing about the internship experience. Those who have mentioned the contract have done so in the context that the contract serves as a way of tracking where students are serving, not necessarily what they are doing (Harcharik, 1993; Mason, 1985; Schmidt, Gardner, Benjamin, Conaway, & Haskins, 1992). Others refer to the contract only tangentially in reference to evaluating the supervised experience (Alexander, 1982; Toohey et al., 1996; Wolf, 1980). We argue that designing the contract is an essential and important learning activity. When done well, developing the contract should enable students to clearly identify goals, create activities that directly link to those goals, and calculate the amount of time it will take to complete those activities. All these actions allow students to practice the planning and time management skills that they will need to succeed as professionals.

The Case of Jane

For purposes of discussing the development of the contract, consider the following scenario. Jane has completed the SAS (Stewart, 1994) and has selected five goals that she would like to achieve through an internship.

1. Jane would like to develop her research abilities, particularly those related to reviewing and interpreting literature.
2. She would also like to improve her marketing skills.

3. She is interested in gaining experience in linking theory to practice.
4. Jane also wants to gain an understanding of the policies and procedures that guide the judicial process on campus.
5. She desires to learn about the overall operation of the Dean of Students office as her career aspirations include working in some capacity in a generalist-type position.

Given these interests, she met with the designated internship supervisor in the Dean of Students office and, with his assistance, identified a possible internship. Now she needs to develop the contract for that experience. A good contract will include eight basic elements: student information; site supervisor information; practicum faculty coordinator information; a purpose statement; objectives, activities, and skills/competencies; site location information; proposed work schedule; and signatures. Some of these elements are more informational while others are instructive in tone. But all the elements are important to a complete contract and are highly recommended to those planning internships. Each is discussed and in Appendix B we have included a sample contract, reflecting Jane's scenario, to provide an example of what a final contract might look like.

The first three elements are informational items. There are three key people involved in the supervised experience: the student, the site supervisor who provides day-to-day supervision to the student, and the faculty supervisor who coordinates the course associated with the internship. Since all three need to interact on a regular basis, it is important that the learning contract include each person's role and their contact information, including title, mailing address, office phone, fax number, and e-mail address. Additionally, it might be useful for the student to report a home address, phone number, and e-mail address because students are not always available during regular business hours.

The purpose statement is an instructive element. It is designed to provide all the parties involved in the experience with a clear, concise overview of what the student intends to do and what the student hopes to achieve from the experience. In Jane's case, the purpose statement suggests that she will conduct research to develop a conflict resolution model that might be used in the adjudication of conduct cases. She also hopes to gain insight into the overall operation of the Dean of Students office. Jane has included three of the skills she hopes to develop as a result of the experience in the purpose statement (research, judicial cases, overall operation of the office). This is generally a good idea. First, it serves to remind Jane of what she wants to focus on during the course of the internship. Second, it assists the site supervisor and faculty supervisor in tracking the progress Jane is making toward achieving her objectives over the course of the academic term.

Objectives, activities, and skills/competencies, the fifth element of the contract, is another instructive component and really represents the substance of the contract. This is the section in which students translate the objectives they hope to achieve during the experience into behaviors in which they will actually engage, and estimate how much time they expect to spend on each activity. Because this is such an important element of the contract, each component merits some discussion here. Objectives are statements that students develop to describe the general tasks they will perform during the experience. In this sense, they describe outcomes the student hopes to achieve by the conclusion of the internship. Objectives should be clear and easily understood by all parties. In Jane's case, three objectives were identified. First, Jane plans to assist with the development of a conflict resolution model that the Dean of Students staff might use in adjudicating certain types of conduct cases. Second, Jane plans to conceptualize the logistics associated with implementing that model. Finally, she hopes to gain an understanding of the overall operation of the Dean of Students office. In each case, Jane has provided her site supervisor and faculty supervisor with a clear idea of what she plans to accomplish during the internship experience.

The next component, *activities*, are typically the most difficult for students to identify. Activities are descriptions of behaviors in which students will engage in order to accomplish the objectives cited in the contract. It is critical, therefore, that the activities represent behaviors that, if successfully completed, will lead the student to achieve the relevant objective. Consider Jane's first objective of developing a conflict resolution model. The activities she has identified that are associated with achieving that goal include conducting research on conflict resolution models, consulting with her site supervisor, and conferring with other Dean of Students staff members about components of the model. All three activities (behaviors) can be directly connected to the outcome Jane hopes to achieve—developing a conflict resolution model. Moreover, each activity can be related to one of the skills she hopes to develop through the experience. Researching the literature on conflict resolutions relates to her objective of developing her research skills, particularly those associated with interpreting literature. Consulting with her site supervisor and other staff members in the office relates to her objective of understanding the overall function of the office.

In the skills/competencies section of the contract, Jane has summarized the skills she believes she will develop as a result of engaging in the activities she has related to her first objective. Again, there are direct connections between the behaviors she will engage in and the skills she will develop as a result of those activities. She notes in this section that she will hone her research skills and collaborate with staff in the office, all skills that she might reasonably develop through the activities she has planned.

The final component of this section is frequently the most challenging for students when designing contracts. A good contract will report how much time the student plans to spend on each activity. This requires that the student calculate time in as specific a manner as possible. For example, Jane has indicated she plans to spend approximately 15 hours consulting with her site supervisor. In this case, Jane's experience will occur during a 15-week semester. Her estimate suggests she plans to spend an hour per week with her site supervisor in individual sessions, a realistic estimate of how much time will be devoted to this activity. The same is true for meeting with other staff members. In this case, there are five other professionals in the office. Jane's plan suggests she will spend an hour with each over the course of the semester, a realistic expectation for this portion of the contract. Estimating research time may be more difficult, but by reporting her plan to spend 20 hours on this task, and assuming all research will need to be conducted before she can start on her second objective, conceptualizing the model, Jane is suggesting that she spend about 4 hours per week conducting research during the first 5 weeks of her experience. In total, Jane estimates she will spend about 40 hours on the activities related to achieving her first objective. These kinds of accurate estimates can be very useful to students when they examine all the objectives they hope to achieve in a given experience. In some cases, students identify too few or too many objectives to reasonably achieve in a given academic term. Good time estimates help students identify when such problems might occur.

Jane repeated these steps in developing the second and third objectives of her contract. In each case, the activities she proposes directly relate to the relevant objective. In each case, she has described skills and competencies that she can reasonably assume she can develop if she engages in those activities. Finally, she has allocated time to each activity based on realistic expectations about how much time it will take to complete those activities. She has also indicated the total amount of time she plans to spend in the supervised experience over the course of the academic term. This is an important consideration when developing contracts. Most graduate preparation programs have internal, departmental standards associated with supervised experiences. These standards normally include a specified number of hours students should expect to spend at the site. Students should consult those guidelines when developing contracts so they can design experiences that not only meet their objectives but meet departmental expectations as well.

It is also important to note that Jane has included language in her contract that reflects all five of the objectives she identified through her assessment as important to achieve. Research skills are included in the first objective. Linking theory to practice and developing marketing skills are described in the activities associated with the second objective in the contract.

Understanding the policies and procedures that guide the judicial process, and gaining an understanding of the overall operation of the Dean of Students office are reflected in the activities associated with the third objective in the contract. Overall, then, Jane has designed an experience that will not only provide a valuable service to the site where she will work but will also allow her to acquire skills in the five areas she identified through the assessment process.

The remaining three sections of the contract are instructive elements. In the site location section, students should report where they plan to conduct the activities described in the contract. In most cases, the site supervisor will need to provide space to the student. Some activities, like conducting research, may be conducted at other locations, but it is essential that the student have a space somewhere on-site if the student expects to be a contributing member of the staff.

The proposed work schedule is another important component for all parties involved in the contract. Students need to balance the expectations of the supervised experience with the other obligations they assume each academic term, including other classes, jobs, GA positions, studying time, and personal life. The site supervisor needs to have a general idea of when to expect the student in the office. In many cases, interns share office space with other employees, and the site supervisor may need to juggle various demands on office space to accommodate the student. Knowing when the student plans to work enables the site supervisor to accomplish the necessary planning. Finally, the faculty supervisor will benefit from knowing the proposed schedule. The schedule provides the faculty supervisor with an idea of how much time the student will be spending on site, enabling her or him to evaluate whether the schedule will allow the student to accomplish the objectives of the contract and balance those responsibilities with other academic demands.

The final element includes the signatures of the three parties involved in the experience. This may seem like a minor bureaucratic matter, but signatures suggest that all the parties have reviewed the components of the contract and have agreed to the parameters of the contract. It is also important that the student obtain all signatures prior to starting work at the site. If the student is to meet all the time requirements of the contract, this usually means designing the contract and obtaining signatures prior to the start of the academic term in which the student enrolls for the supervised experience. Obviously, this calls for advance planning on the part of the student. But we would argue that supervised experiences are most meaningful when they are intentionally planned. Intentional planning, including consultation with the site supervisor and identifying clear objectives and activities, requires time that is typically not available to students during the crunch that accompanies the opening weeks of an academic term. Therefore, we encourage students to conduct their assessments and develop their contracts in the weeks preceding the term in which they plan to conduct the experience. Once the contract has been developed and signed, the next step in the process relates to the structure around which the supervised experience is designed.

THE STRUCTURE OF THE SUPERVISED EXPERIENCE

Once students have assessed their skills, targeted those they wish to develop, identified a site for the supervised practice, and designed the contract, they often feel that the only remaining element of the experience is to conduct the work. But that is not necessarily the case. It is important to have an understanding of the structure around which that experience will be built. This structure includes two components: the roles those involved in the experience will play, and the pedagogical approach the experience assumes.

Roles in the Supervised Experience

There are three key players in every supervised experience: the student, the site supervisor, and the faculty supervisor. Each plays a distinctive role in the experience. Each brings certain expectations to the experience and each expects certain outcomes from the experience. Understanding a bit about each of those roles may provide insight into how the structure of the experience works (the roles of the supervisors are dealt with in greater detail in chapter 3).

The student is the first key player in the supervised experience. It is interesting to note that much of the literature focuses on administrative expectations of students in internships. These include meeting certain grade point requirements, completing course prerequisites, enrolling for a limited number of practicum units, and completing the appropriate paperwork (Schmidt et al., 1992). Others have described the steps students should take to ensure they receive any entitlements that might be associated with the experience. For example, Green (1997) suggests that students ask departments for a list of approved sites, verify the type of credit they will receive, inquire about transportation to and from the site, and ask whether they will be paid for their work or reimbursed for the expenses they will incur during the experience. There is also literature that describes how students should behave once they start working at the site, which includes asking questions, repeating instructions to ensure they are clear, being pleasant to coworkers, and adhering to the established work schedule (Green, 1997). Some have gone so far as to suggest that if the experience is not a positive one, that may be the fault of an "inappropriate student" who does not understand the complexity of an organizational setting (Alexander, 1982, p. 130).

From the perspective of this book, the student's role in the supervised experience goes beyond merely meeting administrative or behavioral requirements. Students need to be realistic in their expectations. They bring certain strengths and skills to the setting, including their interest in the work conducted at the site, their enthusiasm for that work, and their interest in the particular projects they will work on during the experience. Moreover, they bring a fresh perspective to the setting, seeing things others who have worked in that setting for longer periods of time may have overlooked. But students should also be prepared to deal with issues they did not expect when they contracted to work at the site. Every organizational setting experiences periods of time when the work is more reactive than proactive, when tasks are highly routine rather than highly challenging, when compliance is more appropriate than creativity. Organizations are also political entities, and in-fighting is apparent at times causing tension among coworkers and between units. Students should expect to encounter such issues during the course of the experience. Perhaps the most important thing they can remember is that they are there to learn about the organization and its functioning in the broadest sense. That learning includes developing an appreciation for the glamorous as well as the underbelly of the setting. If students come away from a supervised experience with a thorough understanding of the organization and its inner workings they can be more realistic about what to expect should they end up working in that, or a similar, setting. This sort of learning can be invaluable when identifying realistic professional aspirations.

The second key player in the supervised experience is the site supervisor, the person with whom the student will have the most contact over the course of the academic term. The literature on the role of the supervisor, to some degree, parallels what has been written about the student roles. Supervisors are directed to ensure that certain administrative functions occur like orienting the student to the functions of the office and documenting the time spent on the experience (Ciafalo, 1992; Fernald et al., 1982). In other cases, the behaviors supervisors are expected to exhibit are identified, including meeting regularly with students, training them on specific tasks, and integrating them into the setting (Fernald et al., 1982, Mason, 1985). But some scholars take a more enlightened approach to the role of the supervisor. They encourage supervisors to realize that they play a dual role when working with students, supervisor and educator. As educators, supervisors need to recognize the stages that are associated with internships. These stages include exhilaration, rejection, integration, and transformation on the part of the student. If supervisors recognize the attributes associated with each stage, they can more effectively work with the student in a stage-relevant manner

(Garvey & Vorsteg, 1992). In another sense, the supervisor serves as an interpreter, connecting the theory students have learned in the classroom with the work that is conducted in the real world (Ramsey, 1974). (Readers are directed to chapter 3 for a more complete discussion about the roles of the site supervisor and a developmental model of the internship experience.)

The final key player in the supervised experience is the faculty supervisor. Surprisingly, most of what has been written about faculty roles focuses on what they are not prepared to do. Many faculty members operate on the assumption that they are experts in their field. Their role in the classroom, therefore, is to impart that knowledge to students. They disdain the idea that they are responsible for job training. Fortunately that is not usually the case in student affairs, because it is an applied field and most faculty members in this area have had experience as practitioners before becoming full-time faculty members. Faculty members, however, may not be up to date on the most recent developments in a functional area or the latest thinking about how to be respond to student wants and needs (see chapter 3 for a detailed discussion of the faculty supervisor's roles and responsibilities).

The Pedagogical Structure

The pedagogical structure of the supervised experience refers to the form the class associated with the internship assumes. There are a number of approaches to the pedagogical component described in the literature. Toohey et al. (1996) offer a particularly insightful discussion of several models. The attendance model describes a minimalist approach in which the class serves primarily as a means of ensuring that students are working at their sites and completing their assigned tasks. Slightly more advanced is the work history model in which the class is designed to demonstrate to students how they can capitalize on the tasks they are completing on site when they conduct a job search. The work history model is grounded in the assumption that since supervised practice experiences vary so much from student to student, there can be no coherent or structured learning experience for all internship students in a given term, so the class focuses on individual accomplishments. A more modified approach is the broad abilities model in which the faculty member identifies broad objectives for the learning component of the internship experience including things like critical thinking and the development of interpersonal skills. These abilities form the focus of the educational program and the instructor strives to ensure that all students make gains in at least some of these abilities. The specific competencies model is a somewhat more structured approach to learning in which the faculty member identifies key competencies that all practicum students should learn on their sites and works to ensure that all students acquire these competencies. The advantages to such an approach relate to the consistency of performance it can ensure for students while the disadvantages relate to the degree of organization it takes to ensure that consistency.

The final model described in the Toohey et al. (1996) framework, the negotiated curriculum model, reflects the model most frequently used for supervised experiences in higher education and student affairs administration. In this model, the student, site supervisor, and faculty supervisor develop a contract that identifies the tasks the student will assume and the knowledge, skills, and competencies the student will gain from accomplishing those tasks. The advantages to this model include the higher levels of commitment and motivation students demonstrate when they are working on individualized agendas. The disadvantages relate to the enormous amount of effort it can take for the faculty member to individually negotiate each contract each academic term for each student.

We advocate for a modified version of the negotiated curriculum model for faculty who teach the supervised experience class. Clearly, we believe that an individually designed contract is the most beneficial approach for the student and is likely the most beneficial approach for the organization in which the student works since the approach identifies specific tasks and responsibilities the intern will assume. But we suggest that the role of the faculty supervisor should extend beyond simply tracking the progress students make on their contracts over the course of the academic term.

RESOURCES NEEDED IN SUPERVISED PRACTICE EXPERIENCES

Although the previous sections in this chapter have focused on the development of supervised practice experiences, there are two other issues students need to consider when they undertake such experiences. The first of these relates to the resources students may need to successfully complete the experience. The breadth and variety of the supervised experiences that students in higher education and student affairs programs design renders it difficult to identify all the resources students may need, but we encourage students to consider their needs in four distinct areas when evaluating potential internship sites: personnel, facilities, equipment, and financial support. Table 2.1 summarizes these resources.

Personnel Resources

The first of these resources, personnel, refers to the types of access students will have to the personnel who will play key roles in the supervised experi-

TABLE 2.1. Resource Checklist

Resource
Personnel Resources
       Site Supervisor
       Faculty Supervisor
       Support Staff
       Other:
Facilities
       Work Space On-Site
       Meeting Rooms
       Classrooms
       Lab Access
       Approval to Work at Home
       Other:
Equipment
       Desk
       Filing Cabinet
       Phone
       Mailbox
       Copier Access
       FAX Access
       Office Supplies
       Computer
       Special Equipment
       Other:
Financial
       Salary/Stipend/Honorarium
       Travel to Site
       Project Travel
       Hidden Costs
       Insurance
       Other:

ence. Perhaps the most important resource in this area is the site supervisor. It is important that students negotiate the frequency and degree of access they will have to their site supervisor. Even though students may feel they need to confer with their supervisor frequently, they also need to recognize that most site supervisors are managing other personnel at the same time they are supervising the intern. Their availability may be limited, a problem that is further exacerbated by the fact that the student is typically only in the office on certain days and during certain hours. Students should also recognize that their need to meet with the supervisor may vary over the course of the academic term. In some cases, frequent contact early in the assignment is necessary. In other cases, where students are working on long-term projects, the need to confer with the supervisor may arise later in the term. We encourage students to discuss in detail the time they will have with their site supervisor when designing the contract, and include that time in the contract so that all parties are clear on the expectations in this regard.

Access to the faculty supervisor is the second form of support students need to consider when designing experiences. Even though students may be assured of some access to the faculty supervisor, both students and faculty members have other obligations they will be meeting during the academic term. For students who have internships at institutions far removed from the home campus (especially during the summer), face-to-face contact may be difficult, if not impossible. During the regular academic year, students may have other classes to attend and jobs or GA responsibilities to fulfill. Faculty are teaching other classes and working on other projects. But faculty supervisors are valuable resources for students in supervised experiences. They can assist students in resolving difficulties they encounter on the job and serve as sounding boards for students' ideas.

The third group of individuals who can serve as a resource for student interns is the support staff at the site, including receptionists, secretaries, accounting technicians, and others. These staff members are frequently overlooked when students and site supervisors design contracts. Although interns may provide valuable services to the units in which they work, they can also create an additional workload for support staff. Receptionists may be expected to take phone messages or schedule meetings for the intern. Secretaries may be expected to type materials or maintain files for the student. Accounting technicians may be expected to manage funding requests or manage budgets associated with the intern's work. If this is the case, support staff members ought to be advised of these expectations. Support staff can serve as powerful allies to students in supervised experiences. They can socialize the intern about the routines and procedures the office employs. They can make a big difference in how quickly the student becomes acclimated to the culture of the office. The services they provide are frequently overlooked or underrated. We urge students and site supervisors to recognize the important contributions these staff resources can provide over the course of the supervised experience (see chapter 3 for additional discussion about working with support staff and potential pitfalls to avoid).

Facilities

Another group of resources students and site and faculty supervisors need to address when designing experiences relates to facilities. There is the space the student will need to conduct the work on the site and, at times, interns may need space elsewhere on campus to complete their assigned responsibilities. Space on most college and university campuses is at a premium. In many cases, departments barely have sufficient space to accommodate their full-time employees. So finding space to house a graduate student intern can be difficult. However, if the experience is supposed to expose the student to the functioning of the department or office, having a designated workspace in the department or office setting is a necessity. At times, this may mean assigning the intern space in an office already occupied by other staff or GAs. Although sharing an office may not be ideal, it assures the intern of a place in the office in which work related to the experience can be conducted. When interns are assigned to shared space, we encourage them to work out suitable arrangements with their officemates and respect the roles that others in the space need to play. Interns also need to remember that to some degree they will always be viewed as visitors by those who work there regularly.

It is also important to consider other facilities that student interns may need in order to successfully meet the terms of their contracts. These may include conference rooms, classrooms, or access to media or other labs on campus. The kinds of facilities that may be needed are directly related to the tasks the student has described in the contract. When additional facilities are needed, the supervisor may need to make arrangements with those who manage the facilities to provide access to the student. Alternatively, they may need to ensure that the intern is listed as an authorized staff member of the department so that she or he can reserve space as needed.

Finally, there may be some occasions or circumstances in which interns can conduct work related to the contract in their homes. Writing reports, making phone calls, or designing programs are activities that interns can conceivably conduct from their home settings. In fact, some students prefer to handle these kinds of assignments from home, particularly if they are sharing office space at the work site. Other students, however, prefer to distinguish their home environment from their work environment and may not be comfortable managing work tasks in the home setting. Obviously, each case is unique. But if students plan to conduct some of their assignments from home, they need to discuss this option with their site supervisor prior to finalizing the contract. It is important to remember that the intern needs to spend a considerable amount of time in the work setting in order to observe and understand the intricate workings of the setting.

Equipment

Another resource that is frequently omitted in the process of planning supervised experiences is equipment. Again, the needs for equipment are directly related to the tasks defined in the contract. This renders it difficult to identify all the types of equipment that may be needed for the varied projects students assume in supervised experiences, but some items come immediately to mind. Interns need to know if they will have a desk, a filing cabinet, a telephone, a mailbox, access to a copier, access to a fax machine, use of a computer, or access to other equipment that they may need to fulfill their responsibilities. Even minor pieces of equipment such as work trays, index cardholders, message boxes, staplers, or tape dispensers can be essential tools for students, depending on the nature of their assignments.

Related to the issue of office equipment is the issue of office supplies. Access to paper, message pads, pens, stencils, or paper clips can affect the student's ability to complete assignments. Even though these may seem like minor matters, supplies are costly, particularly for units that are operating on shoestring budgets. A discussion about what kind of support students can expect to receive with respect to office supplies can help avoid any problems or shortages that arise after the intern starts working. It is particularly important that the site supervisor inform the support staff member who has responsibility for ordering and issuing office supplies regarding which kinds of intern requests should be honored and which require supervisor approval.

A desktop computer is a staple in most college and university offices. But providing students with a computer also involves ensuring that they have the appropriate ancillary equipment (keyboard, printer access, monitor) as well as the appropriate software to operate that equipment and the specialized software that may be necessary to complete the projects designated in the contract. There also may be other forms of specialized equipment that students will need. These may include audio- and videotaping equipment, slide projectors, overhead projectors, LCDs, microphones, movie projectors and screens, or VCRs, among others. If there are costs associated with purchasing or renting that equipment, clear expectations about which party will incur those costs should be established.

Financial Resources

The final resource that students should consider when designing supervised experiences may be the most obvious: financial support. Like other resources, financial support needs should be linked to the activities that students are expected to engage in under the terms of the contract. The first that comes to mind is any form of pay the student might receive in conjunction with the work, including hourly wages, stipends, or honoraria. In most cases, there are institutional or departmental policies that dictate whether students are even eligible for such payments. Institutional policy may dictate whether interns are eligible to receive compensation. Often when interns are also enrolled students at the institution, they may not be eligible for stipends. Internships conducted at colleges or universities other than the intern's home institution, however, often qualify for remuneration. Some internships, typically those sponsored during the summer by professional associations such as Association of College and University Housing Officers-International (ACUHO-I), National Orientation Directors Association (NODA), and American College Personnel Association (ACPA), for instance, carry stipends and sometimes housing and meals .

There are, however, other costs that may be incurred in connection with an internship. For example, students may need to travel to and from the site if the experience is not conducted at the home campus. Gas, mileage, and parking costs associated with such travel should be calculated into the expenses the student anticipates. Other forms of travel may be required to complete the projects identified in the contract. In some cases, travel to conferences, including registration fees, hotel and meal costs, and travel expenses may be incurred. Some site supervisors may offer to cover these expenses, or split the costs with the student, but there is no standard practice in this area. Again, it is imperative that students understand the potential costs associated with the projects they undertake in their supervised experiences.

Finally, there may be other, more hidden costs that students should consider when planning internships. In many cases, working in a professional capacity in an office will require appropriate dress. Many graduate students may not have wardrobes that meet the dress standards of the office. Accessories, including jackets, dress shoes, and briefcases might also be necessary. Depending upon the nature of the contract, liability or some other form of insurance may be warranted. Many institutions require students in a supervised practice experience to have professional liability insurance, which may be obtained at relatively low cost by student members of NASPA and ACPA. Even if not required, interns are strongly advised to secure professional liability insurance before beginning the internship experience. Even though most campuses have policies in place to cover employees, students are urged to find out whether they, in their volunteer capacities, will be covered by such policies. Other expenses such as long distance telephone calls made from home or time spent on-line on the home computer may be incurred. All these issues should be contemplated when designing contracts and discussed with the site supervisor.

Resources are important considerations in the supervised experience but considerations that are frequently overlooked by students and site supervisors. The resources that are available to interns and the costs associated with conducting the projects identified in the contract are concerns that should be addressed in the design stage of the process. We strongly encourage students and site supervisors to spend some time identifying all the resources that may be associated with each proposed project and to determine who will bear the responsibility for providing those resources. Such conversations can prevent misunderstandings between students and supervisors once the student has started working on site.

$\mathscr{E}$**xercise**

- For one week, keep a list of the resources you use in your current assistantship or job.
- At the end of the week, sort the resources into groups of personnel, facilities, equipment, and financial resources.
- Use this list to identify the resources you might need in an internship.
- Identify people you can turn to for advice about resources.

OVERALL MANAGEMENT ISSUES

The final component that needs to be addressed in any discussion of supervised experiences relates to the overall management of the experience. By *overall management*, we mean the balance that students need to achieve both in the context of the experience itself as well as between the experience and their other responsibilities. The individualized nature of the supervised experience, and the concomitant motivation that usually accompanies that experience, can disrupt the normal sense of balance. To this end, students may need to address many of the following issues in relation to the internship.

On-Site Balance

The first group of concerns relates to maintaining a balance within the context of the supervised practice setting. The most obvious of these is the balance that students need to maintain among the various projects they agree to complete as part of the contract. It is not unusual for students to identify projects at the outset that they find are not particularly interesting or challenging once they actually start working on them. In other instances, students may identify some projects that get much more complex than they first anticipated. A tempting response to either of these scenarios is to simply ignore that particular task or project and devote more time to the other components of the contract. This is seldom a judicious path to take. Remember that the purpose of the supervised experience is to provide students with opportunities to learn. Learning does not occur when students avoid certain components of their contracts. (Interns should also remember that evaluation of the intern and awarding of course grades are based to a substantial degree on fulfilling the internship contract.) Students who encounter challenges in balancing projects should discuss their concerns with their site supervisors. Supervisors may be able to provide some guidance that will enable the students to regain a balance among their assignments. It may be that revisions in the contract are warranted. In either case, the resolution ought to be negotiated with the site supervisor as soon as difficulties arise. To raise the issue during the last week of the internship may not lead to a satisfactory resolution of the problems.

The second form of balance students need to maintain within the internship context is the issue of dependence versus independence. By this we mean the degree to which students feel free to act on their own versus the times when they feel obligated to seek close supervision. There is no easy formula to guide students in this endeavor. We can only suggest that there are times when greater dependence may be warranted. For example, many interns need extra guidance when they first start working at the site or when they undertake a new project. As more time is spent on site, it is likely that students will feel more comfortable acting independently or with more limited guidance. We encourage students to ask their supervisors if they are acting appropriately under different circumstances. Particularly early in the internship, interns should request general guidelines from the site supervisor about her or his expectations in this regard (see chapter 3 for the discussion of the developmental process in the intern/site supervisor relationship).

The final issue to be addressed in the context of the internship setting is the balance between training and learning. We have argued here and elsewhere in this book that the supervised practice experience is an important component of the graduate education curriculum. It is relatively easy, however, for both students and site supervisors to focus more on the training element of the experience and less on the educational element. After all, the student is expected to behave as a professional. And supervisors are encouraged to treat the student as they would any other inexperienced professional. These expectations readily lead to treating the supervised experience as a job training experience. From the perspective of this book, an internship should be much more. Even though on-the-job training is certainly a component of the internship experience, it is only one component of that experience. If students or supervisors realize that they have not talked about what the student has learned or have not discussed the relationship between what the student has learned in classes and what the student has learned on the job, it may be time to revisit the issue of balance between training and learning.

Balance Between the Internship and Other Responsibilities

There are also issues of balance between the supervised experience and the other responsibilities students have in any given academic term. The most obvious of these is the balance between the supervised experience and the other classes that the student may be taking. Supervised practice experiences are often taken in the middle or toward the end of the student's program of study after sufficient classroom learning has occurred to prepare the student for the experience. As the student nears completion of the degree, the issue of finding a job becomes more important. It is easy to rationalize that devoting more time and energy to the internship will better serve the student in the job search process. Focusing extensively on the supervised experience, however, diminishes the time and energy the student can devote to other classes. Because completing all courses is required to earn the degree, students need to keep the benefits of the experience in perspective. Finding the proper balance between the internship and other classes enables the student to achieve both the degree and the opportunity to pursue the position of their dreams.

Most students in internships also have responsibilities outside of coursework. Many serve as GAs or hold jobs outside the campus. Again, it is incumbent upon students to remember *all* their obligations, both the internship site and the outside employer. It is important to remember that their supervisors at those other jobs are likely to serve as references when the student searches for a professional position. It is likely that GA or job supervisors have employed the student for a longer period than the internship supervisor. Students need to balance the demands of their competing jobs to ensure that they adequately meet all their responsibilities.

Finally, many of the most frequently ignored responsibilities students in higher education or student affairs graduate programs encounter are personal in nature. Many students have spouses, partners, children, or other family members for whom they provide care. Nurturing such relationships requires time and energy. The basic philosophy that guides student affairs is the holistic development of the student. This involves promoting their development intellectually, socially, emotionally, physically, spiritually, and personally. Yet many successful professionals do not model a well-rounded lifestyle. They work more than 40 hours per week and often devote evenings and weekends to job-related activities. Graduate students may be particularly prone to focusing too much on their studies and campus jobs at the expense of their personal responsibilities or find themselves in time squeezes due to dysfunctional time management skills, poor planning, or inadequate impulse control. Finding a balance between the expectations of the internship and other academic demands and personal demands is not easy. But we would argue that students who try to balance their lives while in graduate school will be much better prepared to balance those competing demands once they finish their degrees and assume full-time professional positions.

$\mathscr{E}$**xercise**

- Identify all the roles you currently play (student, GA, friend, spouse, parent, sibling, etc.).
- For the next week, keep track of how much time you spend in fulfilling each of these roles.
- Review your results and identify the roles that are consuming too much or too little of your time.
- How can you achieve a better balance among your roles and responsibilities?

CONCLUSION

In conclusion, the internship can be nothing more than on-the-job training or it can be one of the most meaningful learning experiences in the student's curriculum. The success of the experience depends to a large extent on how purposefully it is designed. A successful experience is one that is very intentional in its design. Intentional designs are grounded in careful assessments of skills and selective designations of objectives. These objectives should be translated into a carefully crafted contract that clearly delineates what the student will do and what skills and competencies the student should work on developing. Other issues such as the resources needed to complete the terms of the contract should also be addressed before work at the site commences. Finally, it is essential to keep the supervised experience in perspective and to balance the time and energy devoted to the experience with the other responsibilities of the student. If all these components are addressed when designing the supervised experience, students can maximize the benefits of the experience and accrue all of the important learning that can occur through the supervised experience.

REFERENCES

Alexander, J. R. (1982). Institutional design of public service internships: Conceptual, academic, and structural problems. *Teaching Political Science, 9,* 127–133.

Carter, R., Cooke, F., & Neal, B. (1996). Action-centered learning in industry. In J. Tait & P. Knight (Eds.), *The management of independent learning* (pp. 65–73). London: Koga Page Limited.

Ciofalo, A. (1992). What every professor and work-site supervisor should know about internships. In A. Ciofalo (Ed.), *Internships: Perspectives on experiential learning* (pp. 52-73). Malabar, FL: Krieger Publishing.

Featherman, S. (1998). Higher education in the United States: Changing markets and evolving values. In S. M. Natale, R. P. Hoffman, & G. Hayward (Eds.), *Business education and training: A value-laden process: Vol. 5: The management of values: Organizational and educational issues* (pp. 25–33). New York: University Press of America.

Fernald, C. D., Tedeschi, R. G., Siegfried, W. D., Gilmore, D. C., Grimsley, D. L., & Chipley, B. (1982). Designing and managing an undergraduate practicum course in psychology. *Teaching of Psychology, 9,* 155–160.

Garvey, D., & Vorsteg, A. C. (1992). From theory to practice for college interns: A stage theory approach. *The Journal of Experiential Education, 15*(2), 40–43

Green, M. W. (1997). *Internship success: Real-world, step-by-step advice on getting the most out of internships.* Chicago: VGM Career Horizons.

Harcharik, K. (1993). Piaget and the university internship experience. *Journal of Cooperative Education, 29,* 24–32.

Joslin, A. W., & Ellis, N. E. (1990). *Merging leadership theories and the world of practice: Shared responsibility for a successful internship.* (ERIC Document Reproduction Service No. ED 328 986).

Mason, G. E. (1985, April). *Coordinating the internship program: The ins and outs of directing interns.* Paper presented at the annual conference of the Central States Speech Association, Indianapolis, IN.

McCormick, D. W. (1993). Critical thinking, experiential learning, and internships. *Journal of Management Education, 17,* 260–262.

Miller, T. K. (Ed.). (2001). *The CAS book of professional standards for higher education.* Washington DC: Council for the Advancement of Standards in Higher Education.

Ramsey, W. R. (1974). Role of the agency supervisor. In J. Duley (Ed.), *New Directions for Higher Education: No. 6. Implementing field experience education* (pp. 45–54). San Francisco: Jossey-Bass.

Ryan, M., & Cassidy, J. R. (1996). Internships and excellence. *Liberal Education, 82*(3), 16–23.

Saunders, S. A., & Cooper, D. L. (2001). Programmatic interventions: Translating theory to practice. In R. B. Winston, Jr., D. G. Creamer, & T. K. Miller (Eds.), *The professional student affairs administrator: Educator, leader, and manager.* New York: Brunner-Routledge.

Schmidt, W. V., Gardner, G. H., Benjamin, J. B., Conaway, R. N., & Haskins, W. A. (1992, October). *Teaching the college course series: Directing independent studies and internships in communication.* Paper presented at the annual meeting of the Speech Communication Association, Chicago, IL.

Stewart, G. M. (1994). *Skills analysis survey for graduate students in higher education and student affairs graduate preparation programs.* Unpublished manuscript, University of Maryland at College Park.

Taylor, M. S. (1992). Effects of college internships on individual participants. In A. Ciofalo

(Ed.), *Internships: Perspectives on experiential learning* (pp. 52–73). Malabar, FL: Krieger.

Toohey, S., Ryan, G., & Hughes, C. (1996). Assessing the practicum. *Assessment and Evaluation in Higher Education, 21,* 215–227.

Van Aalst, F. D. (1974). Program design. In J. Duley (Ed.), *Implementing field experience education* (pp. 67–75). New Directions for Higher Education: No. 6. San Francisco: Jossey-Bass.

Winston, R. B., Jr., Lathrop, B. J., Lease, J., Davis, J. S., Newsome, K., & Beeny, C. (2001). Supervised practice in student affairs preparation: State of the art. University of Georgia. Unpublished manuscript.

Wolf, J. F. (1980). Experiential learning in professional education: Concepts and tools. In J. F. Wolf (Ed.), *New Directions for Experiential Learning: No. 8. Developing experiential learning programs for professional education.* San Francisco: Jossey-Bass.

Chapter 3

SUPERVISION
Relationships That Support Learning

Roger B. Winston, Jr.
Don G. Creamer

From our almost 50 years of working with interns, we have concluded that the success of a student's internship experience is determined principally by two factors: the quality of relationships with supervisors, support staff, and the site's clientele and the amount of effort invested in learning. In this chapter we address the realities of the internship setting, site supervision, the development of supervisory roles, building relationships that promote learning, and maximizing the benefits of supervision. We conclude by addressing problems that might arise in the work setting and identify some of the typical challenges that interns can face.

Generally, students enter the internship experience with high expectations. They expect to learn how to run a student activities office, a student disciplinary system, or an admissions program, for example, so that at the end of the internship they will be fully prepared for at least an entry-level position in the functional area. Although they are to be admired for this optimism and enthusiasm, such goals may be too ambitious for the student and too far-reaching for the functional area, and can ultimately lead to disappointment or even disillusionment about the student affairs and higher education fields. What is achieved during the internship, perhaps more than anything, is dependent upon the nature of the relationships that the intern develops with site supervisors, office staff, faculty supervisors, and student clients.

INTERNSHIP SUPERVISION

The internship experience requires that students be actively involved in the ongoing operation of one or more functional areas within an institution. This involvement, however, has more to it than *doing* or *working*. The overriding purpose of the internship experience is for the student to learn. For learning to be optimized, students must observe, read, and collect information, perform professional-level tasks, and receive frequent candid feedback about performance, demeanor, and attitudes. Consequently, supervision is a crucial component in the successful internship experience. Ideally, each intern should receive supervision from two sources: the site supervisor and the faculty supervisor. The site supervisor interacts with the intern frequently at the site, structures the activities in which the intern is involved, and provides support and candid feedback on an ongoing basis. The faculty supervisor has a less directly involved role than the site supervisor, which includes helping interns to reflect on and make meaning from their experiences, providing emotional support, and assisting with problem solving when necessary.

FOUNDATIONAL UNDERSTANDINGS

Before dealing with the multifaceted aspects of internship supervision, it is important that interns understand some basic attributes of higher education institutions and how the internship experience fits in that context.

Realities of the Internship Setting

From the student's perspective, the internship experience generally is eagerly anticipated as one of the first opportunities to actually *do student affairs work*. The internship experience is a vital part of the total professional preparation program, but it differs from classroom-based courses in several important ways. Because these sites are in the *real world*, they are always imperfect and often fall short of the descriptions provided in textbooks and professional journals. Several aspects of internship sites need to be clarified.

Primary Mission of Internship Sites. Internship sites are not created to train interns, unlike classroom-based instruction, which is designed solely for the purpose of educating the enrolled students. Internship sites exist to fulfill institutional responsibilities. As a consequence, should there be a conflict between the needs of interns and fulfilling the site's primary mission, the intern's needs invariably and properly must be given a lower priority. Interns should be thoroughly aware of the primary mission of the chosen site and be adaptable in their expectations of how the site can serve their needs.

Site Supervisors as Working Professionals. From the perspective of professional preparation, site supervisors generally are volunteers who agree to accept interns and to provide supervision as a responsibility above and beyond their customary work assignments. Except in rare instances, site supervisors receive no additional monetary compensation for the work they do in internship supervision. In addition, because supervising interns frequently is not a major part of staff members' *official* job descriptions, they may not receive recognition from the student affairs division for their efforts. Site supervisors usually serve these functions because of a sense of professional responsibility and out of a desire to make a contribution to professional preparation. Realistically, students also must understand that there may be a considerable range in the level of commitment that site supervisors show during the course of the internship and across internship sites.

Dealing with the Unanticipated. One of the hallmarks of work in student affairs is the variability of issues, problems, and concerns that one is called on to address daily. In settings that deal with students' out-of-class life, work in student affairs is seldom routine and cannot be completely anticipated from day to day (even hour to hour on some days). Because of the unpredictability of the challenges that staff members face in their customary duties, sometimes the best-laid plans for internship supervision must be changed on short notice. Flexibility is a highly valued trait in practitioners and interns alike and should be exercised when unexpected demands are placed on sites and the people who manage them.

Levels of Supervisor Expertise and Experience. Seldom do site supervisors have extensive training in supervising staff or interns. Winston and Creamer (1997) found that only about one-half of the staff who responded to their nationwide survey reported having received training in providing supervision to staff. Of those who had received training, only 45% had received any training since completing graduate school. An even smaller number of practitioners have received instruction in supervising student interns. Consequently, most site supervisors are learning as they go or have developed their style and technique through observation of others or trial and error (much in the same way that many college instructors learn to teach). Given this situation, interns need to adjust to supervisors' multiple responsibilities and supervision style and be explicit about their needs and desires. Discerning interns help their supervisors by telling them what they feel they need; sending subtle messages may not be sufficient. On the other hand, interns must be cognizant of the internship limitations; what an intern wants or needs may not be realistic in a given setting or may require more than a site supervisor is able or willing to provide.

In the end, interns have some influence over the quality of supervision if their behavior justifies responsiveness by supervisors. It is important to remember that quality supervision is a two-way responsibility, ideally even synergistic (Winston & Creamer, 1997). Recognition of the realities of supervisor expertise and experience will help the intern seek and receive learning-oriented guidance.

Variability among Sites. Internship sites deal with real people who have real problems and issues, in an institution that has a history of both success and failure, and in a constantly changing society. As a consequence, when students look below the surface, they see that most internship sites have shortcomings and imperfections, as well as hidden excellence. Some sites are doing cutting-edge work and are on the leading cusp of their functional area. Other sites are solid; that is, they are not doing much that can be classified as new or highly innovative, but student evaluations of their programs are positive and they are considered in the mainstream of their functional area. A few sites may be struggling due to a lack of adequate institutional support, frequent turnover in leadership, uncertainty of mission, lack of adequate professional preparation of staff, changing societal conditions, "fossilized" leadership in the site or at higher levels of administration, or shifting demographic characteristics of the student body.

To be an effective internship placement, students do not require assignments only in cutting-edge sites. Valuable learning can be acquired in any of the types of settings described above. The approach to learning and the amount of support received will vary. Just as entry-level professionals often must select among position offers from institutions that are less than a perfect fit, that may not be functioning at the forefront of the profession, so it is with internship selection. In many instances, interns may learn more valuable lessons and skills in settings that require more effort on their part than in more congenial environments. The indisputably valuable professional is one who can come into a less-than-ideal situation and find educationally purposeful activities that allow him or her to learn and to contribute to the unit. In this manner, such professionals may actually change poorly functioning units and help them become more valuable to students.

Thus, the realities of internship settings call upon interns to be cognizant of characteristics, both subtle and overt, of the setting and the actual types of guided experiences available to them. Interns would do well to adopt an attitude of reciprocity in the internship experience that centers on mutuality, with the staff in the site and the intern each contributing to the other to enhance learning.

*ℛ*eflection *𝒫*oint
Consider the supervision you have received in other settings.
- What are some strategies you can use to find "hidden" learning opportunities in the site?
- What should you tell your site supervisor about your learning needs?
- Are there things your supervisors should know about your unique needs and expectations of this experience?

SITE SUPERVISION

Both site supervisors and faculty supervisors play multiple, complementary roles in internships. These roles need to be fully explored. In the sections to follow, we discuss the purposes that site supervision plays in the internship experience and present a model of developmental stages through which many intern–supervisor relationships progress. Following that, we address the faculty supervisor's roles and functions.

A Definition

Supervision for the purposes of this book is a method of training and teaching in which experienced professionals provide guidance, opportunities for skill development, crucial feedback, and general support in a field setting to graduate students who are enrolled in a professional preparation program. It is an interactive, collaborative process in which both the supervisor and intern make vital contributions. Ideally, it is a synergetic process in that the total effect of the supervision process is greater than the sum of individual contributions (see Winston & Creamer, 1997 for a complete discussion of this process in professional staff supervision). High quality supervision is essential if interns are to have an optimal learning experience. Usually, the quality of supervision is the central determinant of the educational value of the internship and is far more important than opulent facilities, large unit budgets, a large number of staff members, or size and type of institution.

Supervision That Promotes Learning

Good supervision is based on: (a) a trusting and supportive relationship between supervisor and intern; (b) an organizational structure that permits interns to observe widely and to assume some responsibilities normally associated with professionals in the site; (c) theory-based practice; (d) open communication and candor; (e) mutual respect; (f) practice that emphasizes observance of professional ethical standards; and (g) accountability.

From our experience, the quality of the relationship between supervisor and intern is the single most important factor in determining the ultimate success of the internship experience. Several things need to be kept in mind about this relationship: (a) it is unequal in terms of power, status, and expertise; (b) even though friendly interactions are necessary for optimum learning, it is important to maintain certain boundaries to avoid development of dual relationships and to permit the exchange of critical evaluations; and (c) it is purposive, that is, the supervisory relationship serves to facilitate accomplishment of the internship learning goals. For the supervisor to guide and direct the intern, a trusting relationship with the intern must be established that allows both parties to have open, honest, and nondefensive interactions.

For an internship site to offer the greatest number of opportunities for interns to learn, it must be open to the intern's observations and limited participation. Sites that are very compartmentalized or have an atmosphere of mistrust and suspicion generally do not offer interns sufficient opportunities to see below the surface, and, therefore, do not offer good learning potential. In some sites, because of fear of job loss or hostile interactions among staff or between the staff and the supervisor, interns are viewed with distrust.

The best learning opportunities are commonly found in sites that base their practice on relevant theory and data based research. In such sites, staff can assist interns in more clearly understanding the connections between the theories and research findings they have been reading and discussing in class and actual practice. Sites that operate atheoretically or without the benefit of grounded research about their operations are unable to explain clearly the basis of practice and may confuse interns or cause doubt in their minds about the value of the classroom learning experience. Ideally, class learning and internship learning should complement each other and help interns integrate their professional education experience. Achieving this integration is a hallmark of successful internships.

Open communication in a site makes the intern's learning easier and less frustrating. In sites that have communication deficits or obstructions, interns may need to rely more heavily on their faculty supervisors, who should be functioning in concert with site supervisors, to help the interns decipher what is going on in the organization. "Shortcomings in communication can give rise to a variety of misunderstandings and faulty assumptions that undermine the intern–supervisor relationship and impede its effectiveness" (Chiaferi & Griffin, 1997, p. 29). Ideally, interns should feel free to ask questions about anything pertinent to the learning experience without fear of causing emotional distress or hostile replies. On the other hand, however, interns should construct their questions in ways that are diplomatic and professional and that do not degrade the work of the site.

Internships are more likely to flourish in ethical environments and languish in dishonest environments. In ethical environments, professional ethics are frequently discussed and professional standards statements explicitly influence actions. In these environments, interns are involved in discussions of ethical issues facing the unit and, consequently, are exposed to maximum learning potential. Interns should be encouraged to raise ethical questions with site supervisors and staff. They should be a part of the maintenance of ethical relationships with student clients and should be granted the benefits of ongoing dialogue with site colleagues about principles and moral codes that guide practice in the site.

Finally, supervisors can maximize interns' learning through establishment of an accountability process. Interns often need assistance in establishing structure for the internship experience. An effective way to accomplish this is for the supervisor and intern to establish learning expectations and for the supervisor to regularly monitor interns' activities and progress toward accomplishment of agreed upon goals, behavior that is expected of quality supervisors (Arminio & Creamer, 2001). If the interns are unable to properly manage their time or make efficient use of resources, supervisors can stimulate invaluable learning by holding them accountable and working through problems experienced by interns. This ubiquitous involvement should continue systematically throughout the internship so that interns can take corrective action in problem areas and receive positive feedback for doing so. Surprise negative evaluations at the end of the term seldom benefit anyone.

Following in Table 3.1, is a checklist of topics that students should discuss with their site supervisors within the first two weeks of the internship— the earlier the better. Read the materials for a better understanding of many of the topics in the list.

STAGES IN THE DEVELOPMENT OF THE SUPERVISORY RELATIONSHIP

Most, although not all, successful relationships between interns and site supervisors go through identifiable developmental stages. It is not possible to present a highly prescriptive model because:

> [This relationship] involves an unique combination of professional and life experiences, personal qualities, similarities, and differences. It re-

quires an interweaving of teaching and learning styles and active communication on a regular basis. Each of the individuals involved brings strengths and weaknesses to the project of constructing a working relationship that will be of mutual benefit. (Chiaferi & Griffin, 1997, p. 25)

This model describes a successful, fully functioning supervisory relationship. In the real world of higher education, however, not all supervisory relationships will progress through all the stages. We believe that the model describes optimal functioning that is achieved in many internships, although not all. Table 3.2 offers an overview of the schema.

Induction Stage

The first stage involves gaining entrée into the internship setting. This includes learning one's way around, meeting professional and support staff, setting learning outcomes, negotiating the specifics of the internship

---

TABLE 3.1. Suggested Topics to Discuss with Supervisor Early in the Internship

- Learning expectations (e.g., what do you expect and what does your supervisor expect of you?)
- Nature of work (e.g., inquire about projects and special assignments)
- Working conditions (e.g., determine desk space, use of telephone, computer, e-mail account if needed)
- Internship schedule (Make sure supervisor knows the number of hours you will be in the setting each week. Inform site supervisor if there are dates when you plan to be away from campus or have other commitments during regularly scheduled hours/days)
- Discuss how and with whom you should communicate should you be running late or unable to be in the setting when scheduled
- Schedule supervision sessions. It is important that sessions occur at least weekly
- Dress (both in and out of the office) and behavior code (e.g., socializing with students (when, where, and how) and means of address for professionals and support staff; that is, Dr., Mr., first name?)
- Dates of special events in the unit and your anticipated involvement, if any
- Relationships with others in the unit (e.g., support, professional, and paraprofessional staff, and students)
- Reporting lines (Find out to whom you report for what. In some settings, you may report to different people for differ projects or activities)
- Readings and other information sources (Ask supervisor to identify resources that can help you understand the functional area better)

TABLE 3.2. Developmental Stages, Needs, Tasks, and Strategies of the Supervisory Relationship

Stages	Intern Needs	Tasks	Supervision Strategies
Induction Stage	• Entrée • Information • Structure • Emotional support • Exploration of role of novice	• To know and become known by others in site and in areas of usual interaction • To learn about the host institution and its mission, history, and aspirations • To learn about the internship site—its goals, procedures, history, and policies—as quickly as possible • To learn about the functional area in a general or generic sense (regionally and nationally) and in different types of institutions (e.g., community colleges, research universities, liberal arts colleges) • To establish supervisor expectations and have clear guidelines governing responsibilities, authority, and operating procedures • To feel "at home" • To feel competent	• Spend as much time as possible with intern and getting to know on personal level • Introduce intern to staff, students, and others with whom he or she is likely to have interactions • Inform other staff about intern's assignments and lay ground rules for interactions • Clearly spell out expectations, written and unwritten rules of conduct, deadline for completion of assignments or projects • Assist intern to operationalize internship learning outcomes • Establish a trusting, mutually respectful, warm, caring relationship
Acclimation Stage	• Increased self-awareness • Confidence in abilities • Feedback about attitudes and performance • Clarification about culture, history, and issues that affect practice	• To deal with dependency–autonomy conflicts • To take on limited professional roles • To take initiative • To be accountable • To become conversant with the literature of the functional area	• Begin to remove some structure • Offer praise for good performance (look for things to commend) • Gently confront attitude problems or performance shortfalls • Share insights into the culture and teach intern how to read culture • Give intern assignments with clear responsibility and considerable autonomy

(Continued)

TABLE 3.2. Continued

Stages	Intern Needs	Tasks	Supervision Strategies
Application Stage	• Exploration of using theory in practice • Greater autonomy • Opportunity to apply knowledge and skills acquired in the classroom	• To analyze programs and services from theoretical perspectives • To complete complex assignments • To solidify professional identity in the functional area	• Initiate discussion of theory use in specific activities • Assign intern project/task with near total autonomy • Move relationship more toward that of peer-to-peer/professional colleague • Confront shortcomings more assertively
Closure Stage	• Closure • Detailed feedback about performance • Fit learning from internship experience into career plans	• To integrate learning • To finish projects and assignments • To bring closure to relationships • To pass information and materials to whoever will assume the intern's responsibilities	• Treat intern as colleague • Provide opportunities to say "good-bye" • Provide thorough, behaviorally anchored evaluation • Assist intern in devising a professional development agenda

experience, and perhaps becoming acquainted with the geographic region if the internship is in an area with which the intern is unfamiliar. At this stage, interns need to ask for structure (what to do, when, and how) and for emotional support as they face many new challenges in a short period of time. If the site has an internship handbook, much of the factual information can be placed where interns can consult it as the need arises. Like most people, many interns have a heightened level of anxiety and self-doubt when entering a new situation.

Interns should be clear and specific about what they most want to learn as a result of the internship experience. They should not expect the site supervisor to be a mind reader. Interns should not be hesitant to tell the supervisor when suggested or planned activities do not address internship learning goals. Interns should be prepared to do some things, however, that they may not particularly enjoy or find exciting because it is important that interns experience the full scope of work that goes on at the internship site. Supervisors may insist that interns do certain things simply because it is a major responsibility of the functional area. Also, interns can expect to do a certain amount of work that is not intellectually challenging or personally rewarding (such as making copies, stuffing envelopes, or answering the telephone) simply because the tasks must be done and everyone in the setting is expected to pitch in. Early in the internship experience, interns may be called on to do more "busy work" simply because they are not yet knowledgeable enough about the site to work with students or to directly help site colleagues fulfill their duties

At this stage, interns need to accomplish several tasks. It is important, for example, that interns become thoroughly familiar with the site and what others expect of it in the institution. Interns need to achieve cultural competence (Kuh, Siegel, & Thomas, 2001), to become fully aware of crucial nuances of the site. They may do this through careful and systematic assessment of the environment, including its people, technologies, goals, policies, procedures, and history. This assessment and this developing cultural competence can be accomplished simultaneously with establishing clear expectations between the site supervisor and the intern.

Supervisors must accomplish several crucial goals during this stage also. It is incumbent upon them, for example, to begin the investment of time with an intern that is essential to the type of relationship that will optimize learning. During this time, supervisors must ensure that others know interns in the office and all site personnel understand the purpose and goals for the internship. Groundwork should be laid to enable all within the site to contribute to the intern's learning experiences. Expectations of both the supervisor and the intern should be clear and explicit and should be established during this stage. The supervisor should show the intern the ways of accomplishing goals within the site (the ways of doing business in the office) and should promote an open, trusting, and mutually respectful relationship. When the proper grounds for the learning oriented relationship have been established, the relationship can move to the acclimation stage.

Acclimation Stage

This stage evolves from the induction stage as the intern becomes comfortable in the setting and comes to know his or her way around the site and institution. The intern is less dependent on the supervisor and other staff for direction or basic information. Self-confidence increases as the intern experiences success in completing assigned tasks and as he or she is given positive feedback for good work or constructive criticism for inadequate performance. An intern can assume greater responsibility and feel less of a need for continuous feedback and encouragement from the supervisor. Through conversation with staff and reading of the professional literature, the intern becomes adept at using the functional area's jargon. The intern begins to see himself or herself less as a student than as a professional practitioner, in at least some areas.

During this stage, the intern takes definitive steps toward accountability with the office, taking the initiative toward becoming a fully functioning professional as he or she becomes familiar with the literature and other professional artifacts of the office and becomes more autonomous in professional and other work-related relationships.

The supervisor during this stage, gives the intern more responsibility. The supervisor should have established a pattern of feedback that results in more professional behavior by the intern who should be allowed more autonomy in organizing and carrying out duties and assignments. Supervisors during this stage should instruct the intern in cultural nuances of the office and the institution and generally help the intern feel more confident in her or his skills.

Application Stage

This stage might be called the *optimal working stage* and occurs when the intern is fully acclimated to the site, knows all the players and their personalities, understands something of the recent history of the site and the institution, and can see the site's strengths and weaknesses. The conversations between intern and supervisor become more philosophical and theoretical in nature; intern and supervisor can openly communicate without fear of offending and can honestly analyze program successes and failures—taking into account theory, institutional politics, personalities, and institutional culture. The relationship becomes truly collegial. The content of conversations is treated as confidential. Because the relationship is built on trust and mutual respect, the supervisor can give the intern sensitive, frank feedback, accompanied by offers of assistance to address difficulties. The intern is also empowered to give the supervisor frank, critical feedback as well. The intern's needs are met through this process and the expected stage-related tasks become integrated into routines within the site.

Closure Stage

The final stage of the relationship centers on closure. The content of supervisory sessions focuses on terminating the intern–supervisory relationship, taking stock of what has been learned and what still needs to be learned, exploration of the intern's career plans, and where the internship experience fits into the overall preparation experience. Ideally, interns should leave the on-site experience with a professional development agenda, which they plan to pursue in the next few months or years. The final stage of the relationship also should focus on assisting the intern to integrate fully what has been learned during the experience into the intern's professional life.

BUILDING RELATIONSHIPS THAT PROMOTE LEARNING

In most settings, the extent and quality of the learning experience is greatly affected by the nature of the relationships interns have with others. Of particular importance are the relationships with supervisors, support staff, the site's clients (usually undergraduate students), and higher level administrators. Learning may be greatly enhanced or it may be jeopardized by these relationships.

In student affairs internships, students usually receive two types of supervision from two different individuals: the site supervisor and the faculty supervisor. Each is important and fulfills complementary, but different, roles and functions.

Site Supervisor's Roles and Functions

Site supervisors play multiple roles in the life of the intern (Kiser, 2000; Stanton & Ali, 1994). Foremost, site supervisors are *teachers*. In that role, they seek to create conditions that will allow the intern to (a) experience the full range of activities associated with the setting; (b) acquire necessary knowledge and information about the area; (c) gain insight into the formal and informal organizational functioning; (d) develop skills through hands-on experience functioning in a "professional role"; and (e) gain direct experience interacting with the student clientele.

Site supervisors are *limit setters* who establish the parameters of the intern's work. Depending on the setting, there may be functions that are inappropriate, perhaps even illegal, for an intern to have access to without students' written informed consent. This is particularly true in areas such as student financial aid, student discipline, and student records. Some areas or functions of a site may require greater skill and knowledge than beginning interns typically possess. Site supervisors may require that interns become more knowledgeable or experienced before undertaking certain activities. There also may be some activities that are too politically or legally sensitive for interns to play significant roles. It is the site supervisor's responsibility to protect interns from situations that carry high risks for legal entanglements, political infighting within the institution, or situations that are likely to become highly volatile and emotionally charged. It is the responsibility of the site supervisor to set appropriate limits of intern involvement in the work of the site.

Supervisors also are *enablers* who create conditions within the unit that provide the intern with entrée, define the intern's role within the unit, and make it possible for the intern to make use of institutional resources, such as office space, telephones, office supplies, computers, e-mail accounts, copiers, vehicles, and direct services of support staff. In this capacity, they are the key persons to ensure that the internship is a rewarding learning experience.

Through observation of supervisors and other staff in the setting, the intern also can see the use of expertise and experience to solve problems and accomplish the functional area's mission. In this sense, the site supervisor is a *model* of professionalism in the functional area. On occasion he or she also may serve as a negative role model; that is, the intern may see personality characteristics and ways of dealing with situations that are ineffective or counterproductive. Both types of learning are important for the intern to experience as he or she forms the intern's vision of the kind of professional he or she is to become. It may be equally important to decide what one *does not* want to become, as it is to decide what one does want.

Another site supervisor role is that of *sponsor*. Because of their experience and longevity in the field, the supervisors can assist the intern to meet other practitioners within the institution and at other institutions and to become acquainted with leaders in professional associations. Supervisors are well positioned to assist interns in the initial stages of building a professional network.

The site supervisor is also an *evaluator* of intern learning, professional demeanor and behavior, and work performance. An essential function of the supervisor is to give the intern frequent, candid feedback about his or her performance and how the individual is perceived within the unit and other areas of the institution. The supervisor provides the intern with a valuable service when he or she points out behaviors or attitudes that have potentially negative consequences for the intern's future career. Many practitioners in student affairs find it difficult to give negative evaluations. In the internship experience, however, it is essential that the intern receives recurrent and constructive criticism. The criticism needs to be delivered in a timely manner so that the intern has an opportunity to change behavior or attitudes and to receive positive feedback for doing so. Generally, it is not beneficial for the supervisor or intern to "save up" critical evaluations until the end of the internship experience, because that usually appears as vindictive faultfinding; that is, there is insufficient time to process the information and take corrective action on the part of either party to the relationship.

Some writers have ascribed mentor roles to the site supervisor. If one accepts the Levinson, Darrow, Klein, Levinson, & McKee (1978) and Levinson (1996) definition of *mentor* as a teacher, sponsor, adviser, guide, exemplar, and facilitator of *the dream*, then it is unrealistic to expect that every site supervisor can fulfill all of these roles for every intern.

For a true mentoring relationship to be formed, there must be mutual attraction and selection between mentor and protégé, somewhat analogous to the initial stages of a romantic relationship. The mentor must see high potential and worthiness in the protégé as a professional practitioner and positive personal characteristics; likewise, the protégé must see qualities and accomplishments in the mentor that he or she admires and wishes to emulate.

---

*E*xercise

Intern Relationship Expectations Inventory

- What three qualities are most important to you in an internship supervisor?

  _____

  _____

  _____

- What do you want most from your internship supervisor?

  _____

  _____

- What kinds of behavior on the part of a teacher or supervisor impede your learning?

  _____

  _____

  _____

- When you disagree with a teacher or supervisor, what do you usually do?

  _____

  _____

  _____

The intern may suggest to his or her supervisor that he or she complete the Supervisor's Relationships Expectations Inventory found in Appendix C. Afterwards, supervisor and intern may exchange responses and use this material as the basis for discussing the intern–supervisor relationship.

Mentoring relationships are characterized by a relatively high degree of non-sexual intimacy, which requires a significant amount of emotional investment by both parties. As Otto (1994) notes, "Mentoring relationships begin with the expectation that . . . [the relationship] will be mutually beneficial to the protégé and the mentor" (p. 18). The mentoring "relationship enables the recipient to identify with a person who exemplifies many of the qualities he [or she] seeks. It enables him [or her] to form an *internal* figure who offers love, admiration, and encouragement in his [or her] struggles. He [or she] reaps the varied benefits to be gained from a serious, mutual, non-sexual loving relationship with a somewhat older man or woman" (Levinson et al., 1978, p. 334). This level of personal affinity cannot be achieved in all internships and should not be expected. Some interns and site supervisors do form mentoring relationships, but such occurrences are relatively rare and should not be presumed as a usual benefit of the internship experience.

FACULTY SUPERVISOR'S ROLES AND FUNCTIONS

Because the faculty supervisor is not present in the internship site frequently, she or he may be seen as less involved than the site supervisor. While this is true, the faculty supervisor still has important roles to play in the internship experience. Depending on the nature and scope of the academic program, there may be an internship coordinator who has overall administrative responsibility for the internship component of the program and an individual faculty supervisor to whom interns are assigned, creating joint responsibility for the internship. In other programs, each major professor is responsible for the internship of advisees and there is no overall coordinator. In yet other programs, the internship is treated as in other classes; each with a faculty supervisor responsible for the instruction and the internship oversight. What follows are descriptions of the roles that need to be fulfilled to assure high quality internships. Whether one or several persons fulfill the role varies from program to program; there is no "best way" for managing the internship program.

    The roles described below need to be filled; interns should seek clarification from the faculty in their program if it is unclear who fills each role.

    Faculty supervisor roles include:

- Placement facilitator
- Sounding board
- Intellectual challenger
- Conflict mediator
- Provider of emotional support

- Information resource
- Hearer of grievances
- Assignor of grades

The faculty supervisor's first responsibility is to assist students in locating suitable placements. A variety of techniques are used effectively in coordinating this matching process and attaining formal agreements with site supervisors. In some programs, students are provided a list of "approved sites" and are instructed to contact site supervisors to inquire about placement—similar to a job search. In other cases, students are expected to locate a suitable site and negotiate terms of the experience with the faculty and site supervisors. (Various sites may use a number of techniques for selecting interns, from formal application processes to informal interviews. Some sites may be highly competitive; others may be open to all students who are interested.) Other programs "assign" students to sites, generally based on expressions of interest by students.

Whatever process is used, the faculty supervisor's responsibility is to determine whether: (a) there is a qualified site supervisor who is willing to have an intern for the particular term; (b) the functional area's practice conforms to the Council for the Advancement of Standards in Higher Education (CAS) standards closely enough that students will be exposed to sound student affairs practices; (c) there are adequate facilities to accommodate an intern (e.g., work space and access to telephones, computers, e-mail, the Internet, and copiers); and (d) the site supervisor is willing to comply with the terms of the internship agreement (e.g., provide regular individual supervision and assign and evaluate relevant projects). It is also the faculty supervisor's responsibility to make sure that the site supervisor understands the academic program's goals for the internship experience and the expectations of students and site supervisors.

Faculty supervisors and interns should maintain regular contact throughout the internship. This may be accomplished in a number of ways— e-mail activity logs, interactive web sites, telephone interviews, face-to-face supervision sessions, or regular seminar meetings with interns. Through whatever means, the faculty supervisor functions as a sounding board. Interns should use the contacts to ask questions that they do not feel comfortable broaching with the site supervisor, putting forth ideas for feedback before presenting them in the placement site, and requesting organizational history that can help the intern understand the unit's dynamics. Faculty supervisors also can be useful in helping interns analyze their feelings and reactions related to events that occur in the site. And, sometimes interns encounter difficulties in the site and need someone to simply listen; faculty supervisors can often fulfill this role.

Faculty supervisors also function as intellectual challengers. Through regular contacts with interns, they challenge students to relate what they have learned in the classroom to what they see happening in the internship site. One of the more difficult tasks students often have is relating theory to practice. Faculty supervisors help students verbalize how they see theory applying and in identifying situations or instances when the theory does not seem to apply and to explore why. Because of the type of professional preparation received or the extent of continuing education they have experienced, site supervisors may have difficulty in assisting students in understanding how theory is used in daily practice. Some sites may operate as if no theory undergirds the work. In such cases, interns will need to diagnosis functioning "theories in use" (Argyris & Schön, 1974, p. 37). Faculty supervisors can assist in this process.

Occasionally, interns become involved in conflict situations with site supervisors, support staff, student-clients, or staff in other institutional units. If the conflict situation becomes too severe, faculty supervisors may be called upon to *mediate*. Faculty supervisors, however, generally resist becoming directly involved because they are not informed about all the factors involved (usually hearing only the intern's perspective) and because it is a much better learning experience for interns to devise ways in which to resolve conflicts. Interns, however, should not hesitate to inform their faculty supervisors when they encounter conflict, but they also should not expect the faculty supervisor to solve their problems for them. Most faculty supervisors defer direct intervention until the intern and his or her site supervisor have unsuccessfully attempted to resolve the conflict.

Faculty supervisors often provide emotional support to interns as they work through difficult or challenging situations. Interns, especially early in their placement, are often called upon to perform tasks that they have never attempted before and which for some interns cause uncomfortably heightened anxiety. Faculty supervisors often provide encouragement, reassurance, and succor, as interns are required to function more independently than they have been required to do in the classroom. As interns gain self-confidence and experience successes in the internship, they generally need less emotional support from others.

Another role that faculty supervisors play is that of *information resource*. Frequently, students encounter questions or are given assignments that require research in the literature. If the typical bibliographic aids such as ERIC do not produce sufficient resources, interns turn to their faculty supervisor for advice in the search process. Because faculty members are ordinarily fairly conversant with the field's literature, they can point interns toward potentially useful information.

The final role that faculty supervisors play is that of *assigning grades* for the internship course. Because faculty members are charged with the responsibility of upholding the academic integrity and standards of the institution, they are the ones with the ultimate responsibility for assigning grades for the internship. In most instances, grades are based on accomplishment of the objectives specified in the learning contract, quality of performance on assignments (such as research or other kinds of projects), completion of assignments made by the site supervisor, attendance in the site, and the recommendation of the site supervisor.

Support Staff

One of the most important allies and resources an intern can have is the support staff, especially secretaries and administrative assistants who have been employed at the institution for at least several years. They generally are rich sources of information, can informally advise interns about who to see for what, but especially what is the best approach to different offices or staff members. Frequently, the support staff members on many campuses have an effective informal communication network that is better (or at least faster) than formal "official" communication. Support staff also can be effective instructors for interns about the informal (unwritten) rules of the workplace—for instance, in some settings one does not bring coffee to one's desk, but are expected to drink it away from the work area; in other offices there is a tradition of people bringing snacks for everyone in the office periodically (interns would be well advised to take their turns in bringing food). Because support staff may be more immediately accessible than site supervisors, they can answer many questions about the institution or unit in a more timely way than the supervisor.

Even though it is very important to develop friendly relationships with members of the support staff, there are several potential pitfalls to avoid.

- Avoid the perception of competition or invasion of territory. Interns need to be sensitive about how they are perceived by the support staff. It is essential that support staff not be threatened by interns taking over responsibilities normally delegated to support staff. If support staff come to view the intern as someone who could take their jobs, they are likely to react defensively to the intern. This is especially true in units that do not regularly host interns.
- Do not become involved in personal lives. Frequently, interns spend a considerable amount of time with the support staff. Through this constant interaction support staff members may come to view the intern as someone with whom they can share their personal prob-

lems. As an administrative intern, he or she should not function as a counselor or therapist. Interns are advised to avoid becoming enmeshed in staff members' personal lives. If that should happen, the potential for learning from the internship experience may be greatly diminished.

- Do not become a "go-between." If the support staff and their supervisor are having difficulty in communicating, it may be tempting for support staff to seek to use the intern as "messenger" to the boss. Interns are advised to avoid becoming entangled in these kinds of supervisory problems, even if it appears that support staff members have legitimate concerns or grievances. From our experience, we have found that interns seldom make positive contributions to these kinds of situations.

- Keep roles clarified. Interns are *special* in that they function as professional or support staff members on some occasions and as students on others. Because of the shifting of roles, authority and responsibility may become blurred in the support staff's eyes. Interns have greater flexibility of work schedules and have "privileges," such as having lunch with the vice president or president, that support staff do not enjoy. This can lead to resentment by support staff unless interns frequently make their role and purpose transparent— the intern's primary purpose is *learning*, not doing the work of another staff member. Even though interns do some of the same kinds of work as others in the setting, the intern's reason for being there is to enhance understanding of the functional area and the field, not to ease others' workloads. Ideally both goals can be realized in the internship.

Student-Clients

Interns sometimes encounter problematic situations when working with the students who constitute a site's clientele. Potential difficulties include: (a) confusion about role and authority; (b) achieving professional identity; (c) age differences; (d) dealing with diversity; and (e) working within the structure.

Confusion about Role and Authority. Students who are the clientele of a particular unit often have difficulty understanding the role and authority of an intern. Is the intern just another professional staff member? Or just another student? Or a spy for the administration? When the intern first arrives in the site, the supervisor can clarify the situation by carefully explaining to students exactly what role the intern will play in the organization. This may not completely eliminate troublesome situations, but it can greatly reduce the probability of misunderstandings.

Generally, it is unwise for interns to be vested with substantial authority because they are inexperienced, their tenure is short term, and introduction of an intern who is perceived as "powerful" may adversely affect the dynamics within the student culture. The more clearly the intern's role and responsibilities are communicated to students the more likely the intern will be able to work with students in positive ways. Interns should resist appearing as if they are intelligence agents for the professional staff. They should also resist being used as "messengers" for students to the professionals.

Achieving Professional Identity. To be effective, interns need to be able to establish good working relationships with the students who have contact with the student affairs unit. Because in many cases there may be small differences in the ages of students and interns, it sometimes becomes a difficult relationship to negotiate. It is important, therefore, that interns dress as "professionals," within the norm established by the practitioners in the site. As a general rule interns should dress slightly more formally than students, which means men should usually wear a dress shirt and tie and women should avoid jeans and shorts during the usual workday. There are obvious exceptions, such as in recreational sports, where attire suitable for sports participation may be the norm for everyone—students and professionals alike. The overall formality of campuses varies greatly. Even though clothes do not make one a professional, interns' work will usually be made easier when everyone can *see* differences in roles. If professionals in the office wear dress shirts and ties or business suits, interns would be well advised to do the same. Equally, if more casual attire is the norm, then interns would be advised to follow suit.

Age Differences. As noted earlier, often interns may be very close in age to the students with whom they have contact. In such situations, it may be difficult for interns to be seen as anything more than just another student. In other cases, interns may be considerably younger than the students who are served by the student affairs unit, especially on commuter campuses. Frequently, older students may question whether younger interns can understand their concerns. In those instances, interns must establish their credibility with the students as possessing knowledge and skills that can be used to the benefit of the older students. In all cases, interns must act as professionals at all times; to do otherwise will undermine their credibility and diminish their usefulness in the internship site.

Dealing with Diversity. Interns may encounter students from academic backgrounds or of ethnicities, sexual orientations, socioeconomic backgrounds, or religious affiliations with which they have had limited interactions. This should be viewed as a valuable opportunity to increase one's multicultural competencies. Some crucial cross-cultural competencies that the student affairs professional needs to develop include "gaining knowledge of other cultures through study and direct experience, developing a greater awareness of . . . [one's] own cultural make-up, decreasing . . . [one's] ethnocentrism, and increasing . . . [one's] respect of other traditions" (Kiser, 2000, pp. 100-101).

Working within the Structure. Usually, the student groups and organizations that interact most frequently with the internship site have a history, established ways of doing things, and entrenched patterns of interpersonal communication. Interns need to be careful that they do not inadvertently disrupt established ways of operating. Many of these structures serve useful purposes such as maintaining continuity between student generations, transmission of values, and negotiated agreements among students with differing points of view. Consequently, interns should be careful that they truly understand the dynamics operating in the setting before intervening. Because interns have a limited amount of time to be at the site, it may be tempting to move to "helping" too rapidly without a full understanding of the entire situation. For example, an intern (Harriet) encounters Jacob in the office frequently and he spends a lot of time talking about his organization's inability to get funds for a project, which sounds worthy and needed by the institution. Once convinced of Jacob's sincerity and the worthiness of his concerns, Harriet might begin exploring ways of getting funds and become an advocate for Jacob's cause. What Harriet does not know, however, is (a) Jacob has been unable to persuade the bulk of his organization of the value of this project; (b) a request for funds were made to the Student Allocations Committee the previous spring and was turned down; and (c) another office on campus is in the process of making a major initiative that will more than adequately address Jacob's concerns. Harriet, because she lacks background and history, may waste time and effort and create friction between the internship site office and another unit on campus that plans to address the issues.

GETTING THE MOST FROM SUPERVISION

There are several things that interns can do to increase the probability that they will get the most possible from supervision.

Insist on Regularly Planned Sessions

At the beginning of the internship, a schedule of supervision sessions should be planned and placed on the supervisor's and intern's calendars. If the supervisor does not suggest this, the intern should request it, explaining that he or she values face-to-face supervision and wants to make sure that there is sufficient time to get such supervision.

Prepare for Sessions

Because time is valuable to both the supervisor and the intern, the supervision sessions should be planned to assure effective use of time. Kiser (2000) suggests that interns prepare written summaries of important events that the interns want to discuss and a list of questions and concerns. It may be necessary to gather data and information relevant to questions and concerns and take them to the meeting as well. If the supervisor does not volunteer it, interns should request feedback about their performance of specific tasks or projects on which they have been working and about their general work performance and attitudes. It may be helpful if the supervisor receives the intern's agenda a few days in advance of the meeting. Ideally, the supervisor and intern can exchange agendas a few days before the meeting.

Be Prepared to Receive and Give Feedback

Supervision is most fundamentally about giving and receiving feedback. Without it, the internship experience loses much of its value. Patterson and Eisenberg (1983) found that (a) feedback is easier to receive when it matches one's self-perception and is most difficult to receive when it conflicts with one's self-perception; that is, feedback is most difficult to accept when it contradicts one's own self evaluation; (b) internalizing feedback requires time and reflection; and (c) feedback is easier to receive if the receiver trusts the source.

Drawing from the literature on interpersonal communication, Kiser (2000, p. 93) offers guidelines for giving effective feedback. Effective feedback is:

- direct and specific, describing specific behaviors or actions;
- offered calmly;
- timely—that is, delivered soon after the experience;

- balanced, recognizing both strengths and weaknesses;
- offered, not forced, allowing the receiver to reflect and respond; and
- helpful in generating ideas for alternative ways of doing things.

Be Assertive

The internship is the intern's learning experience. If interns do not clearly communicate to their supervisor what they want to learn as a result of the experience, they have no legitimate grounds to complain later. Assertiveness is the ability to straightforwardly communicate thoughts and feelings in a manner that respects one's own needs as well as the needs of others (Alberti & Emmons, 1995).

Reflection Point

- How can I make sure that I am being a good supervisee?
- Am I being open to feedback? What is the evidence for this conclusion?

  Am I being honest in my communication? How did that work when you were honest? When is honesty *not* the best policy? Why?

- Am I putting sufficient time into preparing for my supervision sessions?
- Identify two instances in the internship when you were given corrective feedback and changed your behavior. How did you feel when it happened?

Dealing with Problems of the Workplace

Because internships are located in the "real world," there is the potential for encountering the same "evils" found in any workplace, especially sexual harassment, racism, sexism, heterosexism, ageism, and ableism. These "isms" need clarification and should serve as special alerts to student interns. They should neither contribute to nor tolerate them.

- *Sexual harassment.* Almost all colleges and universities in the country have formal statements that define sexual harassment. The National Organization for Women defines it as "Any repeated or unwarranted verbal or physical sexual advances, sexually explicit derogatory statements, or sexually discriminatory remarks made by someone in the workplace, which is offensive or objectionable to the recipient or which causes the recipient discomfort or humiliation or which interferes with the recipient's job performance" (cited in Alle-Corliss & Alle-Corliss, 1998, p. 43). Interns should become familiar with their institution's and the internship-hosting institution's (if different) definitions and policies about sexual harassment.

- *Racism.* Brill (1990) defines racism as "the belief that race determines human traits and capabilities and that particular races are superior to others" (p. 249). Unlawful and unjust discrimination is a logical consequence following acceptance of the premises of racism. Lum (1996, p. 57) maintains that racism is used as an "ideological system to justify the institutional discrimination of certain racial groups against others." The consequences of racism can be viewed as a chain: "*racism* is considered to be the ideological belief that leads to an attitude of prejudism, which in turn results in the behavior of *discrimination*, which leads to the 'expression' of discrimination: oppression, powerlessness, exploitation, acculturation, and stereotyping" (Alle-Corliss & Alle-Corliss, 1998, p. 46). Almost all higher education institutions have formal policies against racial discrimination within the student body and the workplace. Interns need to make themselves familiar with the host institution's policies and procedures for dealing with allegations of racial or ethnic discrimination.
- *Sexism.* Cyrus (1993) asserts that:

Sexism is the subordination of an individual woman or group of women and the assumption of the superiority of an individual man or group of men, based solely on sex. Like racism, sexism is reflected in both individual and institutional acts, decisions, habits, procedures, and policies that neglect, overlook, exploit, subjugate, or maintain the subordination of an individual woman or all women. (p. 219)

Although sexism is most frequently evident in unfair treatment of women, it may also exist as discrimination against men by women or by other men.

- *Heterosexism.* Morales and Sheafor (1995) define heterosexism as "the belief that heterosexuality is or should be the only acceptable sexual orientation" (p. 36). It may also be viewed as a cultural assumption or religious tenet that heterosexuality is natural and the only proper sexual behavior (Cyrus, 1993). The fear of being identified as homosexual or hatred of gays and lesbians is known as homophobia. This fear and the hatred contributes to prejudice, discrimination, harassment, and acts of violence against gay men and lesbian women (Brownsworth, 1993). Most public institutions have official policies against discrimination based on sexual orientation, but actual practice may fall considerably short of the stated policy. When interning in private, especially religiously affiliated, colleges and universities, interns should seek clarification about the institutional policy and *practice* regarding gay, lesbian, bisexual, and transgendered students and staff. Private institutions, unless prohibited by state statute, have the prerogative to legally discriminate against nonheterosexual students and staff because the United States Supreme Court has not deemed sexual orientation a "protected category," as is race and religion.

- *Ageism.* Ageism is the expression of negative attitudes toward older persons (a very relative term) based on unfounded beliefs and erroneous assumptions about the aging process. Similar to sexism and racism, ageism leads to many inaccurate and destructive stereotypes, such as older people think and move slowly, are not creative, cannot grow or change, and dislike innovation and technology (Butler, 1975).

- *Ableism.* Ableism refers to discrimination against persons who have a disabling condition—physical, developmental, mental, social, or economic (Alle-Corliss & Alle-Corliss, 1998). Schmolling, Youkles, and Burger (1993) report that most people who are unaffected by a disability react to persons with disabilities either as if the disability does not exist or matter, or by being overly helpful and reassuring. Neither approach tends to be helpful to persons with disabilities.

How an intern deals with discrimination or wrongful treatment of individuals is a complex issue. Ethically, the American College Personnel Association (ACPA) standards mandate that members seek to halt discriminatory treatment of students and staff. Interns, however, have no power base from which to operate—either formal (as might be vested in someone through his or her professional position in the institution) or informal (through personal clout) because the intern generally is new to the organization with little status. Ultimately, it becomes a personal decision about if, how, or when to confront these complex social issues. Generally, interns should consider informing the site supervisor if they believe the supervisor is unaware of the situation. Interns should also discuss the matter with the faculty supervisor, investigate the host institution's policies and procedures for dealing with the problem situation, weigh the potential benefits, and then made an informed decision about what course of action to take. Sometimes, the discrimination has become so institutionalized that staff in the setting fail to recognize the consequences of their attitudes or actions. In such cases, simply raising the issues to consciousness is sufficient to effect change. This, however, is not always the case.

xercise

Ask your supervisor for a copy of all the important policies and non-discrimination statements related to the issues raised in this session. Review each and be prepared to discuss the policy development process and policy implementation issues with your supervisor.

TROUBLESHOOTING THE INTERNSHIP: ADVICE FOR INTERNS

Like most professional endeavors, no internship is perfect. There are always problems or issues that need to be resolved. Listed below are some problems or issues that interns frequently encounter, along with some suggestions for avoiding or dealing with them.

Poor Match with Supervisor

It is impossible to match all interns' and supervisors' personalities and work styles. Interns must simply accept the fact that these differences exist and that in the world of work one must learn to work cooperatively with all types of people. Instead of being angry or resentful, interns should concentrate on being productive. If it seems that the supervisor is attempting to pressure the intern into being exactly like him or her, the intern should deal with this directly by letting the supervisor know that the attempts to be helpful are appreciated but that the intern has his or her own style (Alle-Corliss & Alle-Corliss, 1998). Even though trying at the time, this can be an excellent learning experience. Consult the faculty supervisor about possible strategies that can be used to create a more helpful situation.

The Vanished Supervisor

Frequently, students seek out internship sites based in large measure on the good reputation a site supervisor may have established based on work with students, inventiveness of programs, personal magnetism, or past supervision of interns. Because of the importance of the supervisory relationship, these may be good reasons for seeking placement in a particular site or at a given institution. It is not uncommon, however, for an intern to discover that, because of changing circumstances, such as taking a new position either within the institution or at another college or university, the supervisor that the student sought is no longer available by the time she or he is ready to begin the internship. (This also may happen to new professionals when taking their first positions.)

The situation has the potential of becoming a major calamity. When the initial supervisor leaves the site on short notice or assumes other duties that preclude following through with the planned supervision, then there may be issues of whom, if anyone, is qualified and available to supervise the internship. If it is too late to seek another site, then the student may be faced with feelings of disappointment and betrayal. We caution students to try to keep the situation in perspective and to resist the temptation of allowing the disappointment to interfere with efforts to make the placement site the best learning situation possible.

We suggest that the student immediately discuss the issues with the faculty supervisor and the originally intended site supervisor (if possible). Students should resist the temptation of immediately withdrawing from the setting before they explore alternative arrangements for supervision and discuss the situation with the faculty supervisor and possibly with the new site supervisor, if one has been identified. In some instances, it may be better to seek another internship site. Or, metaphorically, students may be given a bunch of lemons in the form of dashed plans from which they can work to fashion lemonade. (Such situations *can* prove to be valuable, though not necessarily easy, learning experiences—more valuable in the long run than the originally planned experience.)

Unfortunately, we cannot offer foolproof solutions to these predicaments. The faculty supervisor is likely to be the student's best resource both in deciding whether to seek another site or to create a new plan that can salvage the learning potential of the altered situation. The faculty supervisor may need to assume a more active role in helping the replacement supervisor understand the purpose of the internship and the academic program's expectations of supervisors, interns, and placement sites.

The Absent Supervisor

For a variety of reasons, supervisors may simply spend very little time in their offices during certain periods; this may be typical or may be the result of unusual circumstances. In either case, it can become a significant concern for interns. Alle-Corliss and Alle-Corliss (1998) recommend dealing with this concern as soon as the intern notices a potential problem. "Be clear about . . . [the] need for direct and regular supervision. Use assertiveness skills. If appropriate, use the leverage of . . . academic requirements to substantiate . . . requests and needs" (p. 72). If no satisfactory solution is found, consult the faculty supervisor.

The Overwhelmed Supervisor

Even with the best of intentions, sometimes supervisors become overwhelmed with work or personal/family problems that severely limit their opportunities to interact with interns. Alle-Corliss and Alle-Corliss (1998) recommend that interns be sensitive and supportive to the supervisor's situation, but remain assertive about having needs met. If this is not a short-term situation, inquire about who could help with supervision. It also may be necessary to informally seek out others in the setting who can provide appropriate feedback and guidance. It is also important that the intern consult with the faculty supervisor if the lack of site supervision is negatively affecting the learning opportunities.

Dual Relationships

Dual relationships in this context are those in which the intern and supervisor form kinds of relationships other than supervisory. For example, these relationships can be friendships, romantic/sexual, or financial. In all of these cases, the line between intern and supervisor and other kinds of relationships becomes blurred. If an intern wants to form a friendship with his or her supervisor, or has romantic interests, or wants to form a business arrangement, the intern is best advised to wait until the internship is over. Internships are of relatively short duration.

Fear of Disclosing Mistakes

Sometimes interns are reticent to reveal mistakes they have made to their supervisors because they fear that this will be used against them or will lower their grade. Acknowledging errors or needs for knowledge or skill may be threatening to some interns' fragile self-concepts.

Even though it may be uncomfortable, generally, it is not wise to keep mistakes under wraps because it limits the potential learning and may result in the intern never fully developing his or her potential to be a competent or even outstanding professional practitioner. Most of the leaders in the field with whom we are acquainted can enumerate a long list of mistakes from which they learned important lessons.

Kiser (2000) makes several good points about mistakes. First, everyone makes mistakes sometimes and most are not serious and are relatively easy to repair. "The first step in learning from a mistake is admitting that you have made one" (p. 188). If the intern thinks or feels that she or he has made a mistake, even if not sure, the best course of action is to discuss it with the site supervisor as quickly as possible and to offer to take corrective action as soon as possible.

Interns should also be aware that there are some kinds of mistakes that are not reparable. The kinds of mistakes that would lead to termination of an employee can also lead to the termination of an internship. Some of the kinds of behavior that fall into the *serious* category include: (a) serious violations of professional ethical standards; (b) acts of violence against others; (c) violations of the criminal code; (d) behavior that is damaging to the reputation or functioning of the unit or the institution; (e) violation of unit or institutional policy; (f) violation of safety regulations or policies; (g) violation of the dress code; (h) failure to perform assigned duties; (i) excessive tardiness or unacceptable absences; and (j) insubordination (failure to do as told by legitimate authority).

Interns should also remember that it may be a much more serious offense to attempt to conceal or lie about a situation than it would be if the situation were openly and honestly revealed. Many supervisors will forgive errors but will not accept lying or deceit. Almost without exception, mistakes made, acknowledged, and corrected during the internship results only in positive learning.

Doing "Gofer Work"

From time to time, interns in most settings are called upon to do time-consuming, mundane chores, such as answering the telephone, making copies, stuffing envelopes, or filing. Several things need to be kept in mind when this happens. First, at times of high pressure or crisis, staff at all levels can be expected to pitch in and get tasks done, regardless of how mind-numbing or repetitive. Second, although mundane, if these tasks are not done correctly an office's reputation can be sullied and cause a loss of credibility with its clients. Even though mundane, it may also be important. Third, even though necessary for accomplishing the site's goals, this kind of work by itself has limited educational value for interns.

If an intern feels that she or he is frequently asked to do "gofer work," then she or he should discuss the concerns with the site supervisor. It may be useful to remind the supervisor about the learning goals established for the internship and to respectfully inquire how the "gofer work" promotes goal accomplishment. If difficulties of this nature persist, then it should be discussed with the faculty supervisor.

CONCLUSION

Internship supervision is a key ingredient in the ultimate success of students in preparation for their professions. Because this experience serves to help students integrate all of their learning experiences in their preparation program, its quality goes a long way in defining success for the student. When the internship is accomplished successfully, interns generally feel that their preparation programs also have fulfilled their educational goals. Certainly, internship supervision is vital to this process.

Quality supervision is about promoting learning with student interns. Central to this process is building relationships, especially between the site supervisor and the student intern. Other relationships are important also, such as with the faculty supervisor, support staff in the site, and student clients. When these relationships are built on solid ground, interns generally are successful. They learn what they need to learn to feel self-confident in their abilities and they fully integrate all of their learning experiences.

Building appropriate relationships is developmental and can be characterized in stages that reflect intern needs, tasks to be accomplished by interns, and supervision strategies. These stages depict steps in relationship building from entrée to saying good-bye to site supervisors.

Just as internships are opulent in learning opportunities, they also can be fraught with difficulties. These opportunities and difficulties are discussed in this chapter with a view toward helping interns see ways in which they can play major roles in the ultimate success of the internship experience.

REFERENCES

Alberti, R., & Emmons, M. (1995). *Your perfect right: A guide to assertive living* (7th ed.). San Luis Obispo, CA: Impact.

Alle-Corliss, L., & Alle-Corliss, R. (1998). *Human service agencies: An orientation to fieldwork.* Pacific Grove, CA: Brooks/Cole.

Arminio, J., & Creamer, D. G. (2001). What supervisors say about quality supervision. *College Student Affairs Journal, 21*(1), 35–44.

Argyris, C., & Schön, D. A. (1978). *Theory in practice: Increasing professional effectiveness.* San Francisco: Jossey-Bass.

Brill, N. (1990). *Working with people* (4th ed.). White Plains, NY: Longman.

Brownsworth, V. (1993). Not invisible to attack. In V. Cyrus (Ed.), *Experiencing race, class, and gender in the United States* (pp. 323–326). Mountain View, CA: Mayfield.

Butler, R. N. (1975). *Why survive? Being old in America.* New York: Harper & Row.

Chiaferi, R., & Griffin, M. (1997). *Developing fieldwork skills: A guide for human services, counseling, and social work students.* Pacific Grove, CA: Brooks/Cole.

Cyrus, V. (Ed.). (1993). *Experiencing race, class, and gender in the United States.* Mountain View, CA: Mayfield.

Kiser, P. M. (2000). *Getting the most from your human service internship: Learning from experience.* Belmont, CA: Brooks/Cole.

Kuh, G. D., Siegel, M. J., & Thomas, A. D. (2001). Higher education: Values and culture. In R. B. Winston, Jr., D. G. Creamer, & T. K. Miller (Eds.), *The professional student affairs administrator: Educator, leader, and manager.* New York: Brunner-Routledge.

Levinson, D. J. (1996). *The seasons of a woman's life.* New York: Knopf.

Levinson, D. J., Darrow, C. M., Klein, E. G., Levinson, E. B., & McKee, B. (1978). *The seasons of a man's life.* New York: Knopf.

Lum, D. (1996). *Social work practice & people of color: A process-stage approach* (3rd ed.). Pacific Grove, CA: Brooks/Cole.

Morales, A. T., & Sheafor, B. W. (1995). *Social work: A profession of many faces* (7th ed.). Needham Heights, MA: Simon & Schuster.

Otto, M. L. (1994). Mentoring: An adult developmental perspective. In M. A. Wunsch (Ed.), New directions for teaching and learning, No. 57. *Mentoring revisited: Making an impact on individuals and institutions* (pp. 15–24). San Francisco: Jossey-Bass.

Patterson, L., & Eisenberg, S. (1983). *The counseling process.* Boston: Houghton Mifflin.

Schmolling, P., Youkles, M., & Burger, W. R. (1993). *Human services in contemporary America* (3rd ed.). Pacific Grove, CA: Brooks/Cole.

Stanton, T., & Ali, K. (1994). *The experienced hand: A student manual for making the most of an internship.* New York: Carroll Press.

Winston, R. B., Jr., & Creamer, D. G. (1997). *Improving staffing practices in student affairs.* San Francisco: Jossey-Bass.

Winston, R. B., Jr., Creamer, D. G., & Miller, T. K. (Eds.). (2001). *The professional student affairs administrator: Educator, leader, and manager.* New York: Brunner-Routledge.

Chapter 4
APPLICATION OF THEORY
IN THE SUPERVISED
PRACTICE EXPERIENCE

Sue A. Saunders
Diane L. Cooper

When most students get to the point in their programs at which they start an internship, they are typically excited at finally being able to try out their skills as well as relieved about reducing the challenging academic work of understanding theories and research. The risk for many students is that the joy of being busy and actively involved in the real world of administration takes over and the effort to understand and apply theories at a deeper, more sophisticated, level takes a back seat. For many first-time interns it is tempting to fall into an unreflective way of working, with no time to contemplate the connections between theory and practice and little interest in thinking about what is being learned. The emphasis is on *doing*, not thinking. If interns do not make an intentional effort to analyze how theory informs (or at least could inform) their practice and on how practice can change their view of theory, the internship experience becomes laboring not learning and its ultimate value is, at best, compromised.

This chapter discusses theories and models that can be particularly useful in understanding students and higher education organizations as students begin their internships. First, the focus is on the intern as learner; this is explicated by a discussion of experiential learning models, use of reflection journals, ways that one can become constructively involved in the internship site, and conditions that foster effective learning through practice. Next, we look at the organization: its politics, structures, and ways in which one can scan the environment and respond appropriately. Finally, we address theories that describe the growth of students.

It is important to remember that theory must be implemented with caution. Implementing programs based on inadequate knowledge or understanding of theory is a open invitation to failure. Because of the complexities of the theories discussed here, one could do more harm than good to students and to the institution if programs are created that are grounded in inaccurate or overly simplistic understanding of theory. Interns are advised to review their knowledge of theories or to gain additional knowledge prior to implementing programs. In Appendix D, a list of resources by family of theory is available to assist in this process.

MAXIMIZING LEARNING

One of the first steps to maximize learning is to use a road map with frequently traveled routes and milestones to guide the way. One type of road map for the supervised practice experience is a model of experiential learning, which describes how people gain new knowledge through their experiences and make meaning from them through reflections.

Kolb's Model of Experiential Learning

In the 1970s, David Kolb began work on a model of experiential learning that was consistent with what was known about human cognition and the ways in which individuals grow and develop. The model that emerged from Kolb's research emphasizes the role that experience plays in learning and outlines how experiential learning is the base for concept development, which in turn governs the selection of new experiences. Because the raison d'être of internships is to integrate theory, practice, and self-knowledge, an understanding of Kolb's model provides a basis for students to maximize learning in their internship experience. Kolb (1981) conceived of a four-stage cycle of learning (see Figure 4.1). To assist in understanding this model, a brief case study is presented.

THE CASE OF LATISHA

Concrete Experience

Suppose that Latisha is beginning her admissions office internship during her second year in a college student affairs administration program. During

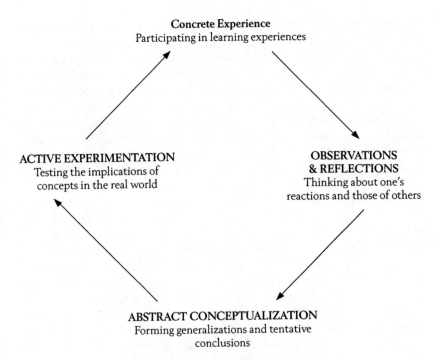

FIGURE 4.1. A Four-Stage Cycle of Learning.

the first visit to the office she has many concrete experiences that can serve as the basis for observation and reflection. As Latisha goes to meet with various admissions counselors, she finds that she is walking up and down many steps to get to the admissions counselors' offices to introduce herself to them.

Observation and Reflection

This concrete experience leads Latisha to move to the observation and reflection stage of Kolb's model. Specifically, Latisha observes that a former private residence (with three floors) located adjacent to the main campus has been designated as the central admissions office where prospective students and their families meet with admissions personnel. She also notices that the central staircase of the admissions building, located just inside the front entryway, contains an automatic stair-climbing device for individuals who need assistance in making their way to the offices of admissions counselors on the upper floors. Finally, Latisha observes that to get close to the receptionist's desk, one must descend two steps and go into what was formerly a sunken living room.

As Latisha is returning to her apartment later that evening, she begins to reflect on what she observed. Initially, she felt troubled about the embarrassment a mobility-challenged student might feel when asking to use the stair-climbing device or having to talk to the receptionist from a distance of six or seven feet. Her early reflections were made from the perspective of the clientele of the admissions office. She also recalled observing that almost all of the parking spaces in the lot adjacent to the building were reserved for individuals with disabilities and that there was a very attractive, accessible, ramp that led to the front door. Latisha's early reflections led her to recall other observations that were consistent with Kolb's theory that links observation and reflection as integrated processes.

Also, in line with the Kolb model, Latisha tried to reflect on her observations from viewpoints other than those of the prospective students. She thought back about her conversations with several staff members. She learned that the location of the admissions office was new and when compared with the former office was more inviting, less cramped, and easier to access by car. She also noticed that counselors and the receptionist did not stay at their desks, but greeted visitors at the door, and she thought about her understanding of the admissions office mission statement, which clearly stated a commitment to diversity in recruiting students from various racial, ethnic, and sexual orientation groups and those with various physical abilities. The admissions office mission statement was disseminated to prospective students in a variety of ways: on the back of business cards, in a prominent place in the viewbook, and in a prominently located place in the building foyer.

Finally, Latisha reflected on the readings from her campus environments class. These readings delved into how a culture of openness to diversity is communicated more by symbols and artifacts (such as diversity of staff, architecture of facilities, and history of the environment) than by what individuals say directly or what is written in policy statements. Latisha had observed that the staff was mostly white, young (age 22–25), and able-bodied, and that the facility was decorated in a traditional fashion, rather like the lobby of an older, elite hotel or 1890s upper middle-class home.

Abstract Conceptualization

As she spent more time reflecting on her experience, Latisha moved to the third stage of Kolb's model: forming abstract concepts and generalizations. In an attempt to integrate her observations and reflections into reasoned conclusions, Latisha believed that she could, at this stage, only draw a tentative conclusion about the degree to which the admissions office communicated an inviting atmosphere to prospective students with mobility problems. Even though Latisha did not have adequate information (such as enrollment and retention data about individuals with mobility limitations or commentary from faculty and other administrators about the environment), she felt that there was a strong possibility that the admissions office was communicating messages that would be discouraging to prospective students with disabilities.

Active Experimentation

The final stage of Kolb's model, testing implications of concepts, is particularly important for the intern. Most internships are relatively short in duration—one term or occasionally an entire academic year. Because of the intricacies of any campus environment, it is nearly impossible to draw conclusions that are reasoned and grounded in appropriate data in such a short time. Moreover, often interns are not privy to all the information available to full-time staff members. For example, on-site supervisors typically try not to burden or bias student interns with information about office politics or the hidden agendas of various administrators who influence the office (especially early in the internship). Therefore, in most cases, interns who delve into the active experimentation stage are testing hypotheses rather than fully formed conclusions.

Latisha wants to test her hypotheses about the openness of the admissions office to mobility-impaired individuals. She wants to raise questions, but does not want to accuse the staff in the admissions office of bias nor does she want to communicate a *know-it-all* attitude after having worked at the site for less than a week. So the way in which Latisha tests her hypothesis is first to determine the enrollment and retention data for various underrepresented populations. She also decides to talk with her faculty supervisor, Tom, about how to bring this issue to the attention of her on-site supervisor in a constructive, nonthreatening way. Since the faculty supervisor knows the on-site supervisor is very open to questions from interns, he advises Latisha to simply ask how mobility-impaired applicants manage to navigate around the admissions office and to share her questions about whether students with mobility limitations respond negatively to the facilities. As in Kolb's model, this active experimentation on Latisha's part (asking the questions of the on-site supervisor) leads to concrete experience (listening to the on-site supervisor's responses) that will in turn lead to further observation and reflection.

Necessary Conditions for Application of Model. For interns to use Kolb's experiential learning model several conditions must be present:

- Concrete experience needs to be approached forthrightly, openly, and without bias.
- Observation and reflection need to incorporate multiple perspectives.
- Abstract conceptualization must include more than personal opinion. It also needs to integrate research-tested theories and seemingly disparate observations into a reasonable hypothesis.
- Active experimentation relies on a willingness to engage in questioning, risk-taking, and reading and responding to the environment.
- Experiential learning requires clear learning goals and continuous monitoring of whether those goals are being achieved.

It is apparent that opportunities to apply Kolb's model of experiential learning occur repeatedly in the course of a busy intern's day. New concrete experiences abound, and the intern is often charged with moving quickly to the active experimentation or problem-solving phase. Because the internship is indeed a learning experience, it is important that interns and their supervisors allow adequate time to work through the middle two stages of Kolb's model—observation and reflection and abstract conceptualization. The questions on the following page should be addressed in written journals that will provide opportunities to reflect and make meaning of concrete experience.

LEARNING STYLES AND EFFECTS ON INTERNSHIPS

Moving through the experiential learning model described by Kolb (1981) requires highly disparate abilities. To be fully open to concrete experience, for example, requires that one suspend the analysis associated with the abstract conceptualization phase. To be truly reflective requires that one refrain from the action and risk taking specified in the active experimentation stage. To be effective in completing the learning cycle requires that one move from observer to actor and from active involvement in the experience to the detachment needed to analyze and draw conclusions about the experience. Kolb contended that individuals, because of their life experience and current environment tend to prefer some learning activities more than others. That is, individuals choose the ways they prefer to take in information, either through concrete experience or abstract conceptualization. They also choose their preference for processing information, either through reflective observation or active experimentation (Evans, Forney, & Guido-DiBrito, 1998).

The Kolb (1981) typology describes four different learning styles. Fail-

*R*eflection *P*oint

Weekly Journal

DIRECTIONS: Fill out this journal on a weekly basis. Discuss it with either your on-site and/or faculty supervisor. Keep these journal entries so that at the end of the term they can form the basis for your evaluation.

1. Describe what you experienced during the past week at your internship (include meetings, tasks accomplished, conversations, services you delivered, etc.). Describe the experiences as fully as possible, without bias, including relevant details.
2. What did you observe about yourself, other people, policies, written materials, and the physical environment during your experience?
3. What did your experience and observations cause you to think about? Use the following perspectives to guide your reflection.

   - How might my experience be perceived by students?
   - How might my experience be interpreted by staff?
   - How might my experience be seen by other elements of the community (faculty, administrators, members of the public, etc.)?
   - What do existing theories/research tell me about my experience?

4. How do my values, experiences, and preferences impact on how I interpret my experience?
5. What tentative conclusions/hypotheses can I draw from my experience, observations, or reflections?
6. What actions do I need to take or what questions do I need to ask either to strengthen or disprove my tentative conclusions?

ing to understand one's preferred learning style and to strengthen one's less preferred learning abilities can prevent students from achieving what they seek from their internships. For example, suppose that Carlos and Caroline are both interns in the judicial programs office. This office is very busy with an increasing number of judicial cases. Interns are expected to participate in a brief orientation designed to teach them the procedural information they need to share with students accused of a conduct code violation. At the close of this orientation, interns are expected to begin sharing this procedural information with accused students. At the close of the orientation, Caroline is very pleased because she has learned exactly what to say to students she will encounter in this office. She now knows the nuts and bolts steps she should follow. Carlos, on the other hand, is highly critical of the orientation because he has little understanding of why students get into trouble and what models he can use to encourage them to avoid violating conduct code rules. Carlos feels unready to begin direct work with students.

Kolb (1981) described four types of learners: (a) convergers, (b) divergers, (c) assimilators, and (d) accommodators. *Convergers'* greatest learning abilities are abstract conceptualization and active experimentation. They prefer technical tasks to interpersonal concerns and like to be involved in problem solving, decision making, and the application of ideas. Caroline could be classified as a converger, given her comfort level in interpreting procedural information to students accused of code violations. *Divergers* are most adept at concrete experience and observation and reflection. In other words, they are the opposites of the convergers. They tend to be highly imaginative, enjoy observing and reflecting, and can generate multiple alternative solutions to a problem. They tend to enjoy interacting with others and are interested in understanding others' feelings. *Assimilators,* whose strengths are in abstract conceptualization and observation and reflection, focus on ideas rather than people. They tend to evaluate the quality of ideas based on logic rather than practicality. They, also, have the ability to create theories by integrating ideas. In the example above, Carlos could be classified as an assimilator. He was uncomfortable explaining procedures to students because he had not been provided with the theoretical underpinnings or assumptions that guided those procedures. *Accommodators* are action-oriented individuals who are adept at concrete experience and active experimentation. They rely on information from others rather than on theories, tend to be very adaptable in new situations, solve problems intuitively, and are at ease in group decision making.

Applying Kolb's (1984) theory to one's learning experience as an intern requires a great deal of flexibility and self-knowledge. The first step is to have a clear understanding of one's learning preferences. The brief descriptions mentioned above as well as the information about Kolb's theory can help one begin this process. Once one has a better sense of one's preferred learning style, one can begin to target those learning tasks that will likely be more challenging. It may be helpful if students seek out more formal ways of determining their preferred learning styles. Faculty supervisors may be able to arrange for interns to complete the third revision of *The Learning Style Inventory* (LSI-3; Kolb, 1999) or university counseling centers may offer this opportunity. (For more information about the *Learning Style Inventory*, including an on-line instrument, consult: www.trgmcber.haygroup.com)

THE CASE OF PATSY

Suppose that Patsy, a masters' student in college student affairs administration, is starting her first internship in the community service office of a community college near her university. Similar to many student affairs master's students (Forney, 1994), Patsy's preferred learning style is that of accommodator. She likes action and new experiences, so her interactions with potential student volunteers are very comfortable and interesting to her.

One of the projects she has undertaken is to create a comprehensive manual for organizations wishing to engage in community service. This project will require gathering manuals from other universities and colleges, analyzing their content, reflecting on the best way to present the information, and determining how to make the manual useful to the students at this community college. This project is not one that particularly interests Patsy initially because it requires more reflection, observation, and technical problem solving than she typically prefers. As she proceeds with the project, she relies more on conversations with student affairs professionals at other schools who created the manuals than on her own ability to analyze. Because she does not spend much time thinking through ways to adapt the manuals to the local student clientele that includes many older students, her supervisor feels that the completed manual is inadequate.

If Patsy had taken the time to adapt her learning style to the requirements needed to complete the tasks before her, it is likely that she would have produced a more acceptable manual. Patsy would have been well advised to spend time reflecting on her work at various stages in the development of the manual and to critique it from the perspective of a student enrolled in that community college. In other words, Patsy should have challenged herself to engage in the learning activities preferred by convergers, divergers, and assimilators. (It could have been helpful, if Patsy had sought out others, students or staff, with different learning styles to critique her plan for the manual.)

Kolb (1984) argued that to be an effective learner throughout the life span, one must integrate disparate learning styles into a flexible approach that recognizes the importance of context and creative approaches to problem solving. Yet learning to integrate one's less preferred learning styles and to adapt one's style to the context of the supervised learning experience requires time, energy, and insight into one's strengths and weaknesses. Typically, when students are asked to adapt their learning styles, they are uncomfortable, less confident, and require more support from others in the setting. The following worksheet is designed to help interns integrate their internship tasks with their learning style.

$\mathscr{R}$eflection $\mathscr{P}$oint

Assessing Your Learning Activities

1. Using Kolb's theory as a guide, describe your learning style. Identify strengths and weaknesses of this style. Give examples of ways in which your learning style has, in the past year, facilitated or impeded progress toward accomplishing important activities.
2. After reflecting on your learning style and its impact on your accomplishment of important activities, determine which activities required for your internship will be most comfortable and interesting? In other words, identify activities that are most congruent with your learning style. Why did you identify these particular activities?
3. After reflecting on your learning style and its impact on your accomplishment of important activities, determine which activities required for your internship will be most challenging? In other words, identify activities that are least congruent with your learning style. Why did you identify these particular activities?
4. What steps might you take to accomplish these challenging tasks? How might you incorporate disparate learning styles to increase the chances of accomplishing these tasks effectively?

ASTIN'S INVOLVEMENT THEORY

Astin's (1984, 1985, 1993) work on the effects of involvement provides another conceptual framework for understanding the steps one might take to get the most out of an internship experience. In this model, involvement is defined as the amount of physical and psychological energy a student devotes to the educational experience (Astin, 1984). Although related to the terms *vigilance, motivation,* and *effort,* involvement connotes a more comprehensive construct that focuses on behavior—on action, rather than on internal psychological states. Involvement has both quantitative and qualitative components. Even though the amount of time spent is certainly important, the level of activity and energy or quality of the investment one devotes to an activity is key.

For example, suppose that two interns (Harry and Janice) are meeting with their faculty supervisor every two weeks. Various topics are discussed in these sessions, including: campus politics, understanding environments, conflict management, ethics, and multicultural diversity. Harry attends all of the sessions, listens quietly to the other intern, rarely participates in the discussions, and does a cursory job on the reflection papers that are submitted at each session. Janice missed two sessions because of illness, but when she is there she initiates relevant discussions, spends considerable time outside of sessions thinking about the implications of her internship, and takes responsibility for talking with her on-site supervisor about issues related to the internship. There is an obvious difference in the level of involvement between the two interns. Winston and Massaro (1987, p. 171) define "intensity of involvement" as a means of combining both time on task and personal investment. In this example, the second intern has a higher intensity of involvement, and therefore, one could hypothesize that Janice's personal development and learning would be affected much more significantly than Harry's.

Astin (1985) described a symbiotic relationship between the theories of student development—such as Chickering and Reisser (1993), Kohlberg (1969), and Perry (1968)—and his own involvement theory. "The theory of student involvement . . . differs qualitatively from these developmental theories. Whereas they focus primarily on developmental outcomes (the 'what' of student development), the theory of student involvement is concerned more with the behavioral mechanisms of processes that facilitate student development (the 'how') of student development" (pp. 142–143).

If an internship is to foster a high intensity of involvement, several critical conditions must be met (Winston & Saunders, 1987). These conditions will help an individual maintain her or his enthusiasm and increase commitment to the intern's own professional development. Perhaps the most significant challenge in promoting a high intensity of involvement is to create incentives for oneself and to make active commitments to personal growth and learning. If interns view their internships simply as a hurdle to be jumped on the road to graduation, then learning is likely to be compromised or negligible. The following conditions will serve as incentives to increase intensity of involvement throughout the learning experience. Similar to the process outlined in chapter 2, from the perspective of theory, following are the conditions most conducive to significant learning in the internship experience.

Create Specific Learning Outcomes Related to Increased Involvement

What knowledge and skills does the student want to learn from the internship? It is important that these outcomes be both detailed and comprehensive. For example, if Stan, an intern in the residence life unit, wants to improve his program presentation skills, he will need to identify what specific elements of effective program presentation he wants to address (one cannot become a great motivational speaker in a single internship!).

Suppose that Stan decides he wants to develop skills in the following areas: creating visual aids, writing comprehensive outlines, and keeping participants engaged. Further, Stan is aware that he is nervous when making presentations, which causes him to be confusing at times when he answers questions. He decides that he wants to decrease the anxiety he feels before and during presentations.

Identify Specific Strategies to Address Learning Objectives

To increase the intensity of involvement, and subsequent learning, from an internship, students need to go beyond the basic course requirements of number of hours on-site or attendance at seminars. They may need to participate in workshops, read additional material, or interview staff or students. In Stan's case, he decides to visit the counseling center to determine how he might reduce his anxiety. He participates in a relaxation workshop offered by the center and reads several articles about public speaking anxiety.

Create Frequent Opportunities for Feedback from Faculty and On-Site Supervisors

A number of studies (Astin, 1993; Baxter Magolda, 1992; Pascarella & Terenzini, 1991) point to the positive developmental effect of faculty and administrators' relationships with students. In general, if faculty and on-site supervisors spend time discussing students' growth and learning, then students will pay more attention to the outcomes of their experience. Regular conversations between faculty or administrators and students about the progress students are making fosters a deeper degree of reflection and encourages students to "actively watch themselves in the process of learning and develop learning strategies that constantly monitor their learning effectiveness" (Cross, 1996, p. 6).

This body of research has implications for interns. The "busyness" of faculty and on-site supervisors can be intimidating to interns seeking opportunities to simply discuss their progress and learning. It is important that interns clearly articulate that they want these discussions to take place, that they schedule these discussions well in advance, that they come to these discussions prepared to talk about their learning, and that they identify specific areas where they desire feedback (see chapter 3 for a more complete discussion of working with supervisors).

Monitor Learning

As stated previously, it is necessary to monitor one's learning and attainment of learning objectives. Without continuous attention to the learning outcomes, it is easy to get caught up in the excitement of completing tasks unaccompanied by an assessment of learning. Interns should ask themselves frequently, "What am I learning from this experience and how can I make it a more powerful developmental experience?" Asking this question on a regular basis will foster the continuous monitoring interns need to assure intensive involvement. Using the reflection form regularly (see previous exercise) will help interns provide a detailed structure through which to monitor their learning. Continuous monitoring will be an incentive to seek feedback from others.

Maintain Involvement through Collaborative Learning

Setting objectives, seeking feedback, and monitoring progress are ways to increase intensity of involvement. Finding opportunities to collaborate with others is another way to accomplish the goal. If possible, it is desirable for interns to work with others (other interns, student-clients, or professional staff) as members of a team. Much of what is done in student affairs is

---

Reflection Point

Critiquing Internship Goals and Objectives

Take a look at your internship goals and objectives. Critique them in the following ways:

1. How do the goals include your learning outcomes?
2. Are your learning outcomes stated in specific terms? If not, how do you change them?
3. Have you identified specific strategies to achieve these outcomes? If not, do so.
4. How are you going to monitor your progress?
5. How might you get others to help you stay on track in achieving your learning objectives?
6. Are there ways in which you can work collaboratively to achieve learning outcomes? If so, what are the opportunities for collaboration?

through group or team efforts. In addition, use group discussions with other interns as a way to do more than "vent" (often perceived by site and faculty supervisors as whining) about the problems on-site. (For many site supervisors, whining interns are to be avoided as much as possible!) These discussions can be valuable means to seek feedback from peers and to identify projects or activities that may lend themselves to collaboration.

ORGANIZATIONAL AND STUDENT DEVELOPMENT THEORIES

Knowing the specific elements of student and organizational development theories is very helpful in accomplishing internship goals and objectives. If the internship is to be successful, students must take advantage of multiple opportunities to apply theory to practice. Success in integrating theory and practice, along with the increased self-knowledge gleaned from reflection allows interns to develop their own philosophy of higher education and student affairs practice based on careful analysis and application and testing of well-founded, relevant hypotheses.

In the last two decades, a plethora of theoretical models has emerged and many of these have been used successfully by student affairs practitioners. Rather than reiterating all of the theories that can be useful in an internship, the remainder of this chapter addresses ways to apply theory to practice, identifies models of organizational development and change that may apply in the internship setting, and discusses several student development theories that have particular utility.

APPLYING THEORY TO PRACTICE: USING PROCESS MODELS

A number of scholars have developed models that help student affairs practitioners apply theory to practice. Rodgers (1991) identified 16 different models that provide structures and steps to help one create programs designed to promote student development. Additionally, there are even more models designed to help practitioners manage and change organizations. If one views management theory as providing models for organizational development, the earliest models were developed shortly after the turn of the 20th century (Creamer & Frederick, 1991). It is clearly beyond the scope of this chapter to reiterate the many models that are available. Readers are encouraged to read the work of Rodgers (1991) and Evans et al. (1998) overview student development theory to practice models and Creamer and Frederick (1991) for an understanding of the ways in which organizational and management theory can be applied to practical student affairs problems. Before using any theory-to-practice model, however, interns should be mindful of several considerations:

- Choose a model based on the issue being addressed. Some models attend more to assessing specific populations to be served (Rodgers & Widick, 1980) while others focus more on alternative modes of service delivery (Morrill, Hurst, & Oetting, 1980).
- Use multiple theories when working with a process model. Most problems faced in a student affairs unit are multidimensional. For example, a concern about student apathy may incorporate Astin's theory of student involvement as well as Creamer's Probability of Adoption of Change model (Creamer & Creamer, 1986).
- Effective translation of theory to practice requires assessment of students or organizational dynamics. All too often interns and new professionals want to quickly get a problem solved without stopping to conduct even a semistructured assessment of student needs and environmental conditions. There are numerous protocols for formal and informal assessment that can be used before charging off to implement theory (Cooper & Saunders 2000; Saunders & Cooper, 2001; Upcraft & Schuh, 1996).
- Revisit the model during the program implementation phase. Even if a workable model was used to plan an intervention designed to foster organizational or student development, it is important to monitor the degree to which the model is being used as the intervention evolves. Additional theories may need to be considered to better understand students or environments as one develops greater familiarity with the problem being addressed.

Understanding Organizations

Interns are faced with a unique challenge in becoming part of the organization in which they work. First, they are typically involved with the site for a relatively few weeks or months and their time in the setting each week is also limited. Second, they are most often seen as "graduate students" without the decision-making authority or long-term commitment of a full-time professional. Third, they may not have had prior experience in analyzing a work environment. Following are considerations about which interns need to be aware as they enter and become adjusted to the internship site.

Politics of the Environment

Faculty and staff in higher education live and work in a political environment. Rules and laws govern how members of the academic enterprise act and interact; social norms dictate how one should conduct oneself within any given setting or group. Moore (1993) stated that politics and specifically political behaviors are " those designed to shape or determine institutional direction and policy and are as rational or irrational, altruistic or self-serving as the people involved" (p. 153). Successful internship experiences often begin with the student taking time to observe and inquire about the politics and corresponding political behaviors in the work setting. There, however, are several precautions related to this process that also need to be addressed.

Generally, the politics of a work environment are subtle and difficult to ascertain without spending time on site observing the interactions among staff and between students and staff. One should also keep in mind that the obvious is not always the most influential factor in understanding organizational behavior. Understanding an organization's history is essential to interpreting the meaning of many current behaviors and activities. Brown and Podolske (1993) described the skills necessary to accomplish this task as "being a good observer, thinker, and politician [and] possessing high-level consultation, negotiation, research design, and measurement abilities" (p. 217). Spending a few days at the work site, preferably prior to beginning the internship, should give the intern an opportunity to watch the interpersonal interactions of staff members with the supervisor, with each other, and with the students or clients who use the service. Observing each of these three types of interactions should provide information from which to formulate hypotheses about the internship site. Examples of some questions one might ask include:

- What is the tone of the discussions subordinates have with the supervisor? Friendly? Formal? Do staff members call each other by first name or by title such as Dr. Smith, Ms. Jones, etc.? Do the staff members have lunch or breaks together frequently? Does it sound as though they socialize with each other away from the workplace? Do staff members seem to know about each about other's lives outside the office?
- Is the supervisor readily available and easily accessible to staff or students? Does one need to make an appointment to talk with certain staff members? Are staff meetings held? If so, how formal are those meetings? Do these meetings deal with significant issues and problems or are they just "show and tell"? Who participates in discussions? How are decisions made? By the supervisor, by consensus, by

some kind of voting? Generally, are decisions finalized or left with obvious ambiguity?

- In what manner are students greeted by staff members upon arriving at the office? Do staff see students as an infringement on their time? How do staff members talk about the students they serve? Do students often get involved in the internal workings of the office? Do students take sides when professionals disagree?

At times it will be important to ask staff members or the site supervisor for their interpretation of what has been observed. It is important, however, to ask more than one person for his or her opinion on the subject at hand. The intern may find that differing opinions exist or that a single event is interpreted by different people to have contrary meanings. It is best to know this at the beginning of the internship experience so that one can further observe and form conclusions of one's own. The answer to these and similar questions should provide the intern with a picture of the political environment of the setting. To best understand politics in an environment, one needs to understand the power structure within the unit. Power is defined by Moore (1993) as "the ability to influence others in such a way that they will more likely do what we prefer" (p. 153). Powerful people within an organization are likely to be able to get things done, even though those with power may not always be individuals with positions of authority on an organizational chart. As interns attempt to gather support for projects or interventions, knowing where power might lie in an organization is helpful. Also, as an intern tries to decipher office politics, reflection about who has power may explain how some (perhaps inexplicable) decisions are made. French and Raven (1959) tried to address the question of what individuals and groups do to have in order to be powerful. Some of the more significant sources of power are:

1. *Authority.* If a person's position is higher in the organization, typically they have more power. One can assume that on most (but not all) issues the senior student affairs officer would have more power than an individual student worker.
2. *Expertise.* People who have information or valuable skills use their expertise as a way to influence an organization. The head of computing technology who can get accurate information about the details of the institution's data management system has considerable power to influence decisions about choice of data systems and policies related to its use. Because this expertise is so specialized, others in the organization are likely to be unwilling to question the computer expert's conclusions.

3. *Control of rewards.* Individuals who deliver resources, political support, performance appraisals, or other valued rewards have the potential to be extremely powerful. The department chair who has a reputation for being able to gain resources for staff in times of scarcity can clearly influence the decisions of staff who report to her.
4. *Coercive power.* The labor union that has the ability to strike is using coercive power and obviously influences decisions. There are more subtle forms of coercive power, however. The student group that writes letters to the editor complaining about unfair treatment or the staff members who can slow down project implementation also have a form of power.
5. *Personal power.* Individuals with charisma, political skills, or the capacity to generate enthusiasm for a vision are also powerful, even if they do not have an obviously powerful position.

It is important to remember that even though all forms of power can be present in an organization, more important is the *perception* that any one person has any of these forms of power. It is that perception, real or not, that actually creates the illusion of power to others in the organization. On the other hand, a person can have a position of authority, have the power to reward or coerce those who report to him or her, and be viewed by others in the organization as completely powerless. Understanding who has power and why can help interns make sense out of what they observe within the setting. For an interesting perspective on how supervisors can intentionally use power to benefit the organization see Winston and Hirt (in press).

Organizational Structures

All colleges and universities are organized somewhat uniquely, usually based on the institutional mission but sometimes arising out of tradition or the power structure within the organization. For example, at some institutions, the senior student affairs officer (SSAO) may report directly to the president whereas at others the head of the student affairs division reports to a provost or chief academic officer. There are a variety of reasons that the institution's mission, history, or leadership preferences of the president would support one of these reporting structures over another (Sandeen, 2001). Barr (1993) pointed out that "no universal reporting structure exists that will assure the effectiveness of the student affairs organization. The informed practitioner must analyze each institutional context prior to making the decision about whether a particular reporting relationship is appropriate" (p. 96).

No matter how much support one finds to justify the existing structure, some aspects of the organization may make no apparent sense. For instance, the intern may find that budgeting for the entire student affairs organization is conducted by a support staff person in student activities, not by a staff member in the SSAO's office. Likewise, one may discover that there is one person who has the title of "Director of Residence Life and Coordinator of Services for Adult Students"—which suggests that she is expected to provide services to two totally different populations of students. Kuh and Whitt (1991) talk about *nonorthodox assumptions* to explain why some structural configurations come into being; and why, no matter how much one tries to anticipate every eventuality, unexpected events occur. Their assumptions include:

1. *Acknowledging that structures within an organization are constantly evolving and are content- (and often person-) specific.* Structures have been put in place to respond to a specific need at a certain time and perhaps have never been changed to something that would be more logical in the present environment. Kuh and Whitt (1991) point out that organizational charts, for example, frequently do not show the true relationships of people or departments to each other.

2. *Understanding that information can come from a variety of sources in the organization and can flow in any direction.* The more information that is passed along, the better informed the organization can be when making important decisions. Too much information or information that is inaccurate, however, can make for an equally unproductive an organization and one with too little information sharing. In organizations where information is thought to be proprietary (owned by certain individuals), accurate information becomes a source of power which is not willingly shared. For individuals lower in the organizational chart, many decisions seem mysterious because they lack sufficient information to understand the context for the decision. Likewise, leadership in these organizations tends to be authoritarian—those lower in the organizational structure cannot participate in decision making *because* they are uninformed.

3. *Recognizing that much of what occurs in organizations cannot be readily predicted or anticipated.* There are so many people, groups, and actions taking place in any given organization (even in small colleges) that it is often difficult, if not impossible, despite planning processes that are in place, to have completely accurate knowledge about the outcome of any event.

4. *Realizing that there are many ways to approach and solve any problem faced by the organization.* The idea that there is one best way to manage people has been abandoned for many years. Yet some still believe that there is a "right answer or outcome" out there for any difficulty.

At best, organizational structures can be established that make it easy for employees to share information, talk about the direction they hope the organization will take in the future, and work together to solve problems as they arise. Interns will no doubt see many instances where Kuh and Whitt's (1991) nonorthodox assumptions come into play.

---

*𝒮*xercise

1. Get a copy of the organizational chart for your internship site and for the larger unit in which your site is housed (e.g., if you work in student activities and that office reports to the vice president for student affairs, get an organizational chart for each).
2. Study the reporting relationships. Do they all seem to fit for the organization? What in the reporting structure would you change? What would be your rationale for those changes? Are there instances where it seems decisions were made in your unit contrary to the formal organizational chart? Why do you think that happened? Is that a singular event or common practice?

ORGANIZATIONAL CULTURE

As an intern watches the staff in the site interact with one another and with outside constituents, she or he will begin to see and feel the culture of the office emerge. Culture in higher education organizations is defined as "the collective, mutually shaped patterns of norms, values, practices, beliefs, and assumptions which guide the behavior of individuals and groups and provides a frame of reference within which to interpret the meaning of events and actions on and off the campus" (Kuh & Whitt, 1988). Kuh and Whitt use the metaphor of an invisible tapestry to describe the processes and products that make up institutional culture. "The summation or end-product of all the social and personal values and the consequences of those values that operate within the organization" (p. iv) comprise the culture of that organization (Fife, 1997, p. xvii).

As the intern continues observing the environment in the site, there are multiple aspects of the culture that should be considered. In particular, he or she should pay close attention to artifacts (structures and processes), values (goals and philosophies espoused by the organization), and basic assumptions (beliefs and feelings the organizations members hold as truths) (Schein, 1985). These three levels of organizational culture can provide the observer with tremendous insight into the environment and the relationships that exist there.

There are a variety of cultural forms that can help one better understand the work environment. Rituals often are used to bring a sense of tradition to the setting. Some institutions have a time each week, for example, when classes are not held so that all-campus meetings and events can take place. Other institutions hold an opening convocation each fall with faculty dressed in academic regalia as a way to welcome new students and their parents to the institution.

Language is another aspect of culture that takes on some unique forms on a campus. Through words, symbols, and metaphors, language creates a method of communication where certain meanings are derived for members of that culture that may not occur for individuals who are external to the culture. "Because colleges and universities are rich in symbolism and ceremony, an awareness of the systems of symbols that mediate meaning between individuals and their culture is important to understanding events and actions" (Kuh & Whitt, 1988, pp. 19–20).

Reflection Point

Consider the following aspects of organizational culture in your internship site:

- Are there any departmental heroes? If so who are they and why are they viewed in that way?
- Are there any institutional myths that stem from past events in your site?
- What are the rituals staff members in the site view as important? Why?
- Are there particular symbols or language that is used in your site to give meaning to the work?

LEADERSHIP

There are many different ideas about what makes a good leader. Some people see leaders as strong, all-knowing individuals who are powerful. At the other extreme, others believe leaders are people whom others admire and respect due to their charismatic personality. Komives, Lucas, and McMahon (1998) define leadership as a "relational process of people together attempting to accomplish change or make a difference to benefit the common good" (p. 31). The administrative head of the internship site, for example, should be encouraging the staff in the department to work as a team toward the common goals they have established to benefit the clients (typically students) who use the service. An intern will be able to watch this process and make judgments about how successful the leader is in fulfilling this definition. There are many myths about the concept of leadership. Some of these include "leaders are born, not made," or "there is only one right way to lead an organization." Komives, Lucas, and McMahon (1998) propose that there are some truths about leadership that one needs to consider including:

- Leaders are made, not born.
- In today's fluid organizations, leadership occurs at all levels.
- Having a charismatic personality is not a prerequisite for leadership.
- There is not one identifiable right way to lead an organization or group.
- Some leaders and scholars believe it is important to make a distinction between the processes of management and leadership.
- Leadership is a discipline that is teachable. (pp. 28–60)

It is important to remember these points as one observes the leaders in the internship site and as the intern becomes the type of leader she or he wants to be as a new professional. Another point to remember is that leaders are not always people designated on an organizational chart. One may find leaders in a variety of positions and at all levels of the organization.

---

*R*eflection *P*oint

After you have been in your internship site for a few weeks, consider the following questions:

- Is the leadership in the workplace well defined? Is the group's leader the head of the department or office?
- If the director of the office is not the 'leader' in your opinion, who is and why?
- What are the approaches to leadership that you feel are happening in an effective way at the site?
- If you were the department head, how would your leadership be different for this site?

ENVIRONMENTAL ISSUES TO CONSIDER

To review, there are several aspects of the internship environment the intern should be observing:

1. The political processes that are in place or under discussion as well as the bases of power that people possess in the organization.
2. Whether the site is organized either to be helpful in completing the tasks at hand or to impede progress toward goal completion.
3. The manner in which the culture has developed at the internship site and the impact that culture has on those working there or served by the staff.
4. How those charged with leadership responsibilities carry out their duties.

Observing these functions within the internship site and learning to listen and ask appropriate questions will provide interns with skills they will need as they become new professionals in student affairs.

USING STUDENT DEVELOPMENT THEORY

In most graduate programs designed to prepare student affairs professionals there is at least one course that teaches prospective practitioners about their clientele. Student development theory, or the application of human development principles to college students, is most often covered in depth. Even though most graduate students in student affairs preparation programs are conversant with the theories of student development, the internship may be one of the first times they have the opportunity to put these theories into practice in a real-world situation. What follows is a brief review of the tenets of three important categories of theory: psychosocial, cognitive-structural, and ethnic identity. In addition, special attention is given to concepts of mattering and marginality (Rosenberg, 1979; Schlossberg, 1984) because these emphasize the effects of the environment on students. Using these theories in practice in an internship site requires that one stop and think about how interventions can be explained in ways that are meaningful to the clientele and supervisors. The final portion of this chapter focuses on practical ways to integrate student development theory into internship projects and how one can use theory to communicate the rationale for plans and actions.

PSYCHOSOCIAL THEORIES

Making an impact on the content of students' development, requires an understanding of the elements of psychosocial theories such as Chickering and Reisser (1993), Erikson (1959/1980), and Marcia (1966).

The Case of Tommy

Suppose that Tommy is an intern who is creating a training program for new members of residence hall judicial boards. He knows that most of these students are sophomores and that many ran for election to the board unopposed. In Tommy's early conversations with board members who were recently elected, he discovers that many are quite reluctant to make judgments about their peers and some feel that they just don't have the communication skills or confidence to ask good questions of those accused of violations.

In reviewing Chickering and Reisser's (1993) theory, Tommy hypothesizes that most of these new judicial board members are dealing with issues of competence. Specifically, Tommy speculates that these board members may need help in developing skills in communication, leadership, and working cooperatively as a judicial board team in order to develop interpersonal competence. Because of his understanding of psychosocial development, Tommy recognizes that the issues surrounding interpersonal competence are the foundation for making fair, compassionate, and consistent judicial decisions or in the words of the Chickering and Reisser theory—developing integrity. Tommy wants the new members to be able to demonstrate integrity by balancing the interests of the residence life program with the interests of individual students, and to develop a congruent sense of social responsibility.

Chickering and Reisser (1993) argue that developing integrity is typically one of the developmental vectors that students address later in their college careers or even after college. Further, developing integrity will not be achieved without addressing the preliminary vectors, such as developing competence and solidifying one's personal identity. Tommy, therefore, decides to focus the first few training sessions on giving students information about and practice in questioning students accused of violations and helping them develop ground rules for discussing cases and making decisions. He also decides that having board members work through challenging hypothetical ethical dilemmas should be scheduled for the latter parts of the training program. Finally, Tommy determines that he should observe the first few judicial cases and provide the board with feedback about their decision-making strengths and weaknesses. Tommy's understanding of psychosocial development theory, along with his informal assessment of new judicial board members, allows him to create a training program with appropriate content and timing more precisely tailored to the needs of new judicial board members.

COGNITIVE-STRUCTURAL THEORIES

Psychosocial theories examine what changes occur in thinking, feeling, and behavior as one matures. In contrast, cognitive–structural theories focus on the processes through which individuals think about challenging content and making decisions. These theories look at the development that occurs in individuals' assumptions about their experiences and environment (Evans et al., 1998). Developed by theorists such as Baxter Magolda (1992), Gilligan (1982/1993), King and Kitchener (1994), Kohlberg (1969), and Perry (1968), cognitive development theories have implications about the ways in which program designers structure and deliver their content.

The Case of Kim

Consider Kim, an intern in the student activities office, is designing and facilitating a series of workshops on leadership skills for sophomore women who want to become more active in campus organizations. The tenets of Baxter Magolda's (1992) conceptualization could help Kim determine the degree of structure and the kinds of interpersonal relationships she wants to foster in the sessions. Assume that the majority of women in the workshops could be classified as transitional knowers. This means participants would accept that some knowledge is uncertain and believe that it is important to emphasize the ways in which learning can be applied to current and future practical situations (Baxter Magolda, 1992). Given such participants, the most effective workshops would emphasize how participants can apply skills to their organizations, and would offer participants multiple opportunities to practice skills. It would also be important for Kim to avoid portraying herself as one who has all of the right answers. Kim's willingness to let participants come to their own conclusions can foster students' movement toward the third stage of the model—independent knowing. Because Baxter Magolda's research suggests that women are more likely than men to use an *interpersonal knowing pattern* during the transitional knowing stage, it would be important for Kim to develop support networks among participants that foster the sharing of ideas among peers. It would be equally important for Kim to overtly demonstrate care and concern for participants. As with Tommy in the previous case, Kim's understanding of developmental theory allows her to tailor her intervention and even her role within that intervention in a more precise way. This greater precision will increase the probability that learning and skill acquisition will occur for participants.

ETHNICITY: IDENTIFYING ROLES

As the student begins the internship, it is important that he or she review the demographics of the institution. One's role in being an active learner is to understand the different types of students represented on the host campus. Interns should understand the types of diversity in terms of ethnicity, culture, gender, religion, sexual orientation, socioeconomic background, physical or emotional challenges, as well as discerning how these differences are celebrated by the student affairs staff and the students themselves. It is important to try to decipher the elements of the organizational culture that facilitate or impede an openness to these differences.

Understanding the culture of the host campus is simply the first step. Becoming a successful change agent who facilitates increased appreciation of differences is much more challenging, partly because of the transitory nature of an internship. This is a challenge worth accepting, however, because most interns and student affairs professionals, even those who have spent decades in the profession, need to continue to refine their abilities to create a more accepting environment for all students.

The Case of Corrie

Recalling identity development models can help as one becomes familiar with the internship setting. Suppose that Corrie is working in an orientation office and begins to wonder how the orientation experience affects students of color as they adjust to the collegiate environment. On the campus where Corrie's internship is located, there appears to be only one ethnic minority visibly evident on the campus—African Americans. Corrie, therefore, would be well advised to think about the Cross (1971, 1991, 1995) model of Nigrescence that describes a sequential process (Cross & Vandiver, 2001) outlining the changes that occur in the psychological lives of African-American individuals as they establish their ethnic identity. According to the model, as one progresses through stages, individuals move from seeing race as unimportant, to an encounter that reminds them of the impact of racial differences, to total immersion in an ethnic culture, often with anger toward the dominant culture. Finally, individuals achieve an integration between their old identity and new ethnic worldview and move on to make meaningful commitments that address problems faced by African Americans and other oppressed groups. Corrie could easily use the Cross model to understand better some of the possible developmental issues African American students might be experiencing as a result of the orientation process. Through that understanding of how they *might* be feeling, Corrie might try to work with African-American students to create some activities that allow them to meet each other and learn about organizations or programs that are focused on their black identity.

As with many white new professionals, Corrie's first reaction to seeing students of color who separate themselves from majority activities, was to adopt a lassiez-faire attitude, assuming that there was no point in trying to get involved with the African-American students because they wanted nothing to do with her. She felt intimidated by the presence of a group of students who are distinct and different from their own race. By stepping into the shoes of those students, and considering some of the factors that she could learn about ethnic identity development, Corrie was able to become an effective and important catalyst who enabled all students, regardless of their differences, to feel comfortable and understood. Some white new professionals fail to incorporate ethnic identity models and therefore cannot begin to appreciate why students of color may seem angry at the majority group or become offended when the campus programs do not take into account their cultural perspectives.

Other identity theories and conceptualizations, such as Helms' (1995) White Identity Development Model, Phinney's (1989) Model of Ethnic Identity Development, Casas and Pytluk's (1995) Model of Hispanic Identity Development, Sodowsky, Kwan, and Pannu's (1995) concepts of ethnic identity in Asian Americans, or Cass's (1979) Model of Homosexual Identity Formation can all serve as guides for practice with diverse ethnic and cultural groups. To some degree, almost all of these theories parallel the stages described by Cross. Students go through a period of separation from the majority or dominant culture to find their identity within their own group and they may express extremely emotional feelings about the larger dominant culture. By using ethnic identity theories to assess where students are in their development, interns can become aware of the needs and possible responses that can be applied to maximize effectiveness as an intern. Again, when interns are new to the campus or office, they can point out observations in forms that help others create bridges and connections for students.

As one acts to facilitate identity development among a diverse array of students, it is important to accept and respect what students who are not from the dominant culture on that campus may be feeling to help them make a transition into a stage of internalization or acceptance. Allowing students to express pride in their differences while recognizing that they may want to share more and feel less fragmented from others, empowers the intern when designing activities that can help students grow and gain confidence. Also, it is important to apply any theory with caution. It is important to recognize that each student may progress through stages in different ways and with a unique timetable that must be respected. Even though interns may be experts on theory, they need to remain humble enough to recognize that they cannot fully understand the life experience of another and are not able, therefore, to make definitive categorizations. To effectively apply theory, one must have an in-depth understanding of the contents of the theory and understand the unique individuals to whom one wants to apply the theory.

As with all issues around cultural difference, an intern needs to understand how the climate may explode into conflict or how sensitivity around specific issues can lead to acts of violence or other inappropriate social behavior. Interns should discuss with faculty and site supervisors the realities of programs being planned, political issues, and the intern's personal comfort zones in working with students from minority communities. It is equally important that interns who are from nondominant populations for the given institution need to exercise caution when planning programs and activities for members of the majority population.

Marginality and Mattering

The psychological and physical environment in which students find themselves play a key role in determining how they develop in college. Schlossberg (1989), using concepts originated by Rosenberg (1979), discusses the notions of marginality and mattering to provide insight for interns as they try to create communities that are inclusive and that foster learning and personal development. As interns approach environments without walls, such as distance learning and computer interactive campus courses, the concept of community on a campus can present a challenge in both practical and conceptual terms. As an intern seeking to understand how to create community within the unit where she or he works, or as a professional desiring to create an inclusive community where students matter and do not feel marginalized or discounted, this concept can be difficult to grasp even when interns are talking with students on a daily basis. Many characteristics in today's society create differences among people. Students of all types are, at least conceptually, sorted into groups for easier or more efficient delivery of services and delineation of programs (e.g., services for students with disabilities, minority student programs, or nontraditional students—adult learners). When interns arrive at a site, it is critical that they try to understand how an institution has defined its students, and how staff have sought to serve them through various organizational structures.

Many professionals have dealt with periods in their lives when they have felt marginalized. Park (1928) defines the marginal person as "one who is living and sharing intimately in the cultural life and traditions of two distinct peoples, never quite willing to break, even if permitted to do so, with past and traditions, and not quite accepted, because of prejudice, in the new society in which the individual seeks to find a place" (p. 892). As a result of coming to a new environment, the intern might even be able to relate to the feeling of being "outside" the office's life. However, interns are "moving through" the process and they are there to gain insight and learn, not necessarily to find a comfortable niche in the unit. For most interns, this is usually a quick and easy transition. For students who feel marginalized, that marginalization may become the focus of their lives on the campus. Their feeling of marginality may thwart academic and social success. The goals of most student affairs divisions are to find ways to help students know they matter and are valued as persons and members of the academic community.

Schlossberg (1989) discusses qualities of a "mattering environment" that encourages involvement and promotes the development of community. She asserts that most individuals, both adolescents and older persons, need to feel that they matter. If a student feels marginalized (as not mattering), she or he may feel unworthy or unwilling to risk involvement because of a fear of rejection or ridicule. The five characteristics that constitute a mattering environment, according to Schlossberg, are briefly discussed.

1. *Attention.* The most fundamental way to encourage a mattering environment is to let students and staff know that they are noticed rather than ignored. Unfortunately, in many environments, it is uncommon to see staff saying hello to students or stopping to ask how a student or colleague is doing. Simple acts like remembering names and something of significance about students and colleagues can go far in showing meaningful, positive attention.

2. *Importance.* It is critical that students and colleagues believe that others care about their opinions, needs, and plans. Students and colleagues alike want to know that their views are important, even if others do not agree or approve. Soliciting the opinions of students about a program proposal, for example, is one way to communicate that students are important members of the community.

3. *Ego extension.* Individuals who believe that they matter instead of being marginalized feel that others in their community are proud of their successes and saddened by their disappointments. Furthermore, ego extension means that individuals believe that their successes are shared and that their failures can burden others. Celebrating students' and colleagues' successes and expressing concern for problems is one way to create a mattering environment. Furthermore, recognizing and reinforcing that an individual's efforts, no matter how seemingly insignificant, have an effect on the health of the community.

4. *Dependence.* It is clear that behavior is affected by dependence on others. For example, students are often reluctant to openly criticize a faculty member for fear of a negative grade. Conversely, behavior is also affected by the perception that others are dependent on an individual. Interns can reinforce the importance of dependence by reinforcing that individuals in a community depend on each other. Since "dependence" can be a double-edged sword where some may be depended upon inappropriately, interns can and

should be role models of how to respond in a healthy way. They should avoid the trap of having too many "dependents," failing to delegate to others, or taking on inequitable shares of the workload.

5. *Appreciation*. Visible, explicit expressions of appreciation are major contributors to a mattering environment. If students and staff members feel that their efforts are appreciated, they will expend extra effort and share feelings of appreciation toward others. A simple thank you, either verbal or in writing, can reap large benefits in terms of helping students and colleagues feel appreciated. For appreciation to be effective, however, it must be genuine.

Schlossberg's (1989) concepts are relatively easy to grasp, but can be challenging to put into practice consistently. When interns believe that they are pressed for time, that their work is not being noticed, that their value to the organization is not appreciated, it becomes much more difficult to create the characteristics of a mattering environment toward others. A faculty member or site supervisor can be an intern's best ally in finding ways to feel important, noticed, and appreciated. Because of the stress associated with the transition of assuming an internship, the intern who perceives him or herself to be part of a mattering environment is more likely to be successful. The same is true for students experiencing transitions.

Reflection Point

Student Development Theory

Think through one of your internship projects from the perspective of student development theory by asking yourself the following questions:

1. What student development theories might guide my creation of this project?
2. Which of these theories seem to be the best fit? Why?
3. What elements of the theory are particularly relevant to my project? Why?
4. In what ways does the theory give me guidance about:

   • Content to be addressed
   • Structure (e.g., timing, who participates, format)
   • My role within the project

CAUTIONS IN APPLYING STUDENT DEVELOPMENT THEORY

As has been stated earlier, interns are staff members working with others who are likely to have considerably more decision-making authority than they do. Interns and young professionals often assume that more experienced professionals in their office share their passion for implementing theory. Yet for many administrators, promoting student development is not their only goal. For some staff or whole administrative units, promoting student development may be a quite low priority. For some, the primary goal is to provide efficient service; for others it may be to keep costs low; and for others, the goal may be to reduce attrition or to promote satisfaction. For interns to create successful interventions that are meaningful for the placement site and its clientele, interns need to couple their assessment of the environment with their desire to apply what they know to the site.

Here are some tips that may be helpful as one actively participates in the internship:

1. Recognize that some of the members of the staff may not know the new theories and research you have learned. Yet these staff members, because of their understanding of the subtleties of the environment, have wisdom from which you can benefit. Unless specifically asked to do so, interns' attempts to be teachers of theory to practitioners will usually not be well received or appreciated.

2. Avoid communicating with other staff members in theoretical jargon that may not be understood by everyone. If you can communicate plans to implement theory in language understood by everyone, you will gain a more precise and useful knowledge of the theory. Furthermore, you can avoid being misunderstood by those who may not possess an extensive knowledge base.

3. Tailor the rationale for programs and interventions to the mission and goals of the unit rather than using theoretical imperatives as the sole or even principal reason for taking initiative in a particular area.

4. Recognize the limitations of theory as explanations of behavior. For example, many commonly used theories are based on the values of Euro-American, middle-class, white, well-educated individuals. Also, there is limited published literature that documents ways in which theory is effectively translated to practice.

CONCLUSION

Multiple opportunities abound for interns to use the literature of student development, organizational development, and student learning in their internship sites, both to better communicate with student-clients and to more fully understand the dynamics of their organization. Also, interns can apply these theories to their own learning and development, thus deepening their understanding of the supervised experience. Using theory as a basis for learning and reflection has several advantages. Theoretical conceptions, because of their complexity and comprehensiveness, can augment both the intern's and supervisor's experience. Theory provides guidance for solving problems and dealing with challenges in a way that promotes self-understanding and learning. Finally, knowing and using theories can help one to anticipate student and organizational concerns, thus allowing interns to more thoroughly address the needs of the institution and those it serves.

REFERENCES

Astin, A. W. (1984). Student involvement: A developmental theory for higher education. *Journal of College Student Personnel, 25,* 297–308.

Astin, A. W. (1985). *Achieving educational excellence: A critical assessment of priorities and practices in higher education.* San Francisco: Jossey-Bass.

Astin, A. W. (1993). An empirical typology of college students. *Journal of College Student Development, 34,* 36–46.

Barr, M. J. (1993). Organizational and administrative models. In M. J. Barr (Ed.), *The handbook of student affairs administration* (pp. 95–106). San Francisco: Jossey-Bass.

Baxter Magolda, M. B. (1992). *Knowing and reasoning in college: Gender-related patterns in students' intellectual development.* San Francisco: Jossey-Bass.

Brown, R. D., & Podolske, D. I. (1993). A political model for program evaluation. In M. J. Barr (Ed.), *The handbook of student affairs administration* (pp. 216–229). San Francisco: Jossey-Bass.

Casas, J. M., & Pytluk, S. D. (1995). Hispanic identity development: Implications for research and practice. In J. G. Ponterotto, J. M. Casas, L. A. Suzuki, & C. M. Alexander (Eds.), *Handbook of multicultural counseling* (pp. 155–180). Thousand Oaks, CA: Sage.

Cass, V. C. (1979). Homosexual identity formation: A theoretical model. *Journal of Homosexuality, 4,* 219–235.

Chickering, A. W., & Reisser, L. (1993). *Education and identity* (2nd ed.). San Francisco: Jossey-Bass.

Cooper, D. L., & Saunders, S. A. (2000). Program assessment skills needed by student affairs administrators. In D. Liddell & J. Lund (Eds.), New Directions for Student Services, No. 90. *Powerful programming for student learning* (pp. 5–20). San Francisco: Jossey Bass.

Creamer, D. G., & Creamer, E. G. (1986). Applying a model of planned change to program innovation in student affairs. *Journal of College Student Personnel, 27,* 19–26.

Creamer, D. G., & Frederick, P. M. (1991). Administrative and management theories: Tools for change. In T. K. Miller & R. B. Winston, Jr. (Eds.), *Administration and leadership in student affairs: Actualizing student development in higher education* (2nd ed., pp. 135–158). Muncie, IN: Accelerated Development.

Cross, K. P. (1996). New lenses on learning. *About Campus, 1*(1), 4–9.

Cross, W. E., Jr. (1971). Toward a psychology of black liberation: The Negro-to-black conversion experience. *Black World, 20*(9), 13–27.

Cross, W. E., Jr. (1991). *Shades of black: Diversity in African American identity.* Philadelphia: Temple University Press.

Cross, W. E., Jr. (1995). The psychology of Nigrescence: Revising the Cross model. In J. E. Ponterotto, J. M. Casas, L. A. Suzuki, & C. M. Alexander (Eds.), *Handbook of multicultural counseling* (pp. 93–122). Thousand Oaks, CA: Sage.

Cross, W. E., Jr., & Vandiver, B. J. (2001). Nigrescence theory and measurement: Introducing the Cross Racial Identity Scale. In J. G. Ponterotto, J. M. Casas, L. M. Suzuki, & C. M. Alexander (Eds.), *Handbook of multicultural counseling* (2nd ed., pp 371–393). Thousand Oaks, CA: Sage.

Erikson, E. H. (1980). *Identity and the life cycle.* New York: Norton. (Original work published 1959)

Evans, N. J., Forney, D. S., & Guido-DiBrito, F. (1998). *Student development in college: Theory, research and practice.* San Francisco: Jossey-Bass.

Fife, J. D. (1997). Foreword. In R. H. Fenske, C. A. Geranios, J. E. Keller, & D. E. Moore (Eds.), *Early intervention programs: Opening the door to higher education.* ASHE-ERIC Higher Education Reports, 25(6). Washington, DC: The George Washington University, Graduate School of Education and Human Development.

Forney, D. S. (1994). A profile of student affairs master's students: Characteristics, attitudes, and learning styles. *Journal of College Student Development, 35,* 337–345.

French, J. R., & Raven, B. H. (1959). The bases of social power. In D. Cartwright (Ed.), *Studies in social power.* Ann Arbor: Institute for Social Research, University of Michigan.

Gilligan, C. (1993). *In a different voice: Psychological theory and women's development.* Cambridge: MA: Harvard University Press. (Original work published in 1982)

Helms, J. E. (1995). An update of Helms's white and people of color racial identity models. In J. E. Ponterotto, J. M. Casas, L. A. Suzuki, & C. M. Alexander (Eds.), *Handbook of multicultural counseling* (pp. 181–198). Thousand Oaks, CA: Sage.

King, P. M., & Kitchener, K. S. (1994). *Developing reflective judgment: Understanding and promoting intellectual growth and critical thinking in adolescents and adults.* San Francisco: Jossey-Bass.

Kohlberg, L. (1969). Stage and sequence: The cognitive developmental approach to socialization. In D. A. Goslin (Ed.), *Handbook of socialization theory and research* (pp. 347–480). Chicago: Rand McNally.

Kolb, D. A. (1981). Learning styles and disciplinary differences. In A.W. Chickering (Ed.), *Modern American college: Responding to the new realities of diverse students and a changing society* (pp. 232–255). San Francisco: Jossey-Bass.

Kolb, D. A. (1984). *Experiential learning: Experience as the source of learning and development*. Englewood Cliffs, NJ: Prentice Hall.

Kolb, D. A. (1999). *The learning style inventory (LSI3) Technical manual*. Boston: McBer.

Kolb, D. A. (2000). *Facilitator's guide to learning*. Boston: TRG Hay/McBer, Training Resources Group.

Komives, S. R., Lucas, N., & McMahon, T. R. (1998). *Exploring leadership: For college students who want to make a difference*. San Francisco: Jossey-Bass.

Kuh, G. D., & Whitt, E. J. (1988). The invisible tapestry: Culture in American colleges and universities (ASHE-ERIC Higher Education Report No. 1). Washington, DC: Association for the Study of Higher Education.

Kuh, G. D., & Whitt, E. J. (1991). Organizational theory: A primer. In T. K. Miller & R. B. Winston, Jr. (Eds.), *Administration and leadership in student affairs: Actualizing student development in higher education* (2nd ed., pp. 135–158). Muncie, IN: Accelerated Development.

Marcia, J. E. (1966). Development and validation of ego-identity status. *Journal of Personality and Social Psychology, 3,* 551–558.

Moore, P. L. (1993). The political dimension of decision-making. In M. J. Barr & Associates (Eds.), *The handbook of student affairs administration* (pp. 152–170). San Francisco: Jossey-Bass.

Morrill, W. H., Hurst, J. C., & Oetting, E. R. (1980). A conceptual model of intervention strategies, In W. H. Morrill & J. C. Hurst (Eds.), *Dimensions of intervention for student development* (pp. 85–95). New York: Wiley.

Park, R. E. (1928). Human migration and the marginal man. *American Journal of Sociology, 33,* 892.

Pascarella, E. T., & Terenzini, P. T. (1991). *How college affects students: Findings and insights from twenty years of research*. San Francisco: Jossey-Bass.

Perry, W. G., Jr. (1968). *Forms of intellectual and ethical development in the college years: A scheme*. New York: Holt, Rinehart & Winston.

Phinney, J. S. (1989). Stages of ethnic identity development in minority group adolescents. *Journal of Early Adolescence, 9,* 34–49.

Rodgers, R. F. (1991). Using theory in practice in student affairs. In T. K. Miller & R. B. Winston, Jr. (Eds.), *Administration and leadership in student affairs: Actualizing student development in higher education* (2nd ed., pp. 203–251). Muncie, IN: Accelerated Development.

Rodgers, R. F., & Widick, C. (1980). Theory to practice. Using concepts, logic, and creativity. In F. B. Newton & K. L. Ender (Eds.), *Student development practice: Strategies for making a difference* (pp. 5–25). Springfield, IL: Thomas.

Rosenberg, M. (1979). *Conceiving the self*. New York: Basic Books.

Sandeen, A. (2001). Organizing student affairs divisions. In R. B. Winston, Jr., D. G. Creamer, & T. K. Miller (Eds.), *The professional student affairs administrator: Educator, leader, and manager* (pp. 181–210). New York: Brunner-Routledge.

Saunders, S. A., & Cooper, D. L. (2001). Programmatic interventions: Applying theory to practice. In R. B. Winston, Jr., D. G. Creamer, & T. K. Miller (Eds.), *The professional student affairs administrator: Educator, leader, and manager* (pp. 309–340). New York: Brunner-Routledge.

Schein, E. H. (1985). *Organizational culture and leadership*. San Francisco: Jossey-Bass.

Schlossberg, N. K. (1984). *Counseling adults in transition.* New York: Springer.

Schlossberg, N. K. (1989). Marginality and mattering: Key issues in building community. In D. C. Roberts (Ed.), *New Directions for Student Services, No. 48. Designing campus activities to foster a sense of community* (pp. 5–15). San Francisco: Jossey-Bass.

Sodowsky, G. R., Kwan, K. K., & Pannu, R. (1995). Ethnic identity of Asians in the United States. In J. G. Ponterotto, J. M. Casas, L. A. Suzuki, & C. M. Alexander (Eds.), *Handbook of multicultural counseling* (pp. 122–154). Thousand Oaks, CA: Sage.

Upcraft, M. L., & Schuh, J. H. (1996). *Assessment in student affairs: A guide for practitioners.* San Francisco: Jossey-Bass.

Winston, R. B., Jr., & Hirt, J. B. (in press). Activating synergistic supervision approaches: Practical suggestions. In S. M. Janosik, J. B. Hirt, D. G. Creamer, & R. B. Winston, Jr. (Eds.), *Supervising new professionals in student affairs: A guide for practitioners.* New York: Brunner-Routledge.

Winston, R. B., Jr., & Massaro, A. (1987). Extracurricular involvement inventory: An instrument for assessing intensity of student involvement. *Journal of College Student Personnel, 28,* 169–175.

Winston, R. B., Jr., & Saunders, S. A. (1987). The Greek experience: Friend or foe of student development. In R. B. Winston, Jr., W. R. Nettles III, & J. H. Opper, Jr., (Eds.), *New Directions for Student Services, No. 40. Fraternities and sororities on the contemporary college campus* (pp. 5–20). San Francisco: Jossey-Bass.

Chapter 5
LEGAL AND ETHICAL ISSUES[1]

Steven M. Janosik
Joan B. Hirt

Internships and assistantships provide students with important opportunities to develop a personal framework for professional behavior. Most often, guidelines for this behavior are provided through the institutions in which they work and the professional associations to which they belong. Although much of what is defined as "professional behavior" is shaped by the culture of the employing organization, a large share of one's professional behavior also is defined by state and federal statutes, courts and the decisions they make, and statements of ethics.

The purpose of this chapter is to highlight a number of important legal and ethical issues that should be addressed early in any supervised experience. By doing so, interns will have a clear understanding of the parameters of acceptable conduct and will be less likely to accidentally breach laws and rules that govern professional practice and will not inadvertently stumble into unethical behavior. It is also likely that field supervisors will be more satisfied with student performance. Finally, this review will help students develop greater confidence in discharging their responsibilities and aid interns in more quickly developing a framework for professional practice. Topics reviewed in this chapter include: formal and informal working relationships, questions of authority and responsibility, liability issues, managing liability, and professional ethics and standards.

---

1. Nothing in this chapter should be construed as legal advice. When legal issues arise one should always seek the counsel of a competent attorney.

FORMAL AND INFORMAL WORKING RELATIONSHIPS

In large measure, the degree of formality evident in a given work setting and the intern-site supervisor relationship is a matter of personality, personal style, and institutional culture. Some site supervisors feel comfortable with a relatively loosely defined work agenda. Others approach the task of supervising a student's field experience with a more explicitly defined structure and expectations. Similarly, the organizational culture of some institutions dictates that everything be written down and signed in triplicate, whereas administrators at other institutions may operate on a "smile and a handshake" basis.

As explained in some detail in chapter 2, regardless of the formality of the relationship created, students and their supervisors should mutually agree upon the tasks to be completed and the learning experiences that are to take place during the internship. Interns who do not establish clear understandings with their site supervisors at the beginning of the practical experience run the risk of discovering near the end of the internship that they have not satisfactorily met the site supervisor's expectations. Even though it is not possible (or even desirable) to specify every minute task or assignment to be performed, a clear understanding set down in writing gives the intern the security of knowing the expectations and frees the site supervisor from the task of having to repeatedly clarify expectations.

In situations where the student is to receive a stipend for the work conducted during the internship, a job description usually identifies the expectations of the supervisor. Absent an employment agreement, other types of documents may serve this purpose. Supervisors may wish to write letters of appointment or memorandums of understanding that outline the nature of the relationship between the student and the supervisor and highlight what is to be accomplished during the course of the internship. In many cases, the faculty member serving as the faculty supervisor for the course will require that a behavioral contract be developed and agreed upon. This learning contract serves the same purpose (see chapter 2 for details about learning contracts).

Regardless of its form, having a document that establishes ground rules for the experience serves to enhance the student's learning and subsequent evaluation. Such a document should include: (a) the goals or the educational objectives to be achieved; (b) the specific work assignments or tasks that will lead to goal attainment; (c) the nature of the supervision to be provided; (d) a statement concerning the work setting; and (e) a statement on the expected number of hours to be worked.

This agreement does three important things for the student. First, it helps to ensure that the activities in which the student will be engaged contribute to what should be an important learning experience. Second, it provides the framework upon which appropriate feedback and evaluation can be made. Finally, in the unlikely event that disagreements over work expectations occur, it serves as an objective source of information that can prove invaluable in resolving the conflict. This document is the key to establishing a good working relationship.

QUESTIONS OF AUTHORITY AND RESPONSIBILITY

Once a field experience agreement has been completed and all parties have agreed to its content, the student and the site supervisor should reread the document carefully to determine what issues of authority and responsibility are created. This is critically important since the nature of the work and the student's relationship with the administrative unit or department create the potential for institutional and personal liability. The following list contains several examples of activities that are commonly found in supervised experiences. Such assignments should not necessarily be avoided, but they do warrant special consideration. The intern should be determining if they will be:

1. Answering phone calls or other inquiries;
2. Handling confidential files or material;
3. Attending meetings where sensitive information is shared;
4. Hiring other student employees;
5. Negotiating or signing contracts;
6. Operating office or other types of equipment, including computers;
7. Supervising others in the department or at events away from the work site.

Each of these activities may carry with it some liability if interns are not appropriately trained or fail to act in a professional manner. This liability may also carry over to the supervisor/employer depending on the line of authority established in the agreement and the degree of supervision given.

The following exercise may help supervisors and interns identify areas of potential liability and ensure that students are provided with adequate training in those areas.

ASSESSING LIABILITY POTENTIAL IN THE INTERNSHIP

1. The intern should ask that the site supervisor complete all of the steps that follow and should schedule a time when the exercise can be discussed.

2. List all the activities identified on the contract in which the intern may be engaged. This may entail identifying some activities that are not listed on the contract but that are associated with accomplishing the tasks listed on the contract.
3. For each activity, rate the potential liability using a 3-point scale where 1 = limited liability potential, 2 = moderate liability potential, and 3 = high liability potential.
4. Rank order those activities placing those with the greatest liability risk at the top of a list.
5. For each activity, identify the training or information that should be provided to the intern to ensure adequate precautions have been taken to minimize liability.
6. Amend the intern's work schedule to ensure that time is provided to receive the training or retrieve the information listed in step 4.

This discussion of authority and responsibility is closely associated with the types of authority that interns might have in the supervised experience setting.

TYPES OF AUTHORITY

Site supervisors and interns alike need to be aware of the kinds and limits of authority that are delegated to interns. From a legal perspective, there are several types of authority. Authority may be *expressed, implied,* or *apparent* (*Brown v. Wichita State University*, 540 P. 2d 66, Kan. 1975). Expressed authority may be found in the plain meaning of any written document establishing authority such as a behavioral contract or job description. For example, an internship contract that states that the student will advise a student group allocates expressed authority to that student to serve in an advisor capacity.

Implied authority emanates from expressed authority and can be defined as that which is necessary or appropriate for exercising express authority. In the example of the intern who has expressed authority to serve as an advisor, implied authority allows the intern to sign forms for the group, chaperone group activities, and represent the group's interests to other constituencies. All such activities are assumed to be appropriate for carrying out the duties of a student group advisor.

Students should take care to act based on their expressed or implied authority. If harm results from the actions of interns acting in good faith within the scope of their responsibilities and the authority granted to them, the liability for the injury or breach of contract becomes the responsibility of the supervisor and institution.

Apparent authority is not authority at all. In this instance, a person creates the illusion of authority where none exists. Students involved in field experiences, as well as all other employee groups, should never act with the apparent authority created by a temporary title, the use of letterhead stationery, or the location of their office space. For example, an intern who is serving as an advisor to a student group should not write a letter on letterhead stationery committing resources of the group. The liability for harm done by those who rely on the appearance of authority or act without authority may now extend to the intern as well as to the supervisor and institution.

Questions of authority and responsibility are especially important if the students in a supervised practice experience are authorized to make decisions independently on behalf on the unit or speak on behalf of other administrators. As a general rule, it is unwise to give interns the responsibility or authority to act as professional practitioners with constituents outside the unit.

LIABILITY ISSUES

To address the potential liability resulting from a failure to discharge assignments, it is important to know about confidentiality and student records, defamation, discrimination, negligence, and sexual harassment.

Confidentiality and Student Records

Most field placement sites in higher education involve students and information about students. This information and resulting student record is regulated by the Family Educational Rights and Privacy Act of 1974 (20 U.S.C. § 1232g),[2] popularly known as the Buckley Amendment or FERPA. The Act and its implementing regulations, 34 C.F.R. Part 99, apply to all public and private educational agencies or institutions that receive federal funds from the U.S. Department of Education or whose students receive such funds under federal loan programs. If a unit and its employees, including interns, engage in compiling or distributing information contained in a student's educational record, they must do so in compliance with this Act. The Act defines what may be included in an educational record and addresses academic, disciplinary, employment, financial, medical, and psychological information. It gives students control of their own records and requires that

---

2. For information about how to read legal citations see Gehring (2001).

institutions receive permission from the student before information can be released. There are exceptions, of course.

The Act exempts "directory information," for example, but even here, the student should be given the opportunity to make a blanket declaration that this personally identifiable information cannot be released. Directory information includes students' names, addresses, phone numbers, dates of enrollment, and in the case of student athletes, height and weight. More generally, information that is collected, stored, or transmitted by those acting on behalf of an institution should be handled in a professional and sensitive manner. Regardless of its nature, information should be shared only with those who have a legitimate need to have it. Leaving office records in plain view of those not connected with the office or discussing office matters with friends and other colleagues as idle gossip are ill advised. Such conduct is highly unprofessional and may be deemed unlawful as well.

Issues surrounding confidentiality and student records are critically important if interns will be involved in answering phone calls and other inquiries or handling confidential files or attending meetings where sensitive information is discussed. Interns should treat all personally identifiable information obtained in the internship site as *confidential* and should not share it with others outside the site, unless required by law or instructed by an organization superior to do so.

Defamation

Defamation can be defined as the act of injuring a person's reputation by the distribution of information (Garner, 1999). Defamation through the spoken word is called *slander*. Defaming someone through a written document is called *libel*. While defamation suits are not common in the higher education setting, disputes may arise when letters of recommendations, phone references, or performance evaluations are perceived to be negative and harm the person who is the subject of such communication. For a person to be found guilty of defaming another person, four requirements must be met: (1) the statement made is false; (2) the information shared identifies the person who is defamed; (3) the information shared causes at least nominal damage to the person defamed; and (4) the falsehood is attributable to the person sharing the information (Kaplan & Lee, 1995).

Allegations of defamation can be avoided by following the best practices and ethical standards discussed later in this chapter.

Discrimination

Those responsible for recruitment, application, interview, and selection processes must exercise great care if they are to avoid liability in the area of employment discrimination. From time to time, students in internships may be involved in these hiring processes. If so, it is important that they know about Title VII of the Civil Rights Act of 1964 (42 U.S.C. § 2000). The statute's basic prohibition is set forth in section 2000e-2(a) which states:

> It shall be an unlawful employment practice for an employer to:
>
> (1) fail or refuse to hire or to discharge any individual, or otherwise discriminate against any individual with respect to his compensation, terms, conditions, or privileges of employment, because of such individual's race, color, religion, sex, or national origin; or (2) limit, segregate, or classify his employees or applicants for employment in any way which would deprive or tend to deprive any individual of employment opportunities or otherwise adversely affect his status as an employee, because of such individual's race, color, religion, sex, or national origin.

Other pieces of federal legislation also address discrimination in employment. For example, the Americans with Disabilities Act (ADA) (42 U.S.C. § 12101) and the Rehabilitation Act of 1973 (29 U.S.C. § 794) (sometimes referred to as Section 504) forbid employment discrimination against individuals with disabilities. The Age Discrimination Act of 1975 (42 U.S.C. § 6101 et seq.) contains a general prohibition of discrimination against individuals age 40 or older in federally funded programs and activities.

Those who hire staff regularly will, more than likely, use office protocols that ensure good hiring practices. These protocols may include guidelines for: (1) placing job advertisements; (2) creating application forms; (3) developing interview questions; and (4) conducting reference and background checks. Those who do not hire staff regularly should consult their human resource officers for such guidance and review suggestions offered by Winston and Creamer (1997). More generally, Title VI of the Civil Rights Act (42 U.S.C. § 2000d) and Title IX of the Higher Education Amendments Act (20 U.S.C. § 1681 et seq.) prohibit discrimination in any education program that receives federal aid. These statutes declare that no person in the United States shall, on the ground of race, color, national origin, or sex, be excluded from participation in, be denied the benefits of, or be subjected to discrimination under any program or activity receiving federal financial aid. These statutes reach beyond employment and cover other important issues such as access and participation by those groups that are protected. Title IX is probably best known because of its application in college athletics. It mandates that opportunities for women in sports programs should approximate their presence in the student body.

Finally, it is also important to remember that states and individual institutions may also protect additional classifications in their nondiscrimination clauses. Sexual orientation, for example, is identified more and more frequently in such statements. Once states or institutions voluntarily grant such protection, they are obligated to provide it.

Suits stemming from allegations of wrongdoing under these federal and state statutes are litigated with regularity. Hiring staff is a complicated process and accommodating the disabled in the myriad of educational programs offered on a college campus can pose a serious challenge to even the most experienced administrator. For these reasons, interns and their supervisors should have a thorough understanding of these statutes, especially if interns will be assisting in any employment function or have responsibility for planning events.

Negligence

Higher education institutions are complex organizations engaged in all kinds of activities that carry some risk. When another person is harmed in some way as a result of these activities, claims of negligence often arise. Examples of these claims might include failing to properly supervise a field trip or classroom activity, allowing the use of equipment without proper training, failing to provide reasonable security of the premises, failing to properly maintain property, or failing to properly warn participants about the risks of an activity.

Colleges and universities face a growing array of negligence suits. Although most students have reached the legal age of majority and are responsible for their own behavior, injured students and their parents are increasingly asserting that the institution has a duty of supervision or a duty based on its "special relationship" with the student (Kaplan & Lee, 1997). An injured party may prevail in a negligence claim if it can be shown that the institution had a duty of care and that the institution failed to operate within an appropriate standard of care to avoid injury (Hendrickson, 1999). These claims may involve the payment of millions of dollars per incident. It is important to remember that interns involved in supervised experiences, regardless of their employment status, are likely to be viewed as "gratuitous employees," so the liability for their actions may very well be extended to their institutions (*Foster v. Board of Trustees of Butler County Community College*, 1991). For this reason, interns involved in supervised experiences should understand their roles and responsibility for supervising others and should know how to report incidents that involve accidents or unsafe conditions.

The liability surrounding the use of alcoholic beverages is a subject that merits special attention. The vast majority of college students consume alcoholic beverages whether or not they have reached the legal age to do so. Serving alcoholic beverages to students who have not reached 21 years of age or serving those who appear to be intoxicated regardless of age is a violation of state law. The provider of the beverage may, in many states, also be held responsible for the accidents and injuries caused by intoxicated persons (Gehring, Geraci, & McCarthy, 1999). This notion of third party liability extends to the provider through social host theories (Kaplan & Lee, 1997). Providing, selling, or allowing alcoholic beverages to be consumed at functions that can be connected with the college or university is *always* a risky business. The appropriateness of such an activity should be carefully discussed *before* the event. If the decision is made to make alcohol part of the activity, it must be carefully managed and monitored. If interns work with student groups that serve or drink alcohol, they should make sure that all institutional policies and state laws are strictly observed. Should a student attending one of the events be injured, the intern and the institution may be held criminally and/or civilly liable.

Sexual Harassment

Sexual harassment is a relatively new issue in higher education. Its origins are found in Title VII of the Civil Rights Act of 1964 that was discussed previously in this chapter. While the Act did not provide for a specific cause of action for sexual harassment, the Fifth Circuit Court of Appeals, in *Rogers v. EEOC* (1971), ruled that workplace harassment was prohibited by law. The key to this ruling was that the harassment took the form of racial discrimination. Five years later, in *Williams v. Saxbe* (1976), sexual harassment of a female employee by a supervisor was recognized as a title VII violation. By 1986, the Supreme Court embraced this concept in its landmark case, *Meritor Savings Bank v. Vinson* and reaffirmed its ban on gender-based harassment in *Harris v. Forklift* (1993).

In the higher education environment, the concept of sexual harassment has been extended to the classroom and the relationship between professors and their students. Even more recently, courts have ruled same-sex sexual harassment (*Nogueras v. University of Puerto Rico*, 1995) and student-to-student harassment (*Davis v. Monroe County Board of Education*, 1999) were covered by federal nondiscrimination statutes.

Sexual harassment is defined as "unwelcomed sexual advances, requests for sexual favors or other verbal or physical conduct of a sexual nature" (29 C.F.R. § 1604.11a). Sexual harassment can take one of two forms: quid pro quo sexual harassment and hostile work environment sexual harassment.

Quid pro quo sexual harassment is the coercion of another into performing an unwelcomed sexual act as a part of a bargain to obtain favors or avoid punitive actions. In the higher education setting, these favors or punitive actions might include promotions, appointments, higher wages or salaries, or grades.

Hostile work environment harassment occurs when individuals, because of their gender, experience a work environment "permeated with discriminatory intimidating, ridicule, and insult which are sufficiently severe or pervasive to alter the conditions of employment and create an abusive working environment" (29 C.F.R. § 1604.11a).

Students who find themselves in new office surroundings should be careful about entering into inappropriate "office banter" or passing along off-color humor to colleagues. These seemingly harmless activities could add to or help create a work environment that others find insulting and harassing.

MANAGING LIABILITY

Interns and their supervisors have an obligation to protect themselves and their institutions from the legal liability that may result from the vast array of activities that may be connected with supervised experiences. The use of a three-step liability management process can help determine and reduce one's exposure to law suits.

Determine the Potential for Harm

First, individuals should examine their administrative decisions, activities, and plans for their *potential for harm to others*. A particular decision may have no potential, some potential, or a severe potential for harm. An example may serve to illustrate the point.

Making a request that an office worker rearrange a stockroom of routine office supplies consisting of paper products, pens, and paper clips carries minimal potential for harm. The materials are lightweight, easy to handle, and pose no real danger in and of themselves. Asking the same office worker to unload and uncrate a shipment of heavy office equipment without the proper safety equipment and some instruction on how to lift heavy objects, on the other hand, carries a greater potential for harm. In the second instance, there is a much greater potential for personal injury such as back strain or for hand or foot injuries if a crate is dropped. Determining the potential for harm is not an exact science but it is a critical first step in managing the liability connected with administrative decisions, activities, or plans.

Determining the Cost of the Potential Lawsuit

The second step in this process is to determine the approximate cost of the lawsuit if one were to result from one's actions. The point of the exercise is not to determine the exact cost of the legal action but to place a reasonable dollar value on a negative outcome. If an institution employs legal counsel as part of a permanent staff, there may be no additional cost to mounting a legal defense since that person is already on staff. If counsel must be retained before the institution can defend itself, these costs could be considerable. Recent court decisions and awards made by juries in similar kinds of cases may serve as helpful guides to estimate the cost of an adverse ruling. In the case of workplace injuries, human resource officers can probably provide cost estimates for workman's compensation claims and lost productivity if an employee is absent from work.

Select a Liability Reduction Strategy

Once these two estimates are obtained, they can be plotted on the matrix drawn below (see Figure 5.1). This visual aid graphically illustrates how much risk is involved in any administrative decision, action, or plan. Where potential for harm is low and the cost of a potential lawsuit is low (quadrant 1), administrators can assume it is safe to act. In all other quadrants, higher levels of professional judgment must be exercised.

If an administrative action falls into quadrant 4 (i.e., high potential for harm and high cost of the potential lawsuit) the most prudent course of action may be to avoid the activity altogether; avoiding is a legitimate liability management strategy. But even in this case, administrators may want to make the decision to plan the activity. If they choose to go forward, they can reduce exposure to their liability by: (a) *transferring* responsibility for the risk; (b) *insuring* themselves against the risk; or (c) *managing* the risk. These strategies may be used alone or in combination with one another. There are times, however, when an institution may elect to proceed with an activity in quadrant 4 if the potential educational benefits are sufficiently great (Winston & Saunders, 1998).

Another example may serve to illustrate how this works. Suppose rep-

High

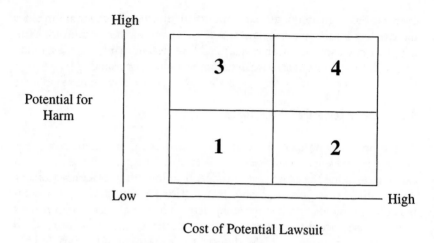

Cost of Potential Lawsuit

FIGURE 5.1. Management Liability Matrix.

resentatives from the senior class approach the administration and request permission to hold a senior party between the last day of exams and graduation. They want to hold the event on campus and serve alcoholic beverages. Even though most of the seniors will be of legal age to consume alcohol, their dates and some family members may not be of age. What could be done to manage the potential liability created by such an event?

Working with representatives of the senior class, administrators could plan to *transfer* some of the liability for serving beverage alcohol by contracting with a catering service. The caterer would have to be licensed to sell beer, wine, and mixed beverages and be trained to serve responsibly. Administrators and the senior class would not purchase or distribute the beverage. The event sponsors could also contract with off-duty police officers to enforce state laws and thus, *transfer* the liability connected with enforcement issues.

In addition, sponsors could *manage* the event so as to reduce the potential for accidents by establishing certain ground rules for the event. They could require that colored wrist bans be worn by event participants so that age could be easily determined, set a maximum drink limit per person, restrict the size of the drink to be served, or limit the time period in which beverages will be served.

Finally, the institution and senior class could obtain special event liability insurance that would cover the costs associated with lawsuits that may result if accidents or injuries occur. Such a policy would *insure* the sponsors from liability. Once these strategies are put in place, the potential for harm and the cost of any potential lawsuit should be recalculated. If the risks have been sufficiently reduced, the event could be held.

Students interested in learning more about risk reduction strategies should read, *Reducing Administrative Liability in Higher Education* (Janosik & Andrews,1985).

PROFESSIONAL STANDARDS AND ETHICS

The first section of this chapter has focused on the law and the implications for failing to adhere to certain federal statutes and the liability that may result from that failure. Although the law provides a good framework for defining professional behavior, it is not, by itself, complete. Even though the law and its standards provide appropriate counsel, everything that is legal is not always ethical. Hate speech is an example that illustrates this principle. Despite the fact that saying hateful things that cause individuals to feel uncomfortable might be protected by the First Amendment of the U.S. Constitution, such behavior would not be condoned by most ethics codes. Consequently, the remainder of this chapter is devoted to ethics and professional standards.

Most professional associations promote ethical behavior through their various codes, principles, or statements. Two such codes are provided in the appendices of this book. The National Association of Student Personnel Administrators' (NASPA) *Standards of Professional Practice* can be found in Appendix E and the American College Personnel Association's (ACPA) *Statement of Ethical Principles and Standards* can be found in Appendix F. Both of these organizations serve large numbers of professionals in the field of higher education administration and student development.

The NASPA statement provides a good general review of the expectations for ethical behavior primarily from an institutional perspective. It addresses 18 different topic areas. ACPA's statement, on the other hand, is more complex and is more focused on the conduct of individual practitioners. It includes a preamble, a mechanism for enforcement, a section on general ethical principles, and a very detailed section on ethical standards.

Other professional associations have developed their own ethical statements around their particular functional area. The Association of College and University Housing Officers—International (AUCHO-I), for example, has its own statement that endorses the ACPA Statement and adds standards specific to housing and residence life professionals.

Once students are placed at a field site, they should ask about any ethical statements or principles that may exist for the institution, student affairs division, or functional area. Individual institutions and departments may also develop policies that govern professional behavior. These should be reviewed thoroughly at an early stage in the supervised experience. Such statements serve as excellent guides and highlight important professional issues that should be discussed with the site supervisor.

ETHICAL PRINCIPLES

Even though codes and lists of standards can be very helpful, no standards statement can cover all situations. Consideration of certain ethical principles affords one a helpful degree of flexibility while maintaining consistency. Kitchener (1985) offers a list that is frequently cited in the ethics literature and also can be found in the ACPA Statement of Ethical Principles and Standards. This list suggests professionals should: (1) respect autonomy, (2) do no harm, (3) benefit others, (4) be just, and (5) be faithful.

Respecting autonomy means allowing others to decide how they live their own lives so long as their actions do not interfere with the rights and welfare of others. In the context of student development, respecting autonomy allows students the freedom to make their own mistakes and learn from them. For example, the intern who is serving as a group advisor might learn that the group's president has decided to invite a certain speaker to address the group without seeking input from the group's membership before issuing the invitation. The advisor thinks this is ill-advised and will prompt reactions from group members that could lead to the president's virtual or literal removal from office. However, since it is within the president's purview to invite speakers to the group's meetings and the president's decision does not interfere with the rights or welfare of the group, the advisor *may* elect not to interfere and allow the president to learn from this experience.

Doing no harm means that individuals have an obligation to avoid behavior that would cause physical or psychological injuries to others. An intern working with new students in an orientation program, for example, should avoid making blanket statements about certain types of students (e.g., those who are very bright, those who participate in athletics). There may be students in the audience who are members of such groups who would be embarrassed or feel demeaned by the comments.

Acting to benefit others means that individuals should act in good faith with one another. Actions that are helpful do not always have to be pleasant. For example, the intern who works in a Judicial Affairs Office may be required to inform students that they have violated campus policy and are to be sanctioned. Explaining this in a professional manner and discussing the learning that can accrue from such sanctions models the behaviors the intern hopes to see in the students who are in violation of the code.

Being just means being fair or treating those with whom we come in contact in an even-handed fashion. This does not mean that there will always be an equal outcome, but it does mean that everyone will be judged using the same criteria. Consider interns who work with students in the residence halls. One group of residents may be making an excessive amount of noise by playing rap music on a boom box while another group of students may be making excessive noise by playing gospel music on their stereo. While the intern's taste may favor one type of music over the other, both groups are making excessive noise and need to be dealt with accordingly.

Being faithful means that professionals keep their promises, tell the truth, and are loyal to their colleagues and institutions. This may seem to be a straightforward assumption. If the intern says he or she will have the report on hazing in the Greek system completed on a certain date, that report should be submitted. But what if the intern learns in the process of gathering data for the report that publishing what really goes on in Greek chapters will result in a lot of negative press for the institution, particularly for the intern's supervisor who advises the Greek system on campus? Dilemmas like this are more frequent than might be expected and aspiring practitioners need to hone their values and ethics so they are prepared to cope with the ambiguities of professional practice.

Interns, and professionals as well, can benefit from the following suggestions with respect to ethical dilemmas and professional practice.

1. Always examine the legal requirements and ethical implications surrounding an action.
2. Consult a mentor or trusted colleague who has no stake in the situation when questions or uncertainty arises.
3. Handle ethical concerns quickly with those most directly involved.
4. Discuss ethics and standards regularly as part of your professional routine.

BEING PRACTICAL ABOUT ETHICS

Applying these ethical principles to daily life can be difficult. As noted above, conflicts among ethical principles and ethical standards occur frequently. To continue with the hate speech example, allowing students to engage in hate speech may satisfy the "respect autonomy" principle but would violate the "do no harm" principle. When choices between principles must be made, one ought to be able to articulate a clear rationale for doing so. In allowing hate speech to occur on campus, courts often point to the traditional value of academic freedom held by public higher education, for example. This value suggests that the free exchange of ideas is critical to the educational process even when these views might be unpopular or repugnant to some. Finding a balance in one's ethical practice is not easy. Another common ethical difficulty involves the dual relationship.

Dual Relationships: A Special Case

Before concluding this chapter on legal and ethical issues, we want to address an often-encountered workplace dilemma known as the *dual relationship*. In the workplace, a dual relationship exists when two individuals assume additional roles beyond that of supervisor-supervisee. Such relationships may not be illegal but are unethical in almost every case. Such relationships have the potential to do great harm and at the least create negative or awkward workplace dynamics. Examples of dual relationships are: (1) an employee who views a supervisor as a confident or counselor with respect to non-work-related matters; (2) a supervisor who develops an extremely close personal relationship with a subordinate; or (3) a graduate hall director who becomes sexually intimate with a resident or a resident assistant she or he supervises. When supervisors or those in positions of authority become involved in additional roles such as counselor, best friend, or lover, the ability to remain objective about job performance or to remain impartial becomes difficult if not impossible. Most ethical standards prohibit such relationships and many employers have personnel policies that prohibit these relationships as well.

Many professionals dismiss this concern about dual relationships thinking that they can remain unbiased and objective. Many professionals think that they can compartmentalize their relationships and eliminate any harm to the other party. Graduate assistants, in particular, are prone to adopt such attitudes. They might argue, "If I can't date undergraduates, there would be no one to date." New professionals in student affairs might also share this feeling, especially when living in small college towns where there may be few professionals of similar age or very few young adults who do not work for the institution. But such attitudes fail to take the perceptions of others into consideration. In many instances it might be just as debilitating and just as disruptive, to create the appearance of unethical behavior as it would to engage in unethical behavior. Consider the following example:

An associate director of student activities and a coordinator of leadership development have worked in the same office for three years. They share common interests and hobbies. They work together on assignments, share office space, and share clerical support staff. The department operates as a team and socializes regularly outside the office. The two become good friends. They do not consider themselves a couple but they do spend lots of time together outside the office.

The current assistant director of student activities leaves mid-year and two inside candidates apply for the interim position. The coordinator who shares office space with the associate director is exceptionally well qualified and the much better qualified of the two inside candidates. The director and associate director make the decision to promote the coordinator to the interim position. Shortly after the announcement is made, anonymous flyers are placed in the staff's office mailboxes that read, "Qualifications for Promotion – Have Sex with the Associate Director."

ℛeflection 𝒫oint

1. Did the associate director and coordinator do anything unethical?
2. What could the director, associate director, or coordinator have done to anticipate this difficulty?
3. Would the ethical guides found in the appendices have helped avoid this situation? If so, how?
4. Now that some staff members have read the flyers, what should the director, associate director and coordinator do now?

Office romances are common in student affairs just as they are in other professions. They offer employees some of the most difficult ethical challenges one can face. As a general rule, in the long run such relationships tend to cause problems for all parties concerned and prudence would dictate avoiding them.

Other Sensitive Human Resource Issues

Other personnel decisions such as hiring and firing staff can create various serious ethical dilemmas. Imagine the following circumstance:

You, as a department intern, are supervising a student worker. The student has been chronically late for work, has made long distance and personal phone calls almost daily, and has taken office supplies for her personal use. All of these behaviors have been witnessed and documented by you. After consulting with your site supervisor, your site supervisor fired the student worker.

Several days have past and you hear from a fellow intern that he is considering hiring the same student for another part-time student position in a different office. Your colleague makes the following statement, "This student seems highly motivated, very personable. My only concern is that she has absolutely no work experience so I cannot get a job reference from anyone. I think I am going to go ahead and take a chance on her."

---

*R*eflection *P*oint

Identify the legal and ethical issues connected with this dilemma. Review the Kitchener principles outlined in this chapter. Do they help focus your understanding of the issues associated with this case study? What would you do in this circumstance?

CONCLUSIONS

Supervised experiences are an important part of any professional preparation program. They are designed to complement and enhance classroom learning, aid in the transition from theory to practice, and give the student a first-hand look at the world of work. In most instances, students will be expected to become fully participating members of the staff with all of the responsibilities attached thereto. Depending on the assignment, some of these responsibilities carry a degree of legal liability and all of them carry the expectation that the student will behave in a professional and ethical manner.

This chapter was designed to highlight the legal and ethical issues connected with supervised experiences. Students, who understand these concepts, ask questions, and act on the knowledge gained through their inquiry will ensure their success.

Reflection Point

Interns should give some time and thought to be given to these issues by completing the following tasks:

1. Interns should ask their supervisors to identify the top three legal issues that have the greatest potential for lawsuits and discuss how the department is managing those legal risks.
2. Interns who are unfamiliar with the litigation process, should attend a civil trial in the nearest municipal court.
3. Interns should ask to see the department's procedures for hiring and the institution's policy statement on affirmative action. Then, discuss how they compliment one another.
4. Interns should ask for a copy of the institution's sexual harassment policy and discuss how it was developed. Do its provisions exceed state or federal law?
5. Interns should ask their site supervisors to discussed the most difficult ethical situation they have experienced and talk about how it was resolved.

REFERENCES

Age Discrimination Act of 1975, 42 U.S.C. § 6101 et seq.

Americans with Disabilities Act , 42 U.S.C. § 12101.

Brown v. Wichita State University, 504 P2d. 66 (Kan. 1975).

Davis v. Monroe County Board of Education (1999).

Family Educational Rights and Privacy Act of 1974, 20 U.S.C. § 1232g.

Foster v. Board of Trustees of Butler County Community College, 771 F. Supp. 1122 (D. Kan. 1991).

Garner, B. A. (Ed.). (1999). *Black's law dictionary* (7th ed.). St. Paul, MN: West Group.

Gehring, D. D. (2001). An introduction to legal research. In R. B. Winston, Jr., D. G. Creamer, & T. K. Miller (Eds.), *The professional student affairs administrator: Educator, leader, and manager* (pp. 415–419). New York: Brunner-Routledge.

Gehring, D. D., Geraci, C. P., & McCarthy, T. (1999). *Alcohol on campus: A compendium of the law and guide to campus policy* (Rev.). Ashville, NC: College Administration Publications.

Harris v. Forklift Systems, Inc., 510 U.S. 17 (1993).

Hendrickson, R. M. (1999). *The colleges, their constituencies, and the courts* (2nd ed.). Dayton, OH: Education Law Association.

Janosik, S. M., & Andrew, L. D. (1985). Reducing institutional and individual liability in higher education. *NASPA Journal, 22*(3), 2–9.

Kaplan, W. A., & Lee, B. A. (1995). *The law of higher education* (3rd ed.). San Francisco: Jossey-Bass.

Kaplan, W. A., & Lee, B. A. (1997). *A legal guide for student affairs professionals.* San Francisco: Jossey-Bass.

Kitchener, K. S. (1985). Ethical principles and ethical decisions in student affairs. In H. J. Canon & R. D. Brown (Eds.), *New directions for student services: No. 30. Applied ethics in student services* (pp. 17–29). San Francisco: Jossey-Bass.

Meritor Savings Bank v. Vinson, 477 U.S. 57 (1986).

Nogueras v. University of Puerto Rico (1995).

Rehabilitation Act of 1973, 29 U.S.C. § 794.

Rogers v. EEOC, 454 F. 2d 234 (5th Cir. 1971).

Title VI of the Civil Rights Act, 42 U.S.C. § 2000d.

Title VII of the Civil Rights Act of 1964, 42 U.S.C. § 2000.

Title IX of the Higher Education Amendments Act, 20 U.S.C. § 1681 et seq.

Williams v. Saxbe, 413 F. Supp. 654 (D.D.C. 1976).

Winston, R. B., Jr., & Creamer, D. G. (1997). *Improving staffing practices in student affairs.* San Francisco: Jossey-Bass.

Winston, R. B., Jr., & Saunders, S. A. (1998). Professional ethics in a risky world. In D. L. Cooper & J. M. Lancaster (Eds.), *New directions for student services: No. 82. Beyond law and policy: Reaffirming the role of student affairs* (pp. 77–94). San Francisco: Jossey-Bass.

Chapter 6
EVALUATING THE SUPERVISED PRACTICE EXPERIENCE

Diane L. Cooper
Sue A. Saunders

Frequently, students report that just as they are beginning to feel that they are acclimated to the host institution and the internship site, and are fully equipped to make substantial contributions, they must begin preparing to leave. For some students, the last day of work cannot come fast enough; for others, this is a sad event ending enjoyable activities and good relationships. However, no matter where students fall on this departure continuum, it is vital that they continue to perform at an acceptable level and in a fully professional manner until the experience concludes. No matter whether the functional area is one where the intern would like to pursue a full-time position or the intern learns that she or he is not a good fit for the area, high levels of professionalism are expected. As Baird (1996) pointed out, "future interns depend on the good will of a placement site and staff for their opportunities, [so] it is extremely important that interns attend carefully to how they conclude their placement" (p. 160). Also, as many veterans in the field often point out, student affairs is a very small field. What an intern does in applied practices experiences becomes an indelible part of his or her professional life history.

Most internships are from 8 to 16 weeks in duration; consequently, the evaluation process needs to begin early, in some cases, prior to the first day of work. Learning objectives, learning contracts, and supervisory agreements are all useful in assessing the work experience. However, leaving the site is not only about evaluation and assessment. Departure can also mean leaving new acquaintances, withdrawing from projects before completion, and training new personnel to assume responsibilities.

Brill (1998) identified three tasks related to ending a field-based experience: completing unfinished business (tasks); considering internal feelings about departing and how to appropriately discuss them (including formal and informal evaluation); and planning for the future. All of these opportunities and challenges are addressed in this final chapter. Specifically, this chapter outlines ways to create positive closure with clients, colleagues, and supervisors. Another critical component of this chapter focuses on ways to assess what the intern has learned as a result of the experience and ways to prepare for the supervisor's summative evaluation. Finally, this chapter gives guidance about choosing the next internship or preparing to use internship learnings in the search for a first professional position.

CREATING CLOSURE

Although ending an administrative internship is different from ending a counseling-based field placement, the psychological services discipline provides some lessons about how to terminate relationships with clients that also apply to administrative internships. Student affairs interns often form close interpersonal relationships that are difficult to leave. The termination process, therefore, requires special attention to both task and relationship details.

If the supervised practice site is on the same campus as the student's preparation program, termination of the experience actually can be more difficult than if it is on another campus. This difficulty arises from the fact that the student remains on campus and may experience pressure to complete projects or maintain relationships associated with the site after the formal termination of the internship. Ideally, the student and site supervisor have addressed this issue when establishing learning goals and objectives for the experience, and time limits have been placed on the tasks so that students can leave the site without fear of being viewed as a "nonteam player" who failed to follow through. The decision to continue with an unfinished task should be a joint decision of the site supervisor and student that occurs prior to the close of the supervised practice experience. Preferably, the question of whether the intern continues tasks after the official close of the internship should be decided, with clearly specified parameters, during the first few weeks of the internship.

Unlike colleagues who are counselors, student affairs practitioners typically do not see individual clients or therapeutic groups who require a specialized process for ending the relationship. However, the type of termination of relationships in student affairs still requires that a plan be developed so that "all bases are covered" and the site is ready to proceed without the intern's presence. Sweitzer and King (1999) cautioned that "you need to think carefully about ending your work with them [clients] and saying goodbye, regardless of the label you apply to the process . . . " departure, leaving, termination (p. 200). Again, if the supervised practice experience is on the home campus, the termination process may differ but should be negotiated by the student and site supervisor early in the experience. For example, an intern, Tarek, has been asked to prepare for Welcome Week as part of his internship experience that officially ends on August 1. New students do not actually arrive on campus until August 13 and Welcome Week is August 13 to 20. Even though Tarek's learning goals did not stipulate that he would participate in Welcome Week activities, he may elect to be a volunteer for all or some of those events. In this case, Tarek's termination process would be very different from someone who is permanently leaving a site.

The first step in the departure process is for interns to compile a list of all projects or tasks that they have been involved with since arriving at the site. An example of a series of steps and activities one might use to prepare to end the supervised practice experience is provided in Appendix G. A detailed description of projects should include not only the task but also other staff who worked on the task and their roles as well. Once the list is complete, students should identify the parts of each project that have been completed and the steps that will follow. Interns should include the names of individuals who will take responsibility for any next steps so that the supervisor will know whom to approach for the continuation of the project. It would be helpful to provide any impressions about the project that will be useful to the supervisor in making any additional assignments to permanent staff. Interns should also be sure to set up a meeting with the supervisor near the end of the supervised practice experience to review this list and answer any additional questions the supervisor might have. Interns should leave a good record of what was done, what is to be done, and identification of possible trouble spots. It is also important to keep copies of correspondence, a record of persons contacted in regard to the activities, with telephone numbers and/or e-mail addresses.

Likewise, it is also important to carefully consider ways to say goodbye to students and colleagues in the work site. A number of authors who have explored field experience processes have discussed the importance of closure through rituals. These rituals are a "formal way of marking an event or passage (such as a going away luncheon) . . . [that] can help provide a sense of completion or closure" (Sweitzer & King, 1999, p. 199). Baird (1996) also noted that ritual adds a sense of *specialness* to the event and allows for a formal way to recall the importance of the experience to the intern and important others from the site.

CLOSURE WITH THE SUPERVISOR

The relationship that the intern develops with a site supervisor is often closely tied to the overall success of the supervised practice experience. As with any supervisory relationship, it can be positive and life affirming or negative and inhibiting. Usually, even if the relationship has been less than ideal, the intern has learned something about himself or herself in the process that, with reflection, can be used in the future.

Sweitzer and King (1999) recommended that closure with the site supervisor not only revolve around task status and work performance evaluation but should also include time to discuss lessons learned during the experience. The learning goals and objectives identified in the contract can be used as a starting point for this discussion. Many interns, however, find that the greatest lessons they learned during the experience could not necessarily be anticipated. These serendipitous learnings might include resolving a conflict, taking a risk, or adapting to an unexpected event. It is important to have time to process these activities with the site supervisor prior to ending the supervised learning experience to provide a sense of context to the event that will serve the student. Interns should also consider scheduling time to provide the site supervisor with feedback about the experience. This might include exploring what went well during the experience, providing examples of how the experience could be improved for those who will serve as interns in the future, as well as offering feedback about the supervision received. The latter of these suggestions comes with a word of caution: students may want to give feedback to the supervisor only if the supervisor has asked for that feedback and the relationship is such that it will be received nondefensively. Students often have concerns that supervisors still have some degree of power in the relationship due to the fact that they may be providing a grade for the experience or letters of recommendation in the future. It is best to let the level of trust and strength of the relationship be the guide when making any decision to provide constructive feedback to a supervisor.

EVALUATING THE EXPERIENCE

The main focus of internships, practica, and other field-based experiences is to link theory with practice, a concept that is a foundation of the student affairs profession (Kruger, 2000). The link between theory and practice, however, does not always appear obvious or occur automatically. It requires students to function as reflective practitioners who understand their strengths, weaknesses, preferences, and learning styles, as well as the specifics of the theories. Most important, a reflective practitioner uses his or her own appraisal as a central source of data in determining effectiveness. Even though incorporating evaluation feedback from site and faculty supervisors is essential, depending totally on others to appraise the supervised practice performance renders an incomplete picture that misses the rich and detailed information about individual learning that only the student can provide. Interns' personal appraisals of the supervised practice experience should include both formative and summative approaches.

Formative Assessment

Throughout the course of the internship, students should keep track of their accomplishments and should regularly check on achievement of previously agreed upon learning objectives. Students should continually reflect on their progress and their own personal reactions to what they see, hear, and experience. *Experience alone is not a very effective teacher.* Students' experiences must be "thought about, reflected upon, and analyzed to yield the greatest learning" (Kiser, 2000, p. 55). The site and/or faculty supervisor may have already developed a procedure that fosters this type of broad and meaningful reflection. Without reflection, students generally fail to recognize the interrelationships between the experience, personal knowledge, and individual professional values.

An internship experience may have a procedure already in place that fosters reflection and formative assessment. The procedure may consist of regular journal entries submitted to the faculty supervisor. There is great value in recording reflections and in sharing them with another, more experienced professional. With the "busyness" most interns and professionals experience, it is difficult to stop, sit quietly, and reflect. The structure of writing and sharing helps most interns stay focused on this important process.

The Reflection Journal (outlined on page 103 in chapter 4) is an excellent way to foster the broad, meaningful reflection advocated throughout this book. It is crucial, however, that students take the time to complete their journals thoughtfully. Simply putting down the tasks one accomplished without thinking through the implications is merely making a list, not engaging in reflection. It will take time to complete the reflection journal regularly, but it is time well worth investing.

With whom should students share their reflections? The Reflection Journal discussed in chapter 4 requires a fair amount of honest self-disclosure in order to be effective. Because some students may not have close, trusting relationships with site supervisors, interns may feel more comfortable submitting an abbreviated version of the journal to the site supervisor, which omits some of the most critical evaluations of the site and its staff. At a minimum, students should be writing a report to the site supervisor on a weekly basis that outlines: (1) accomplishments, (2) summary of important learning, (3) challenges faced, (4) identification of help needed, and (5) questions that need answering.

We recommend that students share the Reflection Journal with the faculty supervisor in its entirety. The responsibility of a faculty supervisor is to help students make meaning of their experiences and to integrate theory, practice, and personal/professional development. Sharing broad and meaningful reflections with a faculty member who is knowledgeable about theories and professional development strategies provides students with a powerful opportunity to maximize their learning from the internship.

Summative Evaluation

The summative evaluation at the close of the internship is an important learning opportunity as well. Often at the end of an internship, it is easy to get caught up in rushing to finish last minute tasks, preparing for final exams, and preparing for the next academic term or for a first professional position. In that rush, it is easy to neglect the importance of reflecting on and evaluating the total internship experience. It is tempting to leave the summative evaluation to the discretion of the faculty and site supervisors. The foundation of a summative evaluation of the internship effectiveness, however, depends not on the supervisor's evaluation but on the student's own honest answers to crucial questions, such as:

Reflection Point

1. To what extent did I achieve the learning goals established at the beginning of the internship?
2. What personal attributes helped me to achieve my goals?
3. What elements of my work environment (e.g., supervisor, office staff, and office structure) helped me achieve my goals?
4. What personal attributes, attitudes, or behaviors hindered me in achieving my goals? (Can you envision different outcomes if you had acted or felt differently?)
5. What elements of the work environment impeded progress in achieving my goals?
6. How would I analyze my work performance?
7. Do I meet or exceed the expectations of my site supervisor? If so, why? If not, why not?

8. What did I learn from the site supervisor's and colleagues' feedback about strengths and weaknesses as a new student affairs practitioner?
9. What feedback do I agree with? What do I disagree with?
10. What new skills did I acquire through the internship?
11. Did I learn skills that I didn't expect to acquire? If so what were these? What skills do I need or want to strengthen through subsequent professional experiences?
12. What are at least three things that I learned that I should never do again?

Analysis of Learning Contracts

In chapter 2 of this text, the importance of developing a learning contract that included goals and time lines for the supervised practice experience was explained. An important part of the evaluation process should include a complete review of the learning contracts done jointly with the site supervisor. The sample learning contract in chapter 2 contained specific objectives, activities, skills and competencies, and time requirements for an internship experience. If one now reviewed those objectives from an evaluative standpoint, the following questions could be raised: "Did I accomplish this?" and "What was the outcome?"

From chapter 2, the following was specified: "Objective 1: To assist with the development of a peer conflict resolution model proposal." The specific activities and time requirements that were listed to assist Maria in meeting that objective included:

1. Research conflict resolution models of other universities and suggestions from the National Association of Mediation in Education (20 hours).
2. Meet regularly with the site supervisor to discuss progress (15 hours).
3. Consult with other Dean of Students staff members on model components (5 hours).

In addition, Maria stated in her "Skills and Competencies to be Acquired" section that she would hone her research skills; she would learn to tailor various conflict resolution models to a specific institution, and she would develop skills to collaborate effectively with many student affairs professionals. The following exercise can assist interns to assess the degree to which the learning objectives of their contract were achieved.

ℛeflection 𝒫oint

Analysis of Learning Objectives

1. Review each objective and write a specific description of how you met that objective noting any unanticipated activities that occurred which were not in the original contract.
2. Repeat this process for all objectives.
3. Reflect on the skills and competencies you intended to acquire as a result of the supervised practice experience. You will need to answer in writing the following questions:
   - With which of the skills and competencies am I most confident?
   - What is the evidence that supports this conclusion?
   - Which skills and competencies do I need to further develop?
   - Specifically, what is the evidence that supports this conclusion?

Analysis of Work Performance

Analysis of work performance consists of two parts: (1) the quality of completing tasks assigned and (2) the quality of the students' interactions with students, staff members in the site, supervisors, and external constituents. The learning objectives created at the beginning of the internship should contain some of the tasks to be completed as a part of the internship. However, some of the tasks that were completed may have been unanticipated when the internship began. For example, John designed as a part of his internship a proposal for an emerging leaders program. However, once he arrived on the internship site, he discovered that he needed additional information about successful programs on other campuses. So, John completed a "benchmarking" assessment process in which he looked at other emerging leaders programs available on the Internet and conducted telephone interviews with leadership educators who had developed exemplary programs on other campuses. Even though this assessment was not originally part of the learning objectives, it certainly was a task that consumed time and required development of skills, and should be included as part of the summative evaluation. The following example exercise outlines the steps that should be taken to complete a personal appraisal of the tasks one has accomplished (Kiser, 2000):

ℛeflection ℘oint

Analaysis of Work Performance

Quality of Task Completion.

1. Gather information from your weekly journals, your calendar, "to do" lists, memos or notes from your supervisor. Use this information to construct a list of tasks you have accomplished during the internship. Your list of accomplishments should consist of your substantive tasks, not every telephone call made or e-mail message written. Using your journal, calendar, and "to do" lists serves to remind you of what you have accomplished, rather than relying on your general memories.

2. For each of the accomplishments you identify, grade your performance using the following scale:

    5 = outstanding, far more proficient than I expected
    4 = good, somewhat more proficient than I expected
    3 = average, about as proficient than I expected
    2 = poor, somewhat less proficient than I expected
    1 = inadequate, much less proficient than I expected.

3. For each rating, write a brief, *factually based* statement that supports your rating.

Quality of Interpersonal Relationships. This portion of evaluating one's work performance is considerably more subjective, and therefore, likely to be subject to bias. Yet reflecting on how well you interacted with students, colleagues, supervisor, and other constituents is a critical component of the learning process. The ability to collaborate, incorporate feedback, communicate unpopular decisions, meet the needs of clients, and portray a positive attitude are all essential elements of success in higher education administration. The following steps will assist you in reflecting on your strengths and weaknesses of your interactions with others:

1. Identify the categories of individuals you worked with during the course of your internship. These categories are site specific and may include students, colleagues, supervisors, support staff, faculty, or external constituents.

2. For each of the categories, write a short paragraph outlining your successes and challenges/frustrations in dealing with people in this category. Referring to your Reflection Journal will likely help you in this process. Once you begin to write your paragraphs you may recognize that your category is too broad to be meaningful. For ex-

ample, you may have discovered different challenges dealing with student leaders than in working with student workers in your site. If you find that the categories are too broad, you can divide them into subgroups that are more manageable. If you are having difficulty identifying successes and challenges, think about feedback that you received since you arrived at the site. Or try to imagine how individuals in each category would describe your ability to establish workable interpersonal relationships.

3. Look over your paragraphs and summarize your strengths and weaknesses in terms of developing workable interpersonal relationships at your site.

Seeking and Using Feedback

The site and faculty supervisors' evaluations of the student's performance are a critical component of an effective internship. It also happens to be the element of the internship that gives the most anxiety to interns and supervisors alike. The overall purpose of this supervisory evaluation is to evaluate achievement of outcomes and performance quality. The supervisory evaluation is designed to look at the experience as a whole, identifying strengths and weaknesses (Alle-Corliss & Alle-Corliss, 1998). Even though students should have received regular feedback about their day-to-day performance from the supervisor, the final evaluation allows the supervisor and student to identify patterns, themes, and issues that emerged during the entire course of the internship. It may also present an opportunity for the site supervisor to further explain her or his reasoning behind the evaluation.

It is part of the obligation of professionals to evaluate the performance of those who work for them. In fact, the American College Personnel Association *Statement of Ethical Principles and Standards* (1992) mandates in section 3.11 that professionals "evaluate job performance of subordinates regularly and recommend appropriate actions to enhance professional development and improve performance." Professionals need to be accountable to the public and to their institution that those who are providing services meet specific standards of competence.

The big question, then, is how to prepare for the summative evaluation by the site supervisor, and if appropriate, the faculty supervisor. Students should recognize that evaluation tends to cause anxiety, even if their work was superb. Not only do students experience this type of anxiety, but many professionals at all levels experience it as well. Evaluation is most productive when it is viewed as a process where students take responsibility for honestly appraising their own performance. It is also important to remember that if students desire to grow professionally they need to seek out both positive and critical feedback. If students are engaging in behavior that unwittingly sabotages their effectiveness (even if the sabotage is minor), it is better to know about the problem so they can make changes rather than remaining ignorant. The internship is the best place to begin establishing a productive approach to evaluation. The preceding sections provide a basis for preparing for student self- evaluation. The following steps will help students prepare for their supervisor's evaluation:

ℛeflection 𝒫oint

Preparing for the Supervisor's Evaluation

1. Review your analysis of learning objectives and your appraisal of your work performance (both of which you completed through the previous exercises).
2. Review the evaluation instrument that your site supervisor will use to complete your summative evaluation. Tell your supervisor that you would like to rate yourself on that instrument so that you can better understand any areas of congruence or discrepancy.
3. Rate your own performance using this instrument and write a few facts that support each of your ratings.
4. At your evaluation conference, discuss discrepancies and similarities between your supervisor's ratings and your ratings.
5. After the evaluation conference is completed, take a few minutes to summarize the conversation so that you will remember the major points of your discussion. It is also helpful to reflect on what actions you tried to take to make the evaluation conference successful. Finally, suggest to yourself ways that you could act or attitudes you could adopt which would make future evaluation conferences more productive.

Analysis of Skills Developed

Although students are likely to have identified in their learning objectives some of the skills they wanted to develop as a result of the supervised practice experience, the summative evaluation process is a time when students can look at all of the skills they acquired, even those they didn't anticipate at the outset. There are several sets of skills that students are likely to want to reflect upon. In their study of midlevel staff, Fey and Carpenter (1996) identified leadership and communication skills as two of the most necessary skills for success in student affairs. In a study of chief student affairs officers, clear communication and honesty and candor were the two most important characteristics that they looked for in on-campus interviews when making hiring decisions (Winston, Torres, Carpenter, McIntire, & Petersen, 2001). In addition, Garland and Grace (1994) indicated that in the future it will be important for student affairs professionals to function as "environmental scanner, milieu manager, market analyst, legal adviser, development officer, researcher, and quality assurance specialist" (p. 4). More recently, Kruger (2000) identified new skills that are especially important for student affairs professionals in the new millennium. Specifically, Kruger highlights the importance of technology skill development including (1) using Web programming language tools as a way to maximize student learning and deliver services and (2) using, creating, and manipulating campus information systems to make databased decisions. Kruger also argued that another area of skill development especially relevant for the new millennium is understanding new organizational paradigms that require "faculty and staff who can work effectively in a cross-disciplinary, cross-functional, [and] collaborative environment" (p. 549).

The purpose of assessing skill development is to identify the broad, transferable competencies that have been acquired during the supervised practice experience. Rather than focusing on the specific work tasks or the quality of interpersonal relationships, the assessment of transferable skills requires that one think more globally, synthesizing different elements of the internship experience. "Functional/transferable skills are things that you do, such as teaching, organizing, persuading, assembling, supervising, computing, researching, analyzing, deciding, operating, and designing" (Lock, 2000, p. 213). It is critically important to identify transferable skills, since they are what students can highlight in a job interview or cover letter. Simply saying, "I am good with computers" is not sufficient. One needs to be specific, stating, for example, that in the admissions office internship "I learned to modify recruitment WebPages using the Front-Page web editor." The following structure may help students reflect on the transferable skills acquired and how to communicate them in concrete terms:

Ꞧeflection Ꝓoint

Identifying the Skills You Acquired

1. Review your learning objectives, position description for your internship, analysis of work performance, results of your supervisor's and/or faculty liaison evaluation, and your own self-rating on the supervisory evaluation form.
2. Review your major internship accomplishments and write them in the far left column of the form that follows.
3. For each of your accomplishments, describe the skills that you used. Once again, be certain to state your skills specifically.
4. For each skill, rate your competence using the following scale:
   3 = Very competent
   2 = Somewhat competent
   1 = Minimal or not competent

Identifying the Skills Acquired as a Result of my Internship Example

Accomplishment	Skills	Rating
I organized the curriculum for a one-day midyear training program for Resident Assistants who had served for one semester	Constructed needs assessment	1
	Analyzed needs assessment data	1
	Researched exemplary programs	2
	Created program theme, learning goals, and topics	3
	Identified and briefed program facilitators	3
	Created participant evaluation form	1

FINAL POINTS TO CONSIDER ABOUT DEPARTURE

As interns plan to leave the site, it is important to remember that coworkers during this experience may have invested a good bit of time and energy into creating the learning opportunity for interns. Typically they have assisted the interns without financial compensation. Many supervisors believe that they have an obligation to give back to the profession through serving as site supervisors in much the same way that someone assisted them when they were in a preparation program. Others see the opportunity to serve as a way to teach skills and competencies they view as important for the continuation of the profession. For most individuals, supervising interns is a form of professional generativity and as such they take great personal pride in the students' accomplishments and blame themselves for any bad experiences.

Students should remember basic etiquette by leaving written thank you notes and perhaps a small token of appreciation for site supervisors and others who had influential roles in the supervised practice experience. The small tokens might include an actual gift or something created by the student such as a poem written to symbolize the importance of the relationship. These tokens, however, should not have high monetary value. It is truly the thought that counts. Giving expensive gifts may appear to be bribes or attempts to unduly influence the supervisor's and other staff's evaluations. This is also part of the ritual of leaving discussed earlier in this chapter. It is appropriate to send the thank you letter(s) right after departing the site. However, do not let too much time pass between departure and corresponding with the individuals at the host site.

One other task to accomplish prior to departing an internship involves talking with the site supervisor about providing a letter of recommendation. Students should check to determine the protocols on their home campus for letters of recommendation and use those as a guide when requesting this letter. Some campuses encourage students to establish credential files at the Career Services Center. In this case, students can talk with the supervisor about points they would like addressed in the letter and ask that it be sent directly to that office (it could be a confidential letter, depending on the guidelines established by Career Services). In other cases, interns may want the supervisor to be *on call* to send letters to or receive phone calls from prospective employers as the student become actively involved in the job search process.

Sweitzer and King (1999) provide some important guidelines that include some suggestions from Baird, (1996) as well. These include:

1. Before requesting the letter, ask if the supervisor feels comfortable and is willing to write a letter that will be supportive of you. Just because someone agrees to write a letter it should not be construed to mean that the letter will be positive and glowing. A less than positive letter could hurt a student in a future job search more than no letter at all.

2. In some cases, students may also want to ask other personnel at the site to serve as references in the future. It is important to make the same request to these individuals as you would to the site supervisor.

3. No matter who is asked to write a letter or serve as a reference, it is

important for the intern to give the writer a clear description of future career goals and objectives. This will assist the writer in gearing the letter to the student's personal strengths in relation to the career path they have in mind. It is also generally a good idea to provide the referent a copy of the résumé in order to help the writer refresh his or her memory. In that résumé provide extra detail about the activities and projects the intern was involved with during the supervised experience.

4. Give plenty of notice to those who are writing letters of reference. In the case of those being listed as references on one's résumé, always give them a list of positions to which you are applying as well as a brief description of specific interests.

Supervisors can be an important resource for future job search processes. Time and attention to making the request during the departure period will pay off in the future.

PLANNING FOR THE FUTURE

The final step in evaluating the supervised practice experience is to translate reflections into goals and plans for continued professional development. As higher education changes ever more rapidly, continued professional development is not a luxury but a survival strategy. Even though institutions and supervisors support professional development, the ultimate responsibility for professional growth rests with the individual. With the plethora of professional association conferences and workshops, on-line courses and discussion groups, and each college's or university's professional development offerings, student affairs professionals will need a clear understanding of their learning goals in order to use their limited continuing education time wisely.

A Professional Development Plan

Even though most higher education administrators are generalists who have expertise in a wide variety of areas, Barr and Dessler (2000) argue that if practitioners want to become institutional leaders they will need to develop specific expertise in an area valued by many colleges and universities. In particular, Barr and Dessler recommend that "legal issues, assessment and evaluation, conflict resolution, and leadership development are just a few of the areas where advanced knowledge and expertise are valuable in determining solutions to the complex problems facing higher education" (p. 640).

To use the supervised practice experience as a springboard for the type of future professional development in which to develop specialized expertise, it is crucial to have specific goals and objectives. The reflective activities described in this chapter constitute the needs assessment data that will allow one to create a long-term professional development plan.

The following activities and questions will provide guidance in constructing a long-term plan:

1. Review one's assessment of skill development. Pay particular attention to the areas rated a 1 or 2, since these may constitute areas that require particular attention.

2. For each skill ask whether that skill is desired. For example, one may have given himself or herself a low rating of "1" for the skill of planning social events for potential donors. Even though a low rating is accurate, one may decide that she or he really don't want to work in the development area and have little interest in planning social events. It would be a waste of time, then, to do professional reading and attend workshops concerning event planning for potential donors.

3. Create a list of skills that one wants to strengthen in the future. One may need to add a few important skills that were not addressed directly in the internship setting.

4. Prioritize the list, using future career goals as a foundation. Ask one's self what skills are most crucial for success. Also, in prioritizing include attention to those competencies that are most lacking. For example, a student may decide that even though as a future residence life operations manager he or she will not need to use teaching skills very often, he or she feels so inadequate about these skills, that they should appear high on the list.

5. For each of the prioritized skills, identify several professional development opportunities that might help hone that skill. Be sure to include such activities as reading, research on the web, participation in a listserv, visits to other campuses as well as the more traditional approaches, such as conferences, workshops, and courses.

6. Look at skills and opportunities. Create several broad learning goals and for each construct several objectives. Be sure to include deadlines with objectives and that there is evidence of a commitment to start work on some of the objectives immediately.

WHAT ABOUT THE NEXT INTERNSHIP?

Some students are in preparation programs where they can have multiple supervised experiences at different sites. The reflections from the personal appraisal, site evaluation, skills developed, and professional development plan all provide excellent information to guide the selection of the next internship site. Internships, as has been stated previously, are rich opportunities for skill development and can serve to position students more advantageously for future full-time professional positions. So it is helpful for students to take some time to think through how the next internship options may further their career. The following questions (adapted from Chiaferi & Griffin, 1997, p. 113) are a useful structure for thinking about future internship options.

1. What student groups, functional areas, or organizational structures might one need to experience in order to position himself or herself advantageously for the career search?
2. What type of setting and supervision would allow one to build on strengths and address weaknesses?
3. What new skills, knowledge, or attitudes would one like to learn and what type of setting might afford the greatest opportunity for one to acquire this learning?
4. What important concerns (if any) were overlooked in the current internship?
5. How might one gather the necessary information about potential internship options?

CONCLUSION

Student affairs work can be a tremendously rewarding career. For many practitioners, the supervised practice experience serves as one of the formal orientations to the field.

The supervised practice experience is typical of what many new practitioners encounter when they start their first professional position. The various aspects of orientation, setting goals, establishing good supervisory relations, and planning for evaluation and feedback are all parts of any new job. What has been learned during this time will serve one well in the future.

REFERENCES

Alle-Corliss, L., & Alle-Corliss, R. (1998). *Human services agencies: An orientation to fieldwork.* Pacific Grove, CA: Brooks/Cole.

American College Personnel Association (1992). *Statement of Ethical Principles and Standards.* Available: http://www.acpa.nche.edu/pubs/prncstan.htm

Baird, B. N. (1996). *The internship, practicum, and field placement handbook: A guide for the helping professions.* Upper Saddle River, NJ: Prentice Hall.

Barr, M. J., & Dessler, M. K. (2000). Leadership for the future. In M. J. Barr & M. K. Dessler (Eds.), *The handbook of student affairs administration* (2nd ed., pp. 629–642). San Francisco: Jossey-Bass.

Brill, N. (1998). *Working with people: The helping process* (5th ed.). New York: Longman.

Chiaferi, R., & Griffin, M. (1997). *Developing fieldwork skills: A guide for human services, counseling, and social work students.* Pacific Grove, CA: Brooks/Cole .

Fey, C. H., & Carpenter, D. S. (1996) Mid-level student affairs administrators: Management skills and professional development needs. *NASPA Journal, 33,* 218–231.

Garland, P. H., & Grace, T. W. (1994, June). *New perspectives for student affairs professionals: Evolving realities, responsibilities, and roles.* ERIC Digest Document ED370507.

Kiser, P. M. (2000). *Getting the most from your human services internship: Learning from experience.* Belmont, CA: Wadsworth/Thomson Learning.

Kruger, K. (2000). New alternatives for professional development. In M. J. Barr & M. K. Dessler (Eds.), *The handbook of student affairs administration* (2nd ed., pp. 535–553). San Francisco: Jossey-Bass.

Lock, R. D. (2000). *Taking charge of your career direction: Career planning guide* (Book 1, 4th ed.). Belmont, CA: Wadsworth/Thomson Learning.

Sweitzer, H. F., & King, M.A. (1999). *The successful internship: Transformation and empowerment.* Pacific Grove, CA: Brooks/Cole.

Winston, R. B., Jr., Torres, V., Carpenter, D. S., McIntire, D. D., & Petersen, B. (2001). Staffing in student affairs: A survey of practices. *College Student Affairs Journal, 21*(1), 7–25.

SKILLS ANALYSIS SURVEY FOR GRADUATE STUDENTS IN HIGHER EDUCATION AND STUDENT AFFAIRS GRADUATE PREPARATION PROGRAMS

In order to determine placements that will be beneficial to both you and the agencies you may serve, we would like some information on your skills, past work experiences, and proposed direction. Below are several general skill areas which we would like you to assess with respect to your work experience.

For each of the skills listed, please:

Indicate your general level of competency in the space to the left of each item using the following codes:

1 = high level of competency
2 = moderate level of competency
3 = minimum experience with the skill
4 = no experience

Indicate in the space to the right of each item, the level of competency you wish to have upon receiving your degree using the same codes.

On the line below each item, describe any experience you have had that requires use of this skill including position, date, major functions. If you have no experience, write "no experience."

To the left of the experience line, place an asterisk by the *five* skills you would most like to further develop, if possible, in your supervised experience. (Consider the need for presenting a breadth and diversity of skills to a future employer.)

SAMPLE

1. <u>2 / 1</u>   Display familiarity with the student affairs professional literature, as well as the current issues and trends in the field or specific to an office or population.
   <u>* /</u>   <u>Exp: Conducted literature search on paraprofessional training</u>
<u>for RAs while serving as a GRD in the residence system on cam-</u>
<u>pus</u>.

In the above example, you have indicated that you have a moderate level of
ability in articulating theories and issues, but you would like to have a high
level of competency before you graduate. So, you have selected this as one of
the five skills (by inserting an asterisk) you would like to hone in your supervised practice experience.

Since supervised experience is a collaborative effort between students, instructors, and supervisors, you are encouraged to add skills or modify any
skills listed. This instrument is constantly under revision due to the changing names and demands of student affairs.

1. ARTICULATION

1. <u>/</u>   Articulate familiarity with the student affairs professional literature, as well as the current issues and trends in the field or
specific to an office or population.

   <u>/</u>   _____

2. <u>/</u>   Articulate and interpret the goals of student personnel work to
a wider population either on or off campus.

   <u>/</u>   _____

3. <u>/</u>   Articulate the social, cultural, and philosophical foundations
of higher education.

   <u>/</u>   _____

4. <u>/</u>   Articulate student concerns to other campus populations.

   <u>/</u>   _____

5.　/　Articulate the concerns, goals, and problems of the other campus populations to students.

　　/　_____

6.　/　Recognize and articulate the special needs of the ethnic and racial minorities, disabled and gay/lesbian/bisexual populations.

　　/　_____

7.　/　Recognize and articulate the special needs of men and women.

　　/　_____

8.　/　Articulate the concerns, goals, and problems of one student population to another student population (e.g., African-American students to Greeks, commuter students to resident students).

　　/　_____

9.　/　Articulate requirements, policies, procedures, and deadlines to students and other campus populations.

　　/　_____

10.　/　Articulate theory to practice.

　　/　_____

2. PROCESS SKILLS

Many of our daily process skills are counseling-based behaviors. Review those listed below.

11.　/　Cite and apply theories of organizational development.

　　/　_____

12.　/　Cite and apply theories of personality development.

　　/　_____

13. /   Cite and apply theories of student/adult development.

    /   _____

14. /   Distinguish between theory and practice.

    /   _____

15. /   Work cooperatively with others.

    /   _____

16. /   Manifest well-developed interpersonal relations and communications skills.

    /   _____

17. /   Work effectively with a wide range of individuals.

    /   _____

18. /   Mediate conflicts between individuals and groups.

    /   _____

19. /   Appreciate and internalize professional standards and ethics.

    /   _____

20. /   Recognize and evaluate group dynamics.

    /   _____

21. /   Display competence in individual and group counseling.

    /   _____

22. /   Engage in systematic planning with a department or unit.

    /   _____

23. __/__　Recognize legal issues and understand relevant legislation.

　　__/__　_____

3. SPECIFIC CAREER BEHAVIORS

Because of the diversity of our profession, there are a variety of skills we can assume. Review those listed below:

24. __/__　Formulate and monitor a budget.

　　__/__　_____

25. __/__　Understand the financing of higher education (such as external fund raising, auxiliary agencies, financing issues).

　　__/__　_____

26. __/__　Administer and interpret personality tests.

　　__/__　_____

27. __/__　Advise student groups (e.g., academic, career, activities).

　　__/__　_____

28. __/__　Perform fair and effective discipline of student misconduct.

　　__/__　_____

29. __/__　Formulate and interpret policy.

　　__/__　_____

30. __/__　Manage physical resources and facilities.

　　__/__　_____

31. __/__　Develop or implement staffing procedures (circle those that apply) selection, training, supervision, evaluation.

　　__/__　_____

32. __/__ Design and write public relations materials for a particular unit of a student affairs division.

    __/__ _____

33. __/__ Advise/counsel individual students (personal, social, spiritual, academic).

    __/__ _____

34. __/__ Work with non-traditional population (e.g., women, minorities, commuters, disabled).

    __/__ _____

4. RESEARCH BEHAVIORS AND SKILLS

35. __/__ Interpret research as reported in professional literature.

    __/__ _____

36. __/__ Conduct independent research.

    __/__ _____

37. __/__ Understand the principles of statistical analysis.

    __/__ _____

38. __/__ Conduct a comprehensive literature search.

    __/__ _____

39. __/__ Design an effective research instrument.

    __/__ _____

40. __/__ Write a report on a specific area of research.

    __/__ _____

41. _/_   Verbally present on a specific area of research.

_/_   _____

42. _/_   Ability to analyze the effectiveness and ineffectiveness of a research design.

_/_   _____

5. PROGRAMMING SKILLS

43. _/_   Assess the extra- or cocurricular needs of a specific population.

_/_   _____

44. _/_   Design an extra- or cocurricular program based on the outcome of a population's needs assessment.

_/_   _____

45. _/_   Implement an extra- or cocurricular program design.

_/_   _____

46. _/_   Design and implement an evaluation procedure for an extra- or cocurricular program.

_/_   _____

47. _/_   Redesign an extra- or cocurricular program based on outcome of past evaluations.

_/_   _____

48. _/_   Develop and evaluate programs.

_/_   _____

49. _/_   Develop a written "how-to" programming report of an event or program.

_/_   _____

6. TRAINING AND INSTRUCTION

50. __/__   Design and implement a peer training program.

   __/__   _____

51. __/__   Design and implement a staff development program.

   __/__   _____

52. __/__   Design and implement a paraprofessional training program.

   __/__   _____

53. __/__   Design and implement a communications training program.

   __/__   _____

54. __/__   Instruct undergraduate courses.

   __/__   _____

55. __/__   Serve as a consultant.

   __/__   _____

56. __/__   Design and implement an evaluation of a training program.

   __/__   _____

57. __/__   Present at a professional conference.

   __/__   _____

58. __/__   Develop a written training manual.

   __/__   _____

59. Discuss your future plans. In what ways do you hope your administrative practicum will add to your potential to achieve these plans?

60. Please comment on your preferred or current work environment. Try to address:

a)   types of work you like to do,
b)   supervision styles,
c)   relationships with colleagues, and
d)   nature of student contact.

Reprinted with permission from Greig M. Stewart. May be reproduced under "fair use standard" of the copyright laws.

SAMPLE INTERNSHIP CONTRACT

The following is a sample internship contract. While you should think creatively when creating this document, make sure that you address each item with an asterisk:

SAMPLE

*Student Information

Jane Doe
jdoe@su.edu.
00 Rose Lane, Blacksburg, Virginia 24060
(H) 951-0000
(W) 231-0000

*Internship Site Supervisor Information

Jemal Smith
jsmith@su.edu
Assistant Dean of Students
107 Brodie Hall, State University, Collegetown, VA 24061
(W) 231-0001

Faculty Internship Coordinator Information:
Dale Jones
djones@su.edu
Associate Professor
123 Abner Hall, State University, Collegetown, VA 24061
(W) 231-0002

*Statement of Purpose

The purpose of this internship is to gain a better understanding of the role and function of the Dean of Students office in mediating and student disputes by assisting in the research and development of a new conflict resolution model. This internship will also provide an opportunity to become familiar with the various programs and positions within the Dean of Students office at State University.

*OBJECTIVES AND ACTIVITIES

Objective 1: To assist with the development of a peer conflict resolution model proposal.

   Activities:

a. Research conflict resolution models of other universities and suggestions from the National Association of Mediation in Education. (20 hours)
b. Meet regularly with the site supervisor to discuss progress. (15 hours)
c. Consult with other Dean of Students staff members on model components. (5 hours)

Skills and Competencies: These activities will hone research skills, will contribute valuable information needed to tailor this model to Virginia Tech, and will provide an opportunity for collaboration with many student affairs professionals.

Time Required: 40 Hours

Objective 2: To conceptualize the logistics of the conflict resolution model.

   Activities:

a. Draft curriculum and training outline for staff and students. (30 hours)
b. Determining parameters of the model (size of peer educator population, target organization for recruiting, etc.) (10 hours)
c. Develop a marketing plan for recruiting students for participation. (20 hours)

Skills and Competencies: In using the research of the first objective to determine the logistics of the conflict resolution model, the link from theory to practice that is so crucial in student affairs will be provided in this objective. It will be necessary to weigh available resources, human and financial, in creating the model components and in planning for the implementation of the model. Strategies for creative marketing will also be learned through this objective.

Time Required: 60 Hours

Objective 3: To gain an understanding of the roles and functions of the various positions within the Office of the Dean of Students and the issues that confront each professional staff member.

Activities:

a. Review available policy manuals and other office literature. (5 hours)
b. Attend weekly staff meetings. (30 hours)
c. Interview office staff on their respective roles. (5 hours)
d. Field telephone calls from students and parents and assist in problem-solving. (10 hours)

Skills and Competencies: This objective will provide insight into the problems and issues of Virginia Tech students and the various protocols for handling such issues within the Office of the Dean of Students. This objective will provide opportunities for developing professional relationships within the student affairs field. Completion of this objective will also allow for professional development through the "hands-on" experience of dealing with students and parental concerns.

Time Required: 50 Hours

TOTAL HOURS: 150 Hours

*Site Location

The Office of the Dean of Students will provide office space for the internship student in room 111 Brodie Hall.

*Proposed Work Schedule

The student and supervisor have agreed that the student will be in the office on Mondays and Wednesday from 9:00AM to 12:00 NOON and Fridays from

1:00PM to 5:00PM. Over the course of the 15 week semester, the 150 hour contract will be satisfied. Changes in the schedule will be made as needed.

*Signatures

Student Signature: _____   Date: _____

Site Supervisor: _____   Date: _____

Faculty Internship Coordinator: _____   Date: _____

SUPERVISOR'S RELATIONSHIP EXPECTATIONS INVENTORY

EXERCISE

- What are the most important qualities of a good internship supervisor?

  _____

  _____

  _____

- What are the most important or valuable things a supervisor has to contribute to the learning in an internship?

  _____

  _____

  _____

- What kinds of behavior do you find most disturbing or aggravating by interns?

  _____

  _____

  _____

- How do you approach giving interns negative feedback or evaluations?

  _____

  _____

  _____

- If an intern disagrees with me or others in the site, I expect her or him to:

  _____

  _____

  _____

After you have completed the Intern's Relationship Expectations Inventory (p. 79), we suggest that you request your supervisor to complete this inventory and that the two of you discuss your responses.

SELECTED RESOURCES TO ASSIST IN UNDERSTANDING
THEORIES COVERED IN CHAPTER 4

Maximizing Learning

Astin, A. W. (1985). *Achieving educational excellence: A critical assessment of priorities and practices in higher education.* San Francisco: Jossey-Bass.

Kolb, D. A. (2000). *Facilitator's guide to learning.* (TRG Hay/McBer, Training Resources Group. 116 Huntington Avenue, Boston, MA 02116) Available: http://www.trgmcber.haygroup.com

Understanding Organizations

Bolman, L. G., & Deal, T. E. (1991). *Reframing organizations: Artistry, choice, and leadership.* San Francisco: Jossey-Bass.

Kuh, G. D., & Whitt, E. J. (1988). *The invisible tapestry: Culture in American colleges and universities* (ASHE-ERIC Higher Education Report No. 1). Washington, DC: Association for the Study of Higher Education.

Moore, P. L. (1993). The political dimension of decision-making. In M. J. Barr (Ed.), *The handbook of student affairs administration* (pp. 152–170). San Francisco: Jossey-Bass.

Student Development Theories

Evans, N. J., Forney, D. S., & Guido-DiBrito, F. (1998). *Student development in college: Theory, research and practice.* San Francisco: Jossey-Bass.

Psychosocial

Chickering, A. W., & Reisser, L. (1993). *Education and identity* (2nd ed.). San Francisco: Jossey-Bass.

Cognitive-Structural

Baxter Magolda, M. B. (1992). *Knowing and reasoning in college: Gender-related patterns in students' intellectual development.* San Francisco: Jossey-Bass.

King, P. M., & Kitchener, K. S. (1994). *Developing reflective judgment: Understanding and promoting intellectual growth and critical thinking in adolescents and adults.* San Francisco: Jossey-Bass.

Cultural Diversity

Ponterotto, J. G., Casas, J. M., Suzuki, L. A., & Alexander, C. M. (2001). *Handbook of multicultural counseling.* Thousand Oaks, CA: Sage.

Marginality and Mattering

Schlossberg, N. K. (1989). Marginality and mattering: Key issues in building community. In D. C. Roberts (Ed.), New Directions for Student Services, No. 48. *Designing campus activities to foster a sense of community* (pp. 5–15). San Francisco: Jossey-Bass.

NASPA STANDARDS OF PROFESSIONAL PRACTICE

NASPA: Student Affairs Administrators in Higher Education is an organization of colleges, universities, agencies, and professional educators whose members are committed to providing services and education that enhance student growth and development. The association seeks to promote student personnel work as a profession which requires personal integrity, belief in the dignity and worth of individuals, respect for individual differences and diversity, a commitment to service, and dedication to the development of individuals and the college community through education. NASPA supports student personnel work by providing opportunities for its members to expand knowledge and skills through professional education and experience. The following standards were endorsed by NASPA at the December 1990 board of directors meeting in Washington, D.C.

1. Professional Services
   Members of NASPA fulfill the responsibilities of their position by supporting the educational interests, rights, and welfare of students in accordance with the mission of the employing institution.

2. Agreement with Institutional Mission and Goals
   Members who accept employment with an educational institution subscribe to the general mission and goals of the institution.

3. Management of Institutional Resources
   Members seek to advance the welfare of the employing institution through accountability for the proper use of institutional funds, personnel, equipment, and other resources. Members inform appropriate officials of conditions which may be potentially disruptive or damaging to the institution's mission, personnel, and property.

4. Employment Relationship
   Members honor employment relationships. Members do not com-

mence new duties or obligations at another institution under a new contractual agreement until termination of an existing contract, unless otherwise agreed to by the member and the member's current and new supervisors. Members adhere to professional practices in securing positions and employment relationships.

5. Conflict of Interest

Members recognize their obligation to the employing institution and seek to avoid private interests, obligations, and transactions which are in conflict of interest or give the appearance of impropriety. Members clearly distinguish between statements and actions which represent their own personal views and those which represent their employing institution when important to do so.

6. Legal Authority

Members respect and acknowledge all lawful authority. Members refrain from conduct involving dishonesty, fraud, deceit, and misrepresentation or unlawful discrimination. NASPA recognizes that legal issues are often ambiguous, and members should seek the advice of counsel as appropriate. Members demonstrate concern for the legal, social codes and moral expectations of the communities in which they live and work even when the dictates of one's conscience may require behavior as a private citizen which is not in keeping with these codes/expectations.

7. Equal Consideration and Treatment of Others

Members execute professional responsibilities with fairness and impartiality and show equal consideration to individuals regardless of status or position. Members respect individuality and promote an appreciation of human diversity in higher education. In keeping with the mission of their respective institution and remaining cognizant of federal, state, and local laws, they do not discriminate on the basis of race, religion, creed, gender, age, national origin, sexual orientation, or physical disability. Members do not engage in or tolerate harassment in any form and should exercise professional judgment in entering into intimate relationships with those for whom they have any supervisory, evaluative, or instructional responsibility.

8. Student Behavior

Members demonstrate and promote responsible behavior and support actions that enhance personal growth and development of students. Members foster conditions designed to ensure a student's acceptance of responsibility for his/her own behavior. Members inform and educate students as to sanctions or constraints on student behavior which may result from violations of law or institutional policies.

9. Integrity of Information and Research
Members ensure that all information conveyed to others is accurate and in appropriate context. In their research and publications, members conduct and report research studies to assure accurate interpretation of findings, and they adhere to accepted professional standards of academic integrity.

10. Confidentiality
Members ensure that confidentiality is maintained with respect to all privileged communications and to educational and professional records considered confidential. They inform all parties of the nature and/or limits of confidentiality. Members share information only in accordance with institutional policies and relevant statutes when given the informed consent or when required to prevent personal harm to themselves or others.

11. Research Involving Human Subjects
Members are aware of and take responsibility for all pertinent ethical principles and institutional requirements when planning any research activity dealing with human subjects. (See Ethical Principles in the Conduct of Research with Human Participants, Washington, D.C.: American Psychological Association, 1982.)

12. Representation of Professional Competence
Members at all times represent accurately their professional credentials, competencies, and limitations and act to correct any misrepresentations of these qualifications by others. Members make proper referrals to appropriate professionals when the member's professional competence does not meet the task or issue in question.

13. Selection and Promotion Practices
Members support nondiscriminatory, fair employment practices by appropriately publicizing staff vacancies, selection criteria, deadlines, and promotion criteria in accordance with the spirit and intent of equal opportunity policies and established legal guidelines and institutional policies.

14. References

    Members, when serving as a reference, provide accurate and complete information about candidates, including both relevant strengths and limitations of a professional and personal nature.

15. Job Definitions and Performance Evaluation

    Members clearly define with subordinates and supervisors job responsibilities and decision-making procedures, mutual expectations, accountability procedures, and evaluation criteria.

16. Campus Community

    Members promote a sense of community among all areas of the campus by working cooperatively with students, faculty, staff, and others outside the institution to address the common goals of student learning and development. Members foster a climate of collegiality and mutual respect in their work relationships.

17. Professional Development

    Members have an obligation to continue personal professional growth and to contribute to the development of the profession by enhancing personal knowledge and skills, sharing ideas and information, improving professional practices, conducting and reporting research, and participating in association activities. Members promote and facilitate the professional growth of staff and they emphasize ethical standards in professional preparation and development programs.

18. Assessment

    Members regularly and systematically assess organizational structures, programs, and services to determine whether the developmental goals and needs of students are being met and to assure conformity to published standards and guidelines such as those of the Council for the Advancement of Standards for Student Services/Development Programs (CAS). Members collect data which include responses from students and other significant constituencies and make assessment results available to appropriate institutional officials for the purpose of revising and improving program goals and implementation.

Reprinted with permission of the National Association of Student Personnel Administrators.

AMERICAN COLLEGE PERSONNEL ASSOCIATION
Statement of Ethical Principles and Standards

As presented by the ACPA Standing Committee on Ethics
And approved by the ACPA Executive Council, November 1992

PREAMBLE

The American College Personnel Association (ACPA) is an association whose members are dedicated to enhancing the worth, dignity, potential, and uniqueness of each individual within post-secondary educational institutions and thus to the service of society. ACPA members are committed to contributing to the comprehensive education of the student, protecting human rights, advancing knowledge of student growth and development, and promoting the effectiveness of institutional programs, services, and organizational units. As a means of supporting these commitments, members of ACPA subscribe to the following principles and standards of ethical conduct. Acceptance of membership in ACPA signifies that the member agrees to adhere to the provisions of this statement.

This statement is designed to address issues particularly relevant to college student affairs practice. Persons charged with duties in various functional areas of higher education are also encouraged to consult ethical standards specific to their professional responsibilities.

USE OF THIS STATEMENT

The principal purpose of this statement is to assist student affairs professionals in regulating their own behavior by sensitizing them to potential ethical problems and by providing standards useful in daily practice. Observance of ethical behavior also benefits fellow professionals and students due to the effect of modeling. Self-regulation is the most effective and preferred means of assuring ethical behavior. If, however, a professional observes conduct by a fellow professional that seems contrary to the provisions of this document, several courses of action are available.

- Initiate a private conference. Because unethical conduct often is due to a lack of awareness or understanding ethical standards, a private conference with the professional(s) about the conduct in question is an important initial line of action. This conference, if pursued in a spirit of collegiality and sincerity, often may resolve the ethical concern and promote future ethical conduct.
- Pursue institutional remedies. If Private consultation does not produce the desired results, institutional channels for resolving alleged ethical improprieties may be pursued. All student affairs divisions should have a widely-publicized process for addressing allegations of ethical misconduct.
- Contact ACPA Ethics Committee. If the ACPA member is unsure about whether a particular activity or practice falls under the provisions of this statement, the Ethics Committee may be contacted in writing. The member should describe in reasonable detail (omitting data that would identify the person(s) as much as possible) the potentially unethical conduct or practices and the circumstances surrounding the situation. Members of the Committee or others in the Association will provide the member with a summary of opinions regarding the ethical appropriateness of the conduct or practice in question. Because these opinions are based on limited information, no specific situation or action will be judged unethical. The responses rendered by the Committee are advisory only and are not an official statement on behalf of ACPA.
- Request consultation from ACPA Ethics Committee. If the institution wants further assistance in resolving the controversy, an institutional representative may request on-campus consultation. Provided all parties to the controversy agree, a team of consultants selected by the Ethics Committee will visit the campus at the institution's expense to hear the allegations and to review the facts and circumstances. The team will advise institutional leadership on possible actions consistent with both the content and spirit of the ACPA Statement of Ethical Principles and Standards. Compliance with the recommendations is voluntary. No sanctions will be imposed by ACPA. Institutional leaders remain responsible for assuring ethical conduct and practice. The consultation team will maintain confidentiality surrounding the process to the extent possible.
- Submit complaint to ACPA Ethics Committee. If the alleged misconduct may be a violation of the ACPA Statement of Ethical Principles and Standards, the person charged is unavailable or produces unsatisfactory results, then proceedings against the individual(s) may be brought to the ACPA Ethics Committee for review. Details regarding the procedures may

be obtained by contacting the Executive Director at ACPA Headquarters.

ETHICAL PRINCIPLES

No statement of ethical standards can anticipate all situations that have ethical implications. When student affairs professionals are presented with dilemmas that are not explicitly addressed herein, five ethical principles may be used in conjunction with the four enumerated standards (Professional Responsibility and Competence. Student Learning and Development. Responsibility to the Institution. Responsibility to Society) to assist in making decisions and determining appropriate courses of action.

Ethical principles should guide the behaviors of professionals in everyday practice. Principles, however, are not just guidelines for reaction when something goes wrong or when a complaint is raised. Adhering to ethical principles also calls for action. These principles include the following:

- **Act to benefit others.** Service to humanity is the basic tenet underlying student affairs practice. Hence, student affairs professionals exist to: [a] promote healthy social, physical, academic, moral, cognitive, career, and personality development of students; [b] bring a developmental perspective to the institution's total educational process and learning environment; [c] contribute to the effective functioning of the institution; and [d] provide programs and services consistent with this principle.
- **Promote justice.** Student affairs professionals are committed to assuring fundamental fairness for all individuals within the academic community. In pursuit of this goal, the principles of impartiality, equity, and reciprocity (treating others as one would desire to be treated) are basic. When there are greater needs than resources available or when the interests of constituencies conflict, justice requires honest consideration of all claims and requests and equitable (not necessarily equal) distribution of goods and services. A crucial aspect of promoting justice is demonstrating an appreciation for human differences and opposing intolerance and bigotry concerning these differences. Important human differences include, but are not limited to, characteristics such as age, culture, ethnicity, gender, disabling condition, race, religion, or sexual/affectional orientation.
- **Respect autonomy.** Student affairs professionals respect and promote individual autonomy and privacy. Students' freedom of choice and action are not restricted unless their actions significantly interfere with the welfare of others or the accomplishment of the institution's mission.
- **Be faithful.** Student affairs professionals are truthful, honor agreements, and are trustworthy in the performance of their duties.

- **Do no harm.** Student affairs professionals do not engage in activities that cause either physical or psychological damage to others. In addition to their personal actions, student affairs professionals are especially vigilant to assure that the institutional policies do not: [a] hinder students' opportunities to benefit from the learning experiences available in the environment; [b] threaten individuals' self-worth, dignity, or safety; or [c] discriminate unjustly or illegally.

ETHICAL STANDARDS

Four ethical standards related to primary constituencies with whom student affairs professionals work—fellow professionals, students, educational institutions, and society—are specified.

1. *Professional Responsibility and Competence.* Student affairs professionals are responsible for promoting students' learning and development, enhancing the understanding of student life, and advancing the profession and its ideals. They possess the knowledge, skills, emotional stability, and maturity to discharge responsibilities as administrators, advisors, consultants, counselors, programmers, researchers, and teachers. High levels of professional competence are expected in the performance of their duties and responsibilities. They ultimately are responsible for the consequences of their actions or inaction.

As ACPA members, student affairs professionals will:

1.1 Adopt a professional lifestyle characterized by use of sound theoretical principles and a personal value system congruent with the basic tenets of the profession.
1.2 Contribute to the development of the profession (e.g. recruiting students to the profession, serving professional organizations, educating new professionals, improving professional practices, and conducting and reporting research).
1.3 Maintain and enhance professional effectiveness by improving skills and acquiring new knowledge.
1.4 Monitor their personal and professional functioning and effectiveness and seek assistance from appropriate professionals as needed.
1.5 Represent their professional credentials, competencies, and limitations accurately and correct any misrepresentations of these qualifications by others.
1.6 Establish fees for professional services after consideration of the ability

of the recipient to pay. They will provide some services, including professional development activities for colleagues, for little or no remuneration.

1.7 Refrain from attitudes or actions that impinge on colleagues' dignity, moral code, privacy, worth, professional functioning, and/or personal growth.

1.8 Abstain from sexual harassment.

1.9 Abstain from sexual intimacies with colleagues or with staff for whom they have supervisory, evaluative, or instructional responsibility.

1.10 Refrain from using their positions to seek unjustified personal gains, sexual favors, unfair advantages, or unearned goods and services not normally accorded those in such positions.

1.11 Inform students of the nature and/or limits of confidentiality. They will share information about the students only in accordance with institutional policies and applicable laws, when given their permission, or when required to prevent personal harm to themselves or others.

1.12 Use records and electronically stored information only to accomplish legitimate, institutional purposes and to benefit students.

1.13 Define job responsibilities, decision-making procedures, mutual expectations, accountability procedures, and evaluation criteria with subordinates and supervisors.

1.14 Acknowledge contributions by others to program development, program implementation, evaluations, and reports.

1.15 Assure that participation by staff in planned activities that emphasize self-disclosure or other relatively intimate or personal involvement is voluntary and that the leader(s) of such activities do not have administrative, supervisory, or evaluative authority over participants.

1.16 Adhere to professional practices in securing positions: [a] represent education and experiences accurately; [b] respond to offers promptly; [c] accept only those positions they intend to assume; [d] advise current employer and all institutions at which applications are pending immediately when they sign a contract; and [e] inform their employers at least thirty days before leaving a position.

1.17 Gain approval of research plans involving human subjects from the institutional committee with oversight responsibility prior to initiation of the study. In the absence of such a committee, they will seek to create procedures to protect the rights and assure the safety of research participants.

1.18 Conduct and report research studies accurately. They will not engage in fraudulent research nor will they distort or misrepresent their data or deliberately bias their results.

1.19 Cite previous works on a topic when writing or when speaking to professional audiences.

1.20 Acknowledge major contributions to research projects and professional writings through joint authorships with the principal contributor listed first. They will acknowledge minor technical or professional contributions in notes or introductory statements.

1.21 Not demand co-authorship of publications when their involvement was ancillary or unduly pressure others for joint authorship.

1.22 Share original research data with qualified others upon request.

1.23 Communicate the results of any research judged to be of value to other professionals and not withhold results reflecting unfavorably on specific institutions, programs, services, or prevailing opinion.

1.24 Submit manuscripts for consideration to only one journal at a time. They will not seek to publish previously published or accepted-for-publication materials in other media or publications without first informing all editors and/or publishers concerned. They will make appropriate references in the text and receive permission to use if copyrights are involved.

1.25 Support professional preparation program efforts by providing assistantships, practica, field placements, and consultation to students and faculty.

As ACPA members, preparation program faculty will:

1.26 Inform prospective graduate students of program expectations, predominant theoretical orientations, skills needed for successful completion, and employment of recent graduates.

1.27 Assure that required experiences involving self-disclosure are communicated to prospective graduate students. When the program offers experiences that emphasize self-disclosure or other relatively intimate or personal involvement (e.g., group or individual counseling or growth groups), professionals must not have current or anticipated administrative, supervisory, or evaluative authority over participants.

1.28 Provide graduate students with a broad knowledge base consisting of theory, research, and practice.

1.29 Inform graduate students of the ethical responsibilities and standards of the profession.

1.30 Assess all relevant competencies and interpersonal functioning of students throughout the program, communicate these assessments to students, and take appropriate corrective actions including dismissal when warranted.

1.31 Assure that field supervisors are qualified to provide supervision to graduate students and are informed of their ethical responsibilities in this role.

2. *Student Learning and Development.* Student development is an essential purpose of higher education, and the pursuit of this aim is a major re-

sponsibility of student affairs. Development is complex and includes cognitive, physical, moral, social, career, spiritual, personality, and educational dimensions. Professionals must be sensitive to the variety of backgrounds, cultures, and personal characteristics evident in the student population and use appropriate theoretical perspectives to identify learning opportunities and to reduce barriers that inhibit development.

As ACPA members, student affairs professionals will:

2.1 Treat students as individuals who possess dignity, worth, and the ability to be self-directed.
2.2 Avoid dual relationships with students (e.g., counselor/employer, supervisor/best friend, or faculty/sexual partner) that may involve incompatible roles and conflicting responsibilities.
2.3 Abstain from sexual harassment.
2.4 Abstain from sexual intimacies with clients or with students for whom they have supervisory, evaluative, or instructional responsibility.
2.5 Inform students of the conditions under which they may receive assistance and the limits of confidentiality when the counseling relationship is initiated.
2.6 Avoid entering or continuing helping relationships if benefits to students are unlikely. They will refer students to appropriate specialists and recognize that if the referral is declined, they are not obligated to continue the relationship.
2.7 Inform students about the purpose of assessment and make explicit the planned use of results prior to assessment.
2.8 Provide appropriate information to students prior to and following the use of any assessment procedure to place results in proper perspective with other relevant factors (e.g., socioeconomic, ethnic, cultural, and gender related experiences).
2.9 Confront students regarding issues, attitudes, and behaviors that have ethical implications.

3. *Responsibility to the Institution.* Institutions of higher education provide the context for student affairs practice. Institutional mission, policies, organizational structure, and culture, combined with individual judgment and professional standards, define and delimit the nature and extent of practice. Student affairs professionals share responsibility with other members of the academic community for fulfilling the institutional mission. Responsibility to promote the development of individual students and to support the institution's policies and interests require that professionals balance competing demands.

As ACPA members, student affairs professionals will:

3.1 Contribute to their institution by supporting its mission, goals, and policies.

3.2 Seek resolution when they and their institution encounter substantial disagreements concerning professional or personal values. Resolution may require sustained efforts to modify institutional policies and practices or result in voluntary termination of employment.

3.3. Recognize that conflicts among students, colleagues, or the institution should be resolved without diminishing appropriate obligations to any party involved.

3.4 Assure that information provided about the institution is factual and accurate.

3.5 Inform appropriate officials of conditions that may be disruptive or damaging to their institution.

3.6 Inform supervisors of conditions or practices that may restrict institutional or professional effectiveness.

3.7 Recognize their fiduciary responsibility to the institution. They will assure that funds for which they have oversight are expended following established procedures and in ways that optimize value, are accounted for properly, and contribute to the accomplishment of the institution's mission. They also will assure equipment, facilities, personnel, and other resources are used to promote the welfare of the institution and students.

3.8 Restrict their private interests, obligations, and transactions in ways to minimize conflicts of interest or the appearance of conflicts of interest. They will identify their personal views and actions as private citizens from those expressed or undertaken as institutional representatives.

3.9 Collaborate and share professional expertise with members of the academic community.

3.10 Evaluate programs, services, and organizational structure regularly and systematically to assure conformity to published standards and guidelines. Evaluations should be conducted using rigorous evaluation methods and principles, and the results should be made available to appropriate institutional personnel.

3.11 Evaluate job performance of subordinates regularly and recommend appropriate actions to enhance professional development and improve performance.

3.12 Provide fair and honest assessments of colleagues' job performance.

3.13 Seek evaluations of their job performance and/or services they provide.

3.14 Provide training to student affairs search and screening committee members who are unfamiliar with the profession.

3.15 Disseminate information that accurately describes the responsibilities

of position vacancies, required qualifications, and the institution.
3.16. Follow a published interview and selection process that periodically notifies applicants of their status.

    4. *Responsibility to Society.* Student affairs professionals, both as citizens and practitioners, have a responsibility to contribute to the improvement of the communities in which they live and work. They respect individuality and recognize that worth is not diminished by characteristics such as age, culture, ethnicity, gender, disabling condition, race, religion, or sexual/ affectional orientation. Student affairs professionals work to protect human rights and promote an appreciation of human diversity in higher education.

As ACPA members, student affairs professionals will:

4.1 Assist students in becoming productive and responsible citizens.
4.2 Demonstrate concern for the welfare of all students and work for constructive change on behalf of students.
4.3 Not discriminate on the basis of age, culture, ethnicity, gender, disabling condition, race, religion, or sexual/affectional orientation. They will work to modify discriminatory practices.
4.4 Demonstrate regard for social codes and moral expectations of the communities in which they live and work. They will recognize that violations of accepted moral and legal standards may involve their clients, students, or colleagues in damaging personal conflicts and may impugn the integrity of the profession, their own reputations, and that of the employing institution.
4.5 Report to the appropriate authority any condition that is likely to harm their clients and/or others.

American College Personnel Association
One Dupont Circle Suite 300
Washington, DC 20036-1110 Phone (202) 835-2272 FAX (202) 296-3286

Last Modified September 27, 1996

Reprinted with permission of the American College Personnel Association.

ENDING THE INTERNSHIP EXPERIENCE QUESTIONNAIRE

While preparing to complete the supervised practice experience, take a few minutes to reflect on this experience and to answer the following questions.

1. Thinking back to the beginning or your internship experience, what goals did you set for yourself? Now that you are almost finished with the experience, how have you met those goals?

<u>Goals I set</u>   <u>Ways that I went about meeting each goal</u>

2. What were some ways the staff at your internship site helped you become integrated into your new environment? Please consider the ways in which you were integrated into the social structure as well as how you learned about policies and procedures of the site.

3. How have staff members at your site helped you prepare for leaving the site? Please consider not only ways in which you will terminate with clients but also ways that you will finish up work site tasks, say goodbye to colleagues, and leave the location.

4. What feelings are you experiencing now that you are preparing to terminate this internship experience?

CONTRIBUTORS

Diane L. Cooper is an Associate Professor of College Student Affairs Administration in the Department of Counseling and Human Development Services at the University of Georgia. She received a bachelor's degree in Marketing Management from Miami University, Oxford, OH (1978), an M.Ed. from the University of Missouri-St. Louis in Counseling (1979), and a doctorate from the University of Iowa in Counselor Education (1985), with a concentration in postsecondary education and vocational development. She served for eight years as a Student Affairs Practitioner at the University of North Carolina at Greensboro before joining the Student Development faculty at Appalachian State University from 1992 to 1995. Dr. Cooper served for six years as the Editor for the *College Student Affairs Journal* and on the editorial board for the *Journal of College Student Development* and the *Georgia Journal of College Student Affairs*. She is the coauthor of a New Directions Series monograph (*Beyond Law and Policy: Reaffirming the Role of Student Affairs*, 1997, with James Lancaster), the *Student Developmental Task and Lifestyle Assessment* (1999, with Theodore K. Miller and Roger B. Winston, Jr.), five book chapters, and numerous journal articles. She is currently serving as a SACSA Scholar and has served on the Professional Development Core Council for the American College Personnel Association. Recently, Dr. Cooper received the Melvene Draheim Hardee Award from the Southern Association of College Student Affairs for outstanding research, scholarship, and leadership in student personnel work. In addition, she has received the Annuit Coeptis Award from the American College Personnel Association in 2000 and the D. Parker Young Award for outstanding scholarship and research in the areas of higher education law and judicial affairs from the Association for Judicial Student Affairs in 2001. Her research interests are in program design and assessment, legal and ethical issues in student affairs practice, and in professional issues related to underrepresented groups in higher education.

Don G. Creamer is Professor of Higher Education and Student Affairs and Director of the Educational Policy Institute of Virginia Tech in the Educational Leadership and Policy Studies Department at Virginia Polytechnic Institute and State University. He received a bachelor's degree (1960) in American History, an M.Ed. degree (1961) in Counseling and Guidance from Texas A&M University at Commerce, and an Ed.D. degree (1965) in Higher Education from Indiana University. Prior to assuming teaching duties, he was Dean of Students at El Centro College of the Dallas County Community College District and previously served in several student affairs administrative roles at Texas A&M University at Commerce. He is past president of the American College Personnel Association (ACPA) and president of the Council for the Advancement of Standards in Higher Education (CAS). He is a member of the Editorial Board of the *Journal of College Student Retention*. He is author or editor of four books including *The Professional Student Affairs Administrator: Educator, Leader, and Manager* (with R. B. Winston and T. K. Miller, 2001) and *Improving Staffing Practices in Student Affairs* (with R. B. Winston, 1997). Creamer is an ACPA Senior Scholar Diplomate and holder of the association's two highest awards, the Contribution to Knowledge Award and the Ester Lloyd-Jones Distinguished Service Award. He also received the Robert H. Shaffer Award for Academic Excellence as a Graduate Faculty Member from the National Association of Student Personnel Administrators and the Robert H. Shaffer Distinguished Alumnus Award from the Indiana University Department of Higher Education and Student Affairs. He has supervised students in internships for over 20 years.

Joan B. Hirt is an Associate Professor in the Higher Education and Student Affairs graduate program in the Department of Educational Leadership and Policy Studies at Virginia Tech. She earned her bachelor's degree (1972) in Russian studies from Bucknell University, her M.A.Ed. in Counseling and Personnel Services from the University of Maryland, College Park (1979), and her doctorate in Higher Education Administration and Policy Studies from the University of Arizona (1992). She spent 17 years as a student affairs administrator in housing and dining services in California and in the Dean of Students office at the University of Arizona. A past president of the Western Association of College and University of Housing Officers, she is a reviewer for the *Journal of College Student Retention*. She has authored or co-authored 15 articles in refereed journals and 14 chapters in books and monographs. She has presented over 35 sessions at regional and national conferences and has delivered keynote speeches at more than a dozen conferences. She received the Annuit Coeptis Award from the American College Personnel Association (1997). Her current research interests focus on professionalization issues and administrative culture in higher education. She has served as a faculty member since 1994.

Steven M. Janosik is a Senior Policy Analyst and Associate Professor in the Department of Educational Leadership and Policy Studies at Virginia Polytechnic Institute and State University (Virginia Tech). In addition, he serves as the Co-Director for Educational Policy Institute of Virginia Tech. He received his bachelor of science degree (1973) in business administration from Virginia Tech, his master's degree (1975) in Higher Education and Student Personnel Services from the University of Georgia, and Ed. D. degree (1987) in educational administration from Virginia Tech. Prior to assuming his faculty position, he served as Deputy Secretary of Education for the Commonwealth of Virginia where he worked closely with the State Council of Higher Education for Virginia, the Virginia Community College System, the Council for Information Management, and the State Department of Education. Janosik also has over 20 years of experience in college administration. He has served on the media board of the American College Personnel Association (ACPA), as editor of the *Journal of College and University Student Housing*, and a member of the executive committee of the Association for Student Judicial Affairs (ASJA). He is currently a reviewer for the *Journal of College Student Retention* and the *Journal of Counseling and Development*. He has written over 20 articles on the topics of campus crime, law in higher education, liability and risk management, residence life, and student development. Janosik received the Outstanding Research Award from Commission III of the ACPA and the D. Parker Young Award for outstanding scholarship and research in the areas of higher education law and judicial affairs from ASJA.

Sue A. Saunders currently serves as Dean of Student Affairs at Lycoming College in Pennsylvania. Her career includes service as a faculty member in the College Student Affairs Administration Program at the University of Georgia, Dean of Students at Longwood College in Virginia, and other administrative positions in Georgia and West Virginia. She has served the American College Personnel Association on the Executive Council, as chair of the Core Council for Dissemination and Generation of Knowledge, and as president of the Virginia state division of ACPA. She is also author of more than 30 publications and regularly presents at national conventions and regional workshops. Her research interests include staff supervision, patterns of professional development, and developmental interventions. Her contributions to the profession have been recognized through her selection for ACPA Annuit Coeptis, Leadership Foundation Diamond Honoree program, and Senior Scholars.

Roger B. Winston, Jr. is Professor of College Student Affairs Administration in the Department of Counseling and Human Development Services at the University of Georgia in Athens. He received a bachelor's degree (1965) in History from Auburn University, a master's degree (1970) in Philosophy, and a doctorate (1973) in Counseling and Student Personnel Services from the University of Georgia. Prior to assuming teaching duties at the University of Georgia in 1978, he was the Dean of Men at Georgia Southwestern State University. He has served on the American College Personnel Association's Executive Council and the Council for the Advancement of Standards' and the National Academic Advising Association's Boards of Directors, been editor of *ACPA Developments*, and is currently on the editorial board of the *Journal of College Student Development* and is a reviewer for the *Journal of College Student Retention*. He is author or editor of 11 books and over 100 journal articles and book chapters. His most recent books are *The Professional Student Affairs Administrator: Educator, Leader, and Manager* (2001 with Don G. Creamer and Theodore K. Miller), *Improving Staffing Practices in Student Affairs* (1997 with Don G. Creamer), and *Student Housing and Residential Life: A Handbook for Professionals Committed to Student Development Goals* (1993 with Scott Anchors). Winston is an American College Personnel Association (ACPA) Senior Scholar Diplomate, holder of the Southern Association for Student Affairs Melvene Hardee Award for Contributions to Student Affairs, and recipient of the ACPA Contribution to Knowledge Award and the National Academic Advising Association's Outstanding Researcher Award. He has been a faculty supervisor of master's and doctoral level interns in Student Affairs Administration for over 25 years.

INDEX